ALICE MOORE DUNBAR-NELSON

THE DUNBAR SPEAKER AND ENTERTAINER

THE POET AND HIS SONG

AFRICAN-AMERICAN WOMEN WRITERS, 1910–1940

Henry Louis Gates, Jr. *General Editor*

Jennifer Burton *Associate Editor*

ALICE MOORE DUNBAR-NELSON

THE DUNBAR SPEAKER AND ENTERTAINER

THE POET AND HIS SONG

Introduction by
AKASHA (GLORIA) HULL

G. K. HALL & CO.
An Imprint of Simon & Schuster Macmillan
New York

Prentice Hall International
London Mexico City New Delhi Singapore Sydney Toronto

G. K. Hall & Co.
An Imprint of Simon & Schuster Macmillan
1633 Broadway
New York, NY 10019

Library of Congress Catalog Card Number: 96-17587

Printed in the United States of America

Printing Number
1 2 3 4 5 6 7 8 9 10

Library of Congress Cataloging-in-Publication Data

The Dunbar speaker and entertainer : containing the best prose and poetic selections / Alice Moore Dunbar-Nelson ; introduction by Akasha (Gloria) Hull.
        p.   cm.—(African-American women writers, 1910–1940)
    Includes bibliographic references (p.   ).
    ISBN 0-7838-1423-2 (alk. paper)
        1. Public speaking.   2. Speeches, addresses, etc., American—Afro-American authors.   3. Afro-Americans—Literary collections.   I. Dunbar-Nelson, Alice Moore, 1875–1935.   II. Series.
PN4121.D9238   1996
808.5'1'08996073—dc 20   96-17587
                                                                        CIP

This paper meets the requirements of ANSI/NISO Z39.48.1992 (Permanence of Paper).

C O N T E N T S

GENERAL EDITORS' PREFACE

The past decade of our literary history might be thought of as the era of African-American women writers. Culminating in the awarding of the Pulitzer Prize to Toni Morrison and Rita Dove and the Nobel Prize for Literature to Toni Morrison in 1993 and characterized by the presence of several writers—Toni Morrison, Alice Walker, Maya Angelou, and the Delaney Sisters, among others—on the *New York Times* Best Seller List, the shape of the most recent period in our literary history has been determined in large part by the writings of black women.

This, of course, has not always been the case. African-American women authors have been publishing their thoughts and feelings at least since 1773, when Phillis Wheatley published her book of poems in London, thereby bringing poetry directly to bear upon the philosophical discourse over the African's "place in nature" and his or her place in the great chain of being. The scores of words published by black women in America in the nineteenth century—most of which were published in extremely limited editions and never reprinted—have been republished in new critical editions in the forty-volume *Schomburg Library of Nineteenth-Century Black Women Writers*. The critical response to that series has led to requests from scholars and students alike for a similar series, one geared to the work by black women published between 1910 and the beginning of World War Two.

African-American Women Writers, 1910–1940 is designed to bring back into print many writers who otherwise would be unknown to contemporary readers, and to increase the availability of lesser-known texts by established writers who originally published during this critical period in African-American letters. This series implicitly acts as a chronological sequel to the Schomburg series, which focused on the origins of the black female literary tradition in America.

In less than a decade, the study of African-American women's writings has grown from its promising beginnings into a firmly established field in departments of English, American Studies, and African-American Studies. A comparison of the form and function of the original series and this sequel illustrates this dramatic shift. The *Schomburg Library* was published at the cusp of focused academic investigation into the interplay between race and gender. It covered the extensive period from the publication of Phillis Wheatley's *Poems on Various Subjects, Religious and Moral* in 1773 through the "Black Women's Era" of 1890–1910, and was designed to be an inclusive series of the major early texts by black women writers. The Schomburg Library provided a historical backdrop for black women's writings of the 1970s and 1980s, including the works of writers such as Toni Morrison, Alice Walker, Maya Angelou, and Rita Dove.

African-American Women Writers, 1910–1940 continues our effort to provide a new generation of readers access to texts—historical, sociological, and literary—that have been largely "unread" for most of this century. The series bypasses works that are important both to the period and the tradition, but that are readily available, such as Zora Neale Hurston's *Their Eyes Were Watching God*, Jessie Fauset's *Plum Bun* and *There Is Confusion*, and Nella Larsen's *Quicksand* and *Passing*. Our goal is to provide access to a wide variety of rare texts. The series includes Fauset's two other novels, *The Chinaberry Tree: A Novel of American Life* and *Comedy: American Style*, and Hurston's short play *Color Struck*, since these are not yet widely available. It also features works by virtually unknown writers, such as *A Tiny Spark*, Christina Moody's slim volume of poetry self-published in 1910, and *Reminiscences of School Life, and Hints on Teaching*, written by Fanny Jackson Coppin in the last year of her life (1913), a multi-genre work combining an autobiographical sketch and reflections on trips to England and South Africa, complete with pedagogical advice.

Cultural studies' investment in diverse resources allows the historic scope of the *African-American Women Writers* series to be more focused than the *Schomburg Library* series, which covered works written over a 137-year period. With few exceptions, the authors included in the *African-American Women Writers* series wrote their major works between 1910 and 1940. The texts reprinted include all the works by each particular author that are not otherwise readily obtainable. As a result, two volumes contain works originally published after 1940. The Charlotte Hawkins Brown volume includes her book of etiquette published in 1941, *The Correct Thing To Do—To Say—To Wear*. One of the poetry volumes contains Maggie Pogue Johnson's *Fallen Blossoms*, published in 1951, a compilation of all her previously published and unpublished poems.

Excavational work by scholars during the past decade has been crucial to the development of *African-American Women Writers, 1910–1940*. Germinal bibliographical sources such as Ann Allen Shockley's *Afro-American Women Writers 1746–1933* and Maryemma Graham's *Database of African-American Women Writers* made the initial identification of texts possible. Other works were brought to our attention by scholars who wrote letters sharing their research. Additional texts by selected authors were then added, so that many volumes contain the complete oeuvres of particular writers. Pieces by authors without enough published work to fill an entire volume were grouped with other pieces by genre.

The two types of collections, those organized by author and those organized by genre, bring out different characteristics of black women's writings of the period. The collected works of the literary writers illustrate that many of them were experimenting with a variety of forms. Mercedes Gilbert's volume, for example, contains her 1931 collection *Selected Gems of Poetry, Comedy, and Drama, Etc.*, as well as her 1938 novel *Aunt Sarah's Wooden God*. Georgia Douglas Johnson's volume contains her plays and short stories in addition to her poetry. Sarah Lee Brown Fleming's volume combines her 1918 novel *Hope's Highway* with her 1920 collection of poetry, *Clouds and Sunshine*.

The generic volumes both bring out the formal and thematic similarities among many of the writings and highlight the striking individuality of particular writers. Most of the plays in the volume of one-acts are social dramas whose tragic endings can be clearly attributed to miscegenation and racism. Within the context of these other plays, Marita Bonner's surrealistic theatrical vision becomes all the more striking.

The volumes of *African-American Women Writers, 1910–1940* contain reproductions of more than one hundred previously published texts, including twenty-nine plays, seventeen poetry collections, twelve novels, six autobiographies, five collections of short biographical sketches, three biographies, three histories of organizations, three black histories, two anthologies, two sociological studies, a diary, and a book of etiquette. Each volume features an introduction by a contemporary scholar that provides crucial biographical data on each author and the historical and critical context of her work. In some cases, little information on the authors was available outside of the fragments of biographical data contained in the original introduction or in the text itself. In these instances, editors have documented the libraries and research centers where they tried to find information, in the hope that subsequent scholars will continue the necessary search to find the "lost" clues to the women's stories in the rich stores of papers, letters, photographs, and other primary materials scattered throughout the country that have yet to be fully catalogued.

Many of the thrilling moments that occurred during the development of this series were the result of previously fragmented pieces of these women's histories suddenly coming together, such as Adele Alexander's uncovering of an old family photograph picturing her own aunt with Addie Hunton, the author Alexander was researching. Claudia Tate's examination of Georgia Douglas Johnson's papers in the Moorland-Spingarn Research Center of Howard University resulted in the discovery of a wealth of previously unpublished work.

The slippery quality of race itself emerged during the construction of the series. One of the short novels originally intended for inclusion in the series had to be cut when the family of the author protested that the writer was not of African descent. Another case involved Louise Kennedy's sociological study *The Negro Peasant Turns Inward*. The fact that none of the available biographical material on Kennedy specifically mentioned race, combined with some coded criticism in a review in the *Crisis*, convinced editor Sheila Smith McKoy that Kennedy was probably white.

These women, taken together, began to chart the true vitality, and complexity, of the literary tradition that African-American women have generated, using a wide variety of forms. They testify to the fact that the monumental works of Hurston, Larsen, and Fauset, for example, emerged out of a larger cultural context; they were not exceptions or aberrations. Indeed, their contributions to American literature and culture, as this series makes clear, were fundamental not only to the shaping of the African-American tradition but to the American tradition as well.

Henry Louis Gates, Jr.
Jennifer Burton

PUBLISHER'S NOTE

In the *African-American Women Writers, 1910–1940* series, G. K. Hall not only is making available previously neglected works that in many cases have been long out of print, we are also, whenever possible, publishing these works in facsimiles reprinted from their original editions including, when available, reproductions of original title pages, copyright pages, and photographs.

When it was not possible for us to reproduce a complete facsimile edition of a particular work (for example, if the original exists only as a handwritten draft or is too fragile to be reproduced), we have attempted to preserve the essence of the original by resetting the work exactly as it originally appeared. Therefore, any typographical errors, strikeouts, or other anomalies reflect our efforts to give the reader a true sense of the original work.

We trust that these facsimile and reprint editions, together with the new introductory essays, will be both useful and historically enlightening to scholars and students alike.

INTRODUCTION

By Akasha (Gloria) Hull

In 1954–55 I won the fifth grade oratorical contest at the all-black West Shreveport Elementary School, Shreveport, Louisiana. Under the strict training of my teacher, Mrs. Beulah Williams, and with much encouragement from home, I had committed to memory a practiced delivery of a poem (author unrecorded) called "Rock of Ages" (I don't know if this was its official title). Each of the four or five stanzas began with the first line of the protestant hymn, "Rock of ages, cleft for me," and I sang these, providing a dramatic lead-in and counterpoint to the spoken text. (In those days I hadn't decided that I couldn't sing.) It was an "ages of man" poem, beginning with the "thoughtlessly singing maiden," and proceeding through the weary, mature woman who "every word her heart did know" to the words being "sung above a coffin-lid." Now, looking back over the schoolgirl script—preserved and dug out of a china cabinet drawer by my mother—my favorite stanza is the next to last one:

> "Rock of Ages, cleft for me"
>> Lips grown aged, sung the hymn . . .
>> "Let me hide myself in Thee"
>> Trembling though the voice and low
>> Ran the sweet strain peacefully,
>> Like a river in its flow;
>> Sang as only they can sing
>> What life's thorny path hath prest;
>> Sang as only they can sing
>> Who behold the promised rest.

Clearly, I was given this piece because of its religious piety and the opportunities it provided for effective dramatization of voice and gesture. At one point, the mournful word "Nevermore" (from Edgar Allan Poe's "The Raven") punctuates three successive lines filled with rolling images of wind and tide.

For my triumph, I received a small, gold-plated pin engraved with "Oratory" and the year. I don't remember whom I vanquished in the contest, but I know that later in our school career, as the same core group of us were promoted from class to class, to junior and then to high school, Charlesetta Jackson's rendition of "St. Peter at the Gate" was the quintessential oratorical event. Charlesetta delivered this long narrative poem in an almost droll and understated manner, her features immobile and her vocal inflections doing all the work. After being treated to repeated performances, we could all say "Thirty years" exactly as she did, with the beginning intonational rise dropping to the resignation of the long-suffering husband who finally gets his heavenly reward.

This extracurricular school activity took its place alongside the many other occasions at which we were expected to—and did—verbally perform. As soon as a child could toddle up on the church platform without falling and say "Jesus wept" (sometimes with a maximum of coaxing and minimum of tears), he or she had a part in the Easter program. The number of lines lengthened with each year and with the elders' assessment of how "smart" you were. The quatrain was popular, and one of the most flippant, reserved for just the right age and personality was:

> What you looking at me so hard for
> I didn't come to stay
> I just came to tell you
> That today is _____ Day!

Dressed in new finery, with hands clasped or folded, boys made a proper bow and girls a drop-knee curtsy. We knew "how to act"—in all the meanings of that phrase. Without historicizing or theorizing, this school and church performance was an accepted part of the world we knew—where you were taught to speak up "like you got some sense" when you were spoken to—or when the formal occasion demanded. We were participating in and perpetuating a vast tradition of oratory that helped to define us as a people.

This is the long-standing racial-cultural heritage that gives rise to *The Dunbar Speaker and Entertainer* (1920). Seven years earlier, to commemorate the fiftieth anniversary of President Abraham Lincoln's issuing of the Emancipation Proclamation, Alice Dunbar-Nelson had edited *Masterpieces of Negro Eloquence: The Best Speeches Delivered by the Negro from the Days of Slavery to the Present Time*.[1] That collection had been devoted to one facet of African-American rhetoric—that which was primarily public and political, concerned with burning national issues of slavery and freedom, and with human and citizenship rights. With the *Speaker*, Dunbar-Nelson is broadening her black oratorical field. In a system derived from Aristotle, rhetoric is traditionally classified as (1) epideictic, ceremonial or occasional; (2) deliberative (legislative-type debate); (3) forensic or judicial; and 4) religious or pulpit. All but the last of these are represented in *Masterpieces*. However, among the epideictic selections—the category that is potentially the most inclusive—the range is limited to essentially the same kinds of topics that dominate judicial and legislative debate even if they are given a more practical or in-group orientation. Departing significantly from its predecessor, the *Speaker* adds to the occasions those at which African Americans and their friends congregated for entertainment and adds to the material selections that are literary and humorous. That Dunbar-Nelson returned to the task of assembling yet another oratorical anthology indicates the importance of rhetoric and public speaking to her personally and to her generation of both black and white Americans.

Since the founding of the United States, oratory has played an important role in the history of the nation. During the colonial period, the rhetoric of the Puritan clergy held sway, superseded during the Revolution by the newly emerging profession of law, which established a usually heavy, florid style.[2] Classical rhetoric, oratory, and elocution were taught in the universities, and public display of these skills (originally in Greek) was customary. During the early decades of the nineteenth century, occasions for speaking included court day, legislative sessions, election campaigns, civil resolutions meetings, religious revivals, patriotic celebrations such as the Fourth of July and George Washington's birthday, ceremonial toasts, business gatherings, and public hangings.[3] The expression as well as the possession of knowledge continued to be regarded as a sign of breeding and culture, particularly in the antebellum South. "Sons of the southern aristocracy were sent to Harvard, Yale, or Princeton, or to southern academies and colleges emphasizing Greek and Latin studies"; these young gentlemen were consequently "expected to excel in both public speaking and private conversation."[4]

The antislavery movement galvanized into activity an arsenal of speakers whose agitation on this issue dominated public discourse in the decades immediately preceding the Civil War. Nevertheless, this was only one of the concerns contributing to what Robert T. Oliver calls the "spirit of renovation" sweeping the country after the War of 1812. He lists "communist communities, a newly revealed religion for Latter Day Saints, abolitionism, women's rights, anti-war enthusiasm, dietary reforms, crusades against tobacco, and prohibitionism."[5] All these fueled conversation, debate, and speeches. At the same time, the ranks of speakers were augmented by blacks and women mounting the lecture platform on behalf of themselves and their causes. After the Civil War, oratory was spread even more widely and then commercialized by the lyceum movement and the lecture system. Originally informal discussions and talks, lyceums had given birth by the late 1860s to the professionalization of public speaking for mass consumption. The beginning of Chautauqua, a system of summer tent lectures, further institutionalized this direction.[6] The national appetite for oratorical edification and entertainment was huge. Audiences are the other half of the equation that equals good speaking, and throughout the history of the United States they have been very receptive. In the nineteenth and early twentieth centuries, people listened attentively to speeches that lasted for two or three hours. Clearly, formalized oral discourse was a valuable and highly valued aspect of life.

Inasmuch as oratory was important for white America, it was even more crucial for the black inhabitants of the country and, with this factor of race, assumed additional dimensions. "Life, liberty, and the pursuit of happiness"—and the public discussion of them—had a meaning for African Americans infinitely more literal and compelling than for the white citizenry. One major fact to be noted (lest it be forgotten) is that the black population was generally excluded from active participation—or any participation at all—in the mainstream forms of the oratory that has been discussed. The existence of slavery, racial prejudice, and legal segregation forced black people to express themselves in separate venues and institutions, utilizing their unique cultural heritage and developing parallel traditions. Only a Frederick Douglass or a Booker T. Washington ever made it onto the national lyceum or Chautauqua circuit. Yet, for both blacks and whites, the race and racial progress have been closely linked to oral representation. Two scholars point out that "it is extremely difficult to speak of black leaders without speaking of spokesmen [sic], in the elemental sense." "It is no fluke of history that men of letters or organizational talents have seldom been acclaimed 'black leaders.'"[7]

Furthermore, "unlike the written word, the spoken word excluded no one either as an audience or as a participant."[8] Until educational privilege was democratized, this potentially egalitarian access to the spoken word was important for the entire nation; for African Americans, prohibited by law from reading and writing until Emancipation, speech had to be the primary mode of communication. Even when writing was possible, Philip S. Foner asserts that "perhaps even more than writers, black orators helped to demolish the myth of the natural inferiority of black people."[9] In addition to the negative contingencies placed upon their expressivity, black people operated from strong, positive shaping influences. Smith and Robb have this to say:

> The African brought to America a fertile oral tradition, and the generating and sustaining powers of the spoken word permeated every area of his life. . . . Communication between different ethnic and linguistic groups was difficult, but the almost universal African regard for the power of the spoken word contributed to the development of alternate communication patterns in the work songs, Black English, sermons, and Spirituals, with their dual meanings, one for the body and one for the soul.[10]

Wielded by blacks, the strict categories of classical rhetoric have, of necessity, broken down. Ceremonial (epideictic) occasions that call for graduation speeches or keynote addresses have had to serve as platforms for the discussion of racial and democratic concerns in styles close to the forensic and/or deliberative.[11] Black historian Carter G. Woodson points out that, judged likewise by ancient classical standards, "the Negro orator might be expected to lack most of the essentials. Yet . . . the Negro in his sequestered sphere is much better informed, much more capable than the white man who passes him by supposes."[12] Thus, given the chance to speak, he/she evidences knowledge as well as presentational skill. Woodson also summarizes the contribution black orators have made in each of the categories.[13] He notes that success accrues from the nonverbal aspects of the speaking situation, aspects that cannot be set forth on the printed page when the speech is repeated via that medium: "Their tones were beautiful, and their gestures natural. They could suit the word to the action and the action to the word. Using skillfully the eye and voice, they reached the souls of man."[14]

Despite their talents, black orators have not usually been regarded with seriousness by the white majority. Speaking of the nineteenth century, Robert T. Oliver writes:

> A Negro orator was as much an anomaly as a high school student urging his opinions about current issues to a general community audience. The adults might (and often do) admire the youngster's skill and praise his accomplishments; but this is far from taking seriously the advice he has to offer. What is being judged is a performance rather than an assertion of leadership. Negroes (and, parenthetically, women) who sought to influence public opinion and policies in that time, through the influence of public speaking, were oddities to be observed and in some fashion perhaps even to be admired—but certainly not leaders to be followed.[15]

This hegemonic viewing of black spokespeople in ways that appreciate their oratorical passion and prowess but still marginalize them and their messages has continued into the present—with rare exceptions. African-American rhetors have found their truest and most responsive audiences among their own people. They are received with openness and met with both audible and visible signs of approval or disapproval.[16] This account—which bears quoting in full—is illustrative. The subject of the story, J. Finley Wilson, published the *Advocate-Verdict* newspaper in Harrisburg, Pennsylvania, with Robert J. Nelson, Alice Dunbar's husband-to-be, as editor, and later established the *Washington Eagle*, for which Dunbar-Nelson herself wrote from 1926 to 1930. Wilson was the Exalted Ruler of the Improved Benevolent and Protective Order of Elks (the Black Elks). Known as an "orator par excellence," who "spoke for all Elks in a strident voice, with compelling logic and convincing emphasis," he is shown here in 1933 at the Alabama State Finals of the Elks Oratorical Contest at which a high school student had just won first place with an oration entitled "Frederick Douglass and the Constitution":

> J. Finley Wilson was present and arose to pay tribute to the several student speakers. The contest had lasted two hours, and the audience was becoming restless. Before many minutes had passed, however, the Exalted Ruler had cast a spell over his listeners, and, to use the trite phrase, "they hung onto his every word." He displayed all the tricks of oratory, and the occasion, as it were, set him on fire. First, there was conversation mixed with dramatic pauses for effect. Frequent modulations of his voice were followed by rapid-fire sentences. All the while, the orator was warming up to his subject. When he reached the climax, his Elks fez fell off his head onto the floor. And when he stooped down to pick it up, pandemonium broke loose in the audience. When the clamor subsided, the orator concluded his message in a loud and thunderous voice which brought forth prolonged applause. Wilson then took his seat, and it was some time before the presiding officer could restore order amid shouts of "Go on!" and "Give us more!"[17]

During the early twentieth century, African Americans had a wide range of opportunities to engage in various types of speaking—political rallies and campaigns; state and local fairs (which usually featured a "Negro" day); farmers' and agricultural meetings; literary societies; national and local conventions of race and fraternal organizations; commencement exercises at secondary schools, colleges, and universities; an array of church-related occasions—sermons, Easter and Christmas programs, special day commemorations (Youth, Men's, Women's, Mother's, etc.), conventions and assemblies; special school programs and oratorical presentations; club, fraternal, and sororal meetings and program events; commemoration of national and racially significant holidays; community gatherings for ad hoc purposes, civic or social. For the more public, political, national, and pulpit occasions, male leaders and spokesmen dominated. However, for the others, women were either well represented or more prevalent, as in, for example, their own sex-segregated clubs, organizations, and spheres, and in auxiliary church activities.

One kind of oratory that seems to have been the province of women and girls was dramatic platform reading, otherwise known as oral interpretation, reading aloud, oral reading, or interpretative reading. Edward L. Jones describes the genre thus:

> No matter what the name the interpreter is primarily concerned with the re-creation of literature for an audience. . . . The materials used by the interpreter may be poetry, prose or drama—whatever the audience will like. Oral interpretation requires that the interpreter accepts his material as a work of art, and must be able to communicate that work of art through the voice and body. The interpreter should respond intellectually and emotionally to the work of art, and through empathy elicit a similar response from the audience.[18]

Women who specialized in this field were known as elocutionists. Some insight into precisely what this meant can be gained from Monroe A. Majors's 1893 work, *Noted Negro Women*.[19] Among his many black women achievers in all fields he includes six figures whose claim to fame is that they are elocutionists.

The first of these, Madame Frances E. Preston, was a widow with one child; she owned a large hairdressing business and had received her education from the Detroit Training School in Elocution and English Literature, entering when she was thirty-three years old for a two-and-a-half-year course. In 1882–83 she toured with the Donivan Famous Tennesseans, and the following year, traveled through eastern Virginia, giving programs alone. In April 1891 she secured a position with the Women's Christian Temperance Union lecture bureau, becoming their first literature listing. From newspaper accounts, we learn that she used a reading desk "heaped high with choice floral tributes," and that a novel feature of her program was an introductory Bible reading, deemed "excellent." A Springfield, Ohio, report describes an entertainment at which both Mrs. Preston and her daughter appeared: "One of the most attractive features of the evening entertainment was the 'Aesthetic Gestures,' and 'Lyre Movement,' by Miss Lillie Preston, daughter of the elocutionist. Her gestures expressing profound grief, anguish, supplication and remorse, by turn, were so natural as almost to cause a person to feel as if he were witnessing a dire disaster or calamity" (100).

Miss Henrietta Vinton Davis, "Elocutionist, Dramatic Reader and Tragedienne," began her study of the art early, laying the foundation for her career "by a wide and thorough study of the best masters in classic and dramatic literature" (108). Her April 25, 1883, debut in Washington, DC, was introduced by Frederick Douglass, for whom she was a kind of protégé. Thereafter she visited major cities in New England, New York, Pennsylvania, and Florida under the professional management of gentlemen in the business. She was "not only an elocutionist, but an actress of very decided force," displayed in Shakespearean selections such as the poison scene from *Romeo and Juliet* (106). Louise De Mortie, another speaker, "took high rank in her profession" based on her "handsome presence, engaging manners and richly toned voice" (113). But her work was cut short by her 1867 death as a "Christian martyr" aiding black orphans in New Orleans.

At eight and nine years old, Miss Hallie Quinn Brown gave early-morning orations to the cows, sheep, and birds when she finished milking the cows on a farm in Chatham, Canada. After some years teaching and one year raising funds for her alma mater, Wilberforce University, as a traveling lecturer, she took a course in elocution, thereafter beginning (in the early 1880s) fundraising tours with "The Wilberforce Grand Concert Company." According to Majors, "She has read before hundreds of audiences and tens of thousands of people, and has received nothing but the highest praise from all." The Washington, DC, *Advocate* reports on one of her appearances:

> Miss Brown is quite tall, has auburn hair, a keen eye, a voice of remarkable compass and features of great mobility. Her selections were as follows: "The Last Hymn," "The Love Letter," "How He Saved St. Michael's"—a thrilling story in verse relating how this famous Charleston [SC] church was saved from fire by the daring act of a slave, "Jemima's Courtship," "Curfew Must Not Ring To-night," in which she exhibited intense dramatic power, "Ameriky's Conversion," "Uncle Daniel's Vision," "The Little Hatchet," and "The Creeds of the Bells." Miss Brown stands by far above the readers we are accustomed to hear. (235)

She was, apparently, "the crowning feature of the company." This program shows the mixture of modes and tones—including the dialectical and the humorous—that was usually offered for such readings. Mary Anna Phinney Stansbury's famous "St. Michael's" was in practically every elocutionist's repertoire (Dunbar-Nelson includes it in the *Speaker*) and "The Bells" was another popular piece. It is worth noting that on one occasion Miss Brown rendered an original selection called "The Apple." In 1893 she was appointed professor of elocution at Wilberforce and lived an increasingly active and influential life, especially in the black women's club movement.

Miss Valetta Linden Winslow of Oakland, California, added Delsarte to her study of elocution. Filling a special engagement at the 1892 Pacific Grove Chautauqua, she aroused enthusiasm for her talent in this form: "Her facial expressions were a constant surprise, expressive of the various passions and emotions of the soul, while every movement was grace and beauty" (San Jose *Mercury*); "Her portrayal of the different passions and emotions that ofttimes rack we poor mortals sore were true to the letter, particularly revenge, pain, abject fear, and entreaty" (Pacific Grove *Review*); "She gave forty-nine different expressions, such as anger, horror, bashfulness, ridicule, etc. with appropriate gestures. The gifted young lady created great enthusiasm. The various expressions were to the life, and her gestures were full of charming grace and appropriateness. She was recalled, and recited 'Sister and I,' with powerful expression and gestures" (San Francisco *Call*, 240).

Apparently these Delsarte tableaux became a common part of platform readings. In the *Speaker*, they are included as full-page illustrations. Black girls and young women dressed in white chemise-like dresses with caps, bows, or bands on their heads display "A Bow," "An Evening Prayer," "Pleading," "Supplication," "Fear," "To a Wild Rose," "Coquetry," "Listen," "I'm So Sleepy," "Bashfulness," "Meditation," "Hope," "A Secret (Silence)," "Vanity," and "Longing."

Finally, there is Ednora Nahar, a stunning, wellborn lady from Boston. (Majors's book provides photographs and likenesses for many of the women.) Early in her career (which began in 1887), she decided to act as her own manager, doing so with such success that she became an entrepreneur, who launched programs and managed other artists, including Elizabeth Greenfield, the famous songstress known as the "Black Patti." Miss Nahar's performances featured complementary costuming. She dressed in Egyptian garb for a Cleopatra selection, and in "Indian costume" for the "Sioux Chief's Daughter." For "Low Back Car," she employed a "rich Irish brogue" that was "perfection itself." Her signature piece was the "Chariot Race" from *Ben Hur*, praised by diverse commentators as a "revelation" (247–48). She studied for one season at Dion Boucicault's Madison Dramatic School; Boucicault joined others in recommending that she "forsake the platform for the stage" (249).

These elocutionists enacted at a professional or semiprofessional level a specialized version of what large numbers of black men and women, girls and boys were doing in their churches, communities, and schools. The purpose of *The Dunbar Speaker and Entertainer* was to provide ready-made material for these occasions—even though original compositions were sometimes given. This intent is underscored by the sample programs that Dunbar-Nelson provides at the end of the book. She suggests readings and music for holidays such as Thanksgiving, Memorial Day, and Emancipation Day, for types of occasions focused on "The Young Negro," "Negro Wit and Humor," "Lincoln-Douglass Celebration," and "Quaint Phases of the Life of the Negro." Noting that the programs "are not necessarily to be taken as a whole by anyone arranging an evening's or a morning's entertainment," she hopes that they will open vistas for "any enterprising teacher[s]" who can then "suggest to their schools other programs that will show to the boys and girls the wide range of the writings of the men and women of their own race" (278).

Dunbar-Nelson's explicit targeting of schools probably has its general origin in her lifelong experience as an elementary and secondary school teacher and, more specifically, in her earlier attempts to publish supplementary textbooks for black students. She is guided by a conviction that she articulated in an article, "Negro Literature for Negro Pupils." Too long, she says, have African-American children been forced "to believe that they are pensioners on the mental bounty of another race. . . . for two generations we have given brown and black children a blonde ideal of beauty to worship, a milk-white literature to assimilate, and a pearly Paradise to anticipate, in which their dark faces would be hopelessly out of place."[20] In 1918, two years before the *Speaker* appeared, she had corresponded with the World Book Company about publishing an industrial training text with them, and with Doubleday Page and Company about "a supplementary reader for the seventh and eighth grades of colored schools." The latter rejected her proposal-manuscript with this comment:

> . . . the book should contain a great deal more material of the character of that selection you have given from Booker T. Washington to the exclusion of quite a number of selections you have made. Your own examination of this material in the light of the comparison we have drawn will show you very clearly what we mean.[21]

She was being told in a circumlocutory but still unmistakable way that they did not appreciate the racial spiritedness of her selections.

The inclusions in the finally published *Speaker* are quite broad, depicting black people from varied points of view. The first section, "Juvenile," contains poems about nature and the natural world of plants and animals. Almost all are allegories that inculcate moral lessons. Dialect, both "humorous" and "serious," occupies the next two sections. Paul Laurence Dunbar is generously represented, and other contributors include Ruth McEnery Stuart and James Weldon Johnson. One of the most striking selections is Payne Erskine's "Mammy Clarissa's Vengeance," a first-person narration by the title character of how she allowed her newborn son to be mistaken for the mistress's new baby and reared as lord of the plantation, while the mistress's child was in turn taken to be Mammy Clarissa's and raised as a slave. White authors like Stuart and Erskine are fairly well represented in the volume, their selections starred by an asterisk.

The fourth section, "Dramatic," seems to be where Dunbar-Nelson placed everything that belonged there as well as other pieces that she simply wished to include but that did not obviously fit into any of the other categories. It is by far the largest grouping, including lynching poems, the excellently chosen denouement from Charles Chesnutt's novel *The Marrow of Tradition*, prose excerpts about black soldiers in Europe, the climax of a Dunbar short story, poems about heroic black figures, Walt Whitman's "Ethiopia Saluting the Colors," a moving scene from W. E. B. Du Bois's novel *The Quest of the Silver Fleece*, and so on. Here are the most suspenseful, violent, graphic, and dramatizable selections. There are also many dramatic monologues and much battlefield material, as well as overt depictions of racial cruelty and injustice. The two final sections of the volume, "Oratorical" and "Commemorative," both contain holiday orations and tributes to the usual roll call of white and black leaders. Some of these are fine examples of set pieces that demonstrate the technique and style of classical rhetoric—for example, the carefully balanced consideration of "Lincoln and Douglass." Dunbar-Nelson brings the praise down to earth with her own "The Boys of Howard [High] School" and her poem "To the Negro Farmers." The book closes with two appreciations of Booker T. Washington, the first a poem in neoclassical style by John Riley Dungee and the second a short selection by President Theodore Roosevelt that keeps Washington in his "humble" place.

Congruent with its origins, the dedication of the *Speaker* reads: "To the children of the race which is herein celebrated, this book is dedicated, that they may read and learn about their own people." (This echoes the dedication to her earlier collection, *Masterpieces of Negro Eloquence*.) In his foreword, Leslie Pinckney Hill, president of the Cheyney (Pennsylvania) School for Teachers, stresses the important role of reading for the formation of adult character. With the "highest interests of American democracy and the needs of the war-torn world" as backdrop, Hill asserts that Dunbar-Nelson's volume

> will reveal to the colored youth of the land the mind and heart quality of their own representative men and women. The result ought to be a great increase among them of self-reliance and race pride, a wider spread impulse to noble striving and the placing of a very much higher estimation upon the potential abilities of dark complexioned people everywhere. (13)

Though "speaking" was, in many respects, a kind of entertainment, its intellectual results were frequently emphasized. Hill's remark recalls a statement in the Newport News (Virginia) *Commercial* referring to Madame Frances E. Preston's performance: "One evening with Mrs. Preston will add more intellectuality to our children than many books, and we advise our readers to let no opportunity pass that will do so much for the little folks."[22]

Hill's foreword is followed by a short—only one-page—introduction by Dunbar-Nelson that manages succinctly to say a great deal about effective oratorical delivery. Throughout the text are scattered photographs of Frederick Douglass, "Principal Washington in his private office, Tuskegee Institute," and Abraham Lincoln, as well as many very fine, realistic illustrations by an artist who is not acknowledged in any way other than by his signed drawings. Overall, eleven selections by her late husband, Paul Laurence Dunbar, are included, and eight by Dunbar-Nelson herself. Clearly she took this opportunity to include as much of her own work as possible. And given her additional role as editor and compiler, the "Dunbar" in the title could well be a pun, referring as much to her as to the famous poet.

It is fitting that this assemblage of oratory by and about black people should invoke the name of Dunbar. He was himself a gifted reader. He performed extensively before black and white gatherings, enthralling them with his lithe handsomeness, quick and graceful movements, and rich, colorful voice. In her critical essay about him, "The Poet and His Song," Dunbar-Nelson recounts two anecdotes that are illustrative. While visiting her family in West Medford, Massachusetts, Dunbar was distracted from writing serious poems by his two-year-old niece, "who persisted in hugging his avuncular shoes":

> "How can one work?" he asked fretfully, and then burst laughingly into "How's a poet to write a sonnet, can you tell?" And so dashed off the poem on scrap paper, and read it aloud to the small maiden, who thereupon suggested that the "Woo—oo" of the wind was a "Boogah Man." So that was written immediately, dramatizing it as he wrote, much to her delight.
>
> The dramatic instinct was strong behind the delicate perception of the power of suggestion. One must dramatize the poems as they were written, white hot. So, when "The Dance" and "The Valse" were penned, the metre must be dramatized in order to get it right; anapestic tetrameter admits of no limping lines; so one must waltz, humming the lines in order that there be no faulty rhythm.[23]

When Dunbar read, he did so in this dramatic style.

In the second place, his dialect poetry strikes the heart of something I am tempted to call "authentic" and "enduring" African-American racial sensibility even as I acknowledge variations and historical differences. I grew up hearing the cadences of Dunbar's "A Negro Love Song" from my mother. And when I taught at the University of Delaware during the 1970s, the black studies students in my English classes begged me to read dialect Dunbar, his "honey"s and "chile"s toning seamlessly with their own more current signifying. About three years ago I was honored in my hometown by a black professional sorority composed of beauticians and other independent businesswomen. A retired schoolteacher not far removed from the cohort who tutored me was the hit of the program with her splendid all-stops-out but dignified rendition of Dunbar's "When Malindy Sings"—delivered to an audience that spanned multiple generations and economic–social classes.

Generally, Dunbar's work—and especially his dialect poetry—has provided repertoire for these kinds of cultural occasions despite his own decrying of what he dubbed in his poem "The Poet" his "jingle in a broken tongue." And despite, too, the judgment of critics such as James Weldon Johnson that dialect is a limited genre only capable of two "stops"—pathos and humor (although Johnson himself wrote dialect). In "The Poet and His Song" Dunbar-Nelson takes pains to position herself on the side of those who would downplay the dialect and praise the standard English. They feel—with justification—that white America rewarded Dunbar for the dialect because it fit more comfortably within their stereotypes of black people; they relegated black people's liking it to class affiliation or unprogressive, unenlightened backwardness. She gratuitously digresses in her essay to assert:

> Say what you will, or what Mr. [William Dean] Howells wills, about the "feeling the Negro life esthetically and expressing it lyrically," it was in the pure English poems that the poet expressed *himself*. He may have expressed his race in the dialect poems; they were to him the side issues of his work, the overflowing of a life apart from his dearest dreams. (124)

And time after time in her diary, she notes with disgust how, after she has read what she considered to be Dunbar's best poetry to audiences, they clamored for the dialect poems.[24]

Her position on this issue is consonant with her usual allegiance to high culture and to the dominant norms. This bias totally determines her critical approach in "The Poet and His Song," where she doggedly reads Dunbar according to the tenets of nineteenth-century British Romanticism (a subject she had studied in depth at Cornell University during the summers of 1907 and 1908). She avers that an urban poet is an impossibility and that Dunbar, though born in the city, did not really come alive until he had experienced Nature in its pristine beauty. The essay charts the development of the poet as a series of sojourns in the wild—his first summer at a lake ("Nature had called him, and he had not been able to heed her call, until the Lake told him how"); vacations in the Catskill Mountains (where he "cried aloud for joy" to discover that the light turned violet on the ground beneath potato vines); the country around West Medford; his first acquaintance with the sea; a stay at Arundel-on-the-Bay on the Eastern Shore of Maryland; a winter in rural Colorado, which was

> as much of a revelation of Nature as the sea! But here was a new mother, more stern, less sure, never so capable of intimacy. Magnificent sweep of mountain range . . . Unsurpassed sunsets, wonderful sunrises that flushed the eastern prairies, and reflected back on the snows of the mountains in the west . . . the meadow lark perched on the eaves of the house, tossing golden liquid sweetness to the high clear heavens . . . Here was Nature, untamed, unconfined, unfamiliar, wild. It went to the head like new wine, and ideas came rushing, fulminating, fructifying. (132)

Pushing this schematic, Dunbar-Nelson never mentions the oral influence of the poet's mother, for example, and only alludes to racial motivations: "The darker side of the problems of the race life was being brought home more and more forcibly to him as he grew older, and the stern ruggedness of nature in the Rocky Mountains forced him to a realization of the grim problems of the world's work" (133).

Dunbar-Nelson's essay is most valuable for its intimate look at the scenes and situations that spawned particular Dunbar poems. From her, commentators have learned that one of his most quoted pieces, "Sympathy"—with its line "I know why the caged bird sings"—arose from the poet's feeling of confinement as he fulfilled his job in the bookstacks of the Library of Congress in the oppressive heat of summer. Elsewhere she discloses:

> There was in Washington [DC] a bare, red-clay hill, open to the sun, barren of shade on its highest point, steep of ascent, boldly near the sky . . . Daily walks on the hill fulminate in one line in "Love's Apotheosis," "the sun-kissed hill." The white arc light of the corner lamp, filtering through the arches of the maple on

Spruce street, make for the tender suggestion in "Lover's Lane," where the lovers walk side by side under the "shadder-mekin'" trees. (125)

Here, Dunbar-Nelson is elaborating the point that stored experiences eventually found their way into swiftly phrased lines of poetry—another Romantic tenet.

Without ever using the personal pronoun "I," Dunbar-Nelson accompanies the poet and takes us along with her. Only once does the skillful manner she has devised to do this call attention to itself. Recreating a hike in the Catskills, she tells of merriment "loud and long, because any old dead branch when carried on a walk became dignified by the name of alpenstock, and the leather chatelaine purse of the companion in tramping became a knapsack" in the finished poem. Dunbar-Nelson's powers of description and smooth, impeccably grammatical style are evident throughout the essay. Some of the things she says, however couched, ring true about poetry and the creative process. Near the end she speaks of true poets as thinking "by leaps and bounds . . . Else wherefore think? One might as well ruminate": "And three or four great poems may have the same trivial place of conception, or a great soul-shaking experience may culminate in a line. Else why write poetry?" (134)

Both this critical reminiscence and *The Dunbar Speaker and Entertainer* indicate Alice Dunbar-Nelson's inseparability from the name and fame of her first husband. Married to him in 1898 and then separated in 1902 (four years before his early death from tuberculosis), she benefited for the rest of her life from that association—even as it paradoxically obscured some of her own original accomplishments.[25] Her status as his widow gave her the recognition she needed to project herself as a lecturer. She traveled as often as she was invited to read Dunbar's poetry and talk knowledgeably about him. One of the most commercial flyers screams: "N O T I C E ! ! Mrs. Paul Laurence Dunbar COMING!" After noting her qualifications and "attractive Features and appearance," the text continues: "This is Mrs. Dunbar's first visit to Portsmouth and she says: 'I can give you an "Evening with

Dunbar."' The lecture will be illustrated with Readings from the poet. The program will be interspersed with Music by the Choir."

All were invited to attend this program, held at the Third Baptist Church, admission twenty-five cents.[26] Perhaps her most stellar event was a joint "Recital" with the acclaimed tenor Roland Hayes. Billed as "The Life of Paul Laurence Dunbar Told in His Songs and Lyrics," it took place at the New-Century Club in Wilmington, Delaware, March 21, 1916. These readings place her squarely, if more inconspicuously, within the cadre of black women elocutionists and lecturers. She also gave countless talks about subjects—other than Dunbar—that were race, education, and women related. In her diary the catchphrase "Spoke fine" is the oral equivalent to its counterpart, "Produced lit.," which stood for written work of all types. Her lectures and readings, and publications such as "The Poet and His Song" and the *Speaker*, all represent her need, both psychological and financial, to generate visibility and projects. The latter two, the subject of this volume, reveal her as critic and anthologist, additional facets of the shining contribution she made to African-American life and letters until her 1935 death.

In the final analysis, the tradition preserved in *The Dunbar Speaker and Entertainer* is one place where the oral and scribal meet. Broad sections of black people came together—usually in their churches and schools—for recreation and enlightenment. What they witnessed, what they presented to each other did educate, instill values, and morally uplift through the projection of pleasantly packaged ideals and models of behavior. Referring to the United States as a whole, Robert Oliver writes, "Americans, and all others who 'live' democracy as well as value it, talk out their mutual concerns. There is no substitute for face-to-face confrontation."[27] To confrontation, I would add dialogue and communication. The republication of the *Speaker* helps insure that African Americans talk to each other across the generations (forging a much-needed continuity of historical consciousness) and speak, also, to interested others—such cross-talk being the foundation upon which rests all vital human-social relationships and institutions.

NOTES

[1]It was published in 1914 by the Douglas Publishing Company, Harrisburg, Pennsylvania, as a joint venture of Dunbar-Nelson and her future husband, Robert J. Nelson.

[2]Mabel Platz, *The History of Public Speaking* (New York: Noble and Noble, 1935), 254.

[3]*A History of Criticism of American Public Address*, ed. William Norwood Brigance (New York: McGraw-Hill, 1943), 73–90.

[4]Barnet Baskerville, *The People's Voice: The Orator in American Society* (Lexington: University of Kentucky Press, 1979), 77.

[5]Robert T. Oliver, *History of Public Speaking in America* (Boston: Allyn and Bacon, 1965), 227.

[6]Baskerville, 101–2.

[7]*The Voice of Black Rhetoric, Selections*, ed. Arthur L. Smith and Stephen Robb (Boston: Allyn and Bacon, 1971), 3.

[8]*American Orators Before 1900: Critical Studies and Sources*, ed. Bernard K. Duffy and Halford R. Ryan (New York: Greenwood, 1987), xv–xvi.

[9]Philip S. Foner, *The Voice of Black America* (1972), quoted in *The Rhetoric of Struggle: Public Address by African American Women*, ed. Robbie Jean Walker (New York: Garland, 1992).

[10]*The Voice of Black Rhetoric*, 1, 2.

[11]*The Rhetoric of Struggle*, 2–3.

[12]Carter G. Woodson, *Negro Orators and Their Orations* (Washington, DC: Associated Publishers, 1925), 5.

[13]Woodson, 10–12.

[14]Woodson, 6.

[15]Oliver, 246.

[16]Arthur L. Smith, *Rhetoric of Black Revolution* (Boston: Allyn and Bacon, 1969), 63.

[17]Marcus L. Boulware, *The Oratory of Negro Leaders: 1900–1968* (Westport, CT: Negro Universities Press, 1969), 143. This is Boulware's eyewitness account of the occasion, for which he was present to serve as one of the contest judges. As familiar as he was with black speaking, he pronounced himself "stunned" by this display, which was notable but not singular.

[18]Edward L. Jones, *Black Orator's Workbook* (Seattle: University of Washington Department of Printing, 1982), 37.

[19]Monrow A. Majors, *Noted Negro Women: Their Triumphs and Activities* (Chicago: Donohue and Henneberry, 1893). Page numbers are given parenthetically within the text.

[20]*The Southern Workman* (February 1922): 59–63. Reprinted in *An Alice Dunbar-Nelson Reader*, ed. R. Ora Williams (Washington, DC: University Press of America, 1979), 134.

[21]Correspondence with a friend, "Lu," at the World Book Company, Publishers, 1918. Letter from Edgar D. Hellweg of the Doubleday Page Educational Department to Alice Dunbar-Nelson, February 20, 1918.

[22]Majors, 99.

[23]Alice M. Dunbar, "The Poet and His Song," *A. M. E. Review* (African Methodist Episcopal Church) 31, no. 2 (October 1914): 131. Subsequent references are given parenthetically within the text.

[24]*Give Us Each Day: The Diary of Alice Dunbar-Nelson*, ed. Gloria T. (Akasha) Hull (New York: Norton, 1984).

[25]For a full treatment of Dunbar-Nelson's life and work, see the chapter on her in Gloria T. (Akasha) Hull, *Color, Sex, and Poetry: Three Women Writers of the Harlem Renaissance* (Bloomington: Indiana University Press, 1987).

[26]Undated flyer, *Give Us Each Day*, 148.

[27]Oliver, xviii.

THE DUNBAR SPEAKER
AND ENTERTAINER

ALICE DUNBAR-NELSON

THE DUNBAR
SPEAKER AND
ENTERTAINER

CONTAINING

The Best Prose and Poetic Selections by and about THE NEGRO RACE

With Programs arranged for special entertainments

Edited by

Alice Moore Dunbar-Nelson

And an Introduction by

Leslie Pinckney Hill

Illustrated

Published by

J. L. NICHOLS & CO.

Agents Wanted   Naperville, Ill.

Dedication

*To the children of the race which is herein
celebrated, this book is dedicated, that they
may read and learn about their own people*

TABLE OF CONTENTS

5

*The names marked with an asterisk are the names of members of the Caucasian Race.

FOREWORD

WHAT the children read the fathers will believe. What the fathers believe will constitute the ideals of the race. Therefore nothing is more important to the development of any people than the content of those printed pages on which they form their youthful minds. Bishop Spaulding said, "The voices that spoke to me in my boyhood are now speaking through me to the world." Let those voices speak of self-reliance, noble striving, and ambition for high achievement, and the quality of the adult life will generally be of the same character. Let those voices suggest low self-esteem or mediocre life aims, and the later manhood will be correspondingly low in thought, feeling, and conduct.

So well known is the operation of this principle that the vast machinery of our system of education in America has always revolved about its reading courses. But these reading courses have been almost necessarily one-sided and undemocratic. Devised and executed exclusively by experts of the white race, they have naturally reflected only the ideals of that race. They have set before America and the world only those traditions of heroism, self-sacrifice, delicacy of feeling, high thinking, and noble endeavor which have

9

been exemplified in representative white men and women. The result naturally is a universal and solidified conviction in the minds of all American youth that the progress of the world—industrial, political, intellectual and social—has been exclusively the white man's achievement. Nothing could have been a more reasonable conclusion for the long generations which have been nourished on Livy, Plutarch, Green, Grote, Mommsen, Parkman, Bancroft or Fisk. These have been the historians of the white world just as Homer, Dante, Shakespeare, Milton and Lowell have been its poets, and Thackeray, Eliot, Dickens and Hawthorne its romancers. The massive influence of these great spokesmen has all been on the side of the amazing mind power and outward competency of their exalted race, and their estimation of the white man's superiority has been universally received by public opinion. In vain may you search their pages—those pages upon which all our reading has been founded—for anything other than a patronizing view of that vast, brooding world of colored folk—yellow, black and brown—which comprises by far the largest portion of the human family.

The results of this one-sided reading have long been very clear to see, and they have been very mischievous. The two most important results alone need mention here. The first is a feeling of contempt, tempered with pity, on the part of the white man everywhere for his colored brother. The second is a disastrous, unconscious acceptance on the part of large masses of the colored races themselves of the estimation placed upon them by their white neighbors. These two conditions in turn have bred those misunderstandings between race groups and those misinterpretations of one race by another that lie at the base of all our horrifying modern war. Exactly as Germans have looked with contempt upon Frenchmen or Englishmen, so the whole white world has viewed the darker races. These darker people have consequently been at a tremendous disadvantage in having little or no recognized literature for the expression of their highest ideals and aspirations, and no channels through which their recognized spokesmen might make known to the world the inner heart of the race. Colored boys and girls have not been reading about heroic black warriors and statesmen, martyrs or saints, though the progress of the world has depended largely upon these. They have not seen often enough even the poor reproductions of world famous works of art wrought by bronze or ebony hands. They do not ponder enough the pages of the black man's romance written by the black novelist. They have not stored their minds with the poetry that has sung its way out of the black man's sorrow and travail and made a place for itself among the lasting monuments of the world's music. And not knowing how much they have to be proud of, how much to live for, strive for, and die for, colored people in enormous masses plod on wearily in the path of life discouraged and half efficient. Twelve millions of American Negroes in particular are, to use Mary White Ovington's expression, "half men," because they do not know even so much of the nobility and grandeur of the black man's finer traditions as Doctor DuBois has set forth in his stimulating little book "The Negro."

Surely the highest interests of American democracy and the needs of the war-torn world dictate now that nothing be left undone to awaken to new life, and to call to a high plane of self-reliance and activity, so potent a portion of our population. The great conceptions of liberty, inter-racial and international justice, and of universal democracy are in the air. Now that the insane waste and frightful misery of war are done, the colored races everywhere must be given a just and untrammeled opportunity to contribute all they can to the reconstruction of a new, more liberal and democratic social order.

It is against this background of the world need that Mrs. Alice Dunbar-Nelson's book is seen to have peculiar significance to the colored race in America. Hers is the first attempt I have known of directly on the part of any Negro to frame a speaker composed entirely of literature produced by black men and women, and about black men and women, and embodying the finest spiritual ideals of the Negro race. The selections that make up this volume will reveal to the colored youth of the land the mind and heart quality of their own representative men and women. The result ought to be a great increase among them of self-reliance and race pride, a wider spread impulse to noble striving and the placing of a very much higher estimation upon the potential abilities of dark complexioned people everywhere. Above all things, it ought to mean a better understanding between the races in these States because of the truth which this little volume seeks to prove—that the white man has no fine quality, either of heart or mind, which is not shared by his black brother.

LESLIE PINCKNEY HILL,

The Cheyney School for Teachers,

Cheyney, Pa.

INTRODUCTION

VOLUMES might be written about the manner of presenting the selections in this little volume. Oratorical rules and elocutionary efforts have been written about time out of mind, and it is fairly safe to say that none of them ever made a really good speaker. The one safe guide is one's feelings. Be sure that the selection has become a part of your inner feeling, and the expression, gestures, proper inflections, will come naturally. Stilted gestures, learned by rote, fail to impress an audience, as inflections and modulations learned by rule are mechanical and unpleasant to the hearers.

Before you begin to learn anything to recite, first read it over and find out if it fires you with enthusiasm. If it does, make it a part of yourself, put yourself in the place of the speaker whose words you are memorizing, get on fire with the thought, the sentiment, the emotion—then throw yourself into it in your endeavor to make others feel as you feel, see as you see, understand what you understand. Lose yourself, free yourself from physical consciousness, forget that those in front of you are a part of an audience, think of them as some persons whom you *must* make understand what is thrilling you—and you will be a great speaker.

14

BOOK I.
Juvenile

A Bow

THE BIRDLET

GOD'S birdlet knows,
   Nor cares, nor toils,
   Nor weaves it painfully
An everlasting nest.
Through the long night on a twig it slumbers;
When rises the red sun,
Birdlet listens to the voice of God
And it starts and sings.
When spring, Nature's beauty,
And the burning summer have passed,
And the fog and the rain
By the late fall are brought,
Men are wearied, men are grieved,
But birdlet flies into distant lands,
Into warmer climes beyond the blue sea;
Flies into the spring.

—ALEXANDER POUSHKIN.

THE SPARROW'S FALL

TOO frail to soar, a feeble thing,
It fell to earth with fluttering wing;
But God, who watches over all,
Beheld that little sparrow's fall.

'Twas not a bird with plumage gay,
Filling the air with its morning lay;
'Twas not an eagle bold and strong,
Borne on the tempest's wing along:

Only a brown and weesome thing,
With drooping head and listless wing;
It could not drift beyond His sight
Who marshals the splendid stars of night.

Its dying chirp fell on His ears,
Who tunes the music of the spheres,
Who hears the hungry lion's call,
And spreads a table for us all.

Its mission of song at last is done,
No more will it greet the rising sun;
That tiny bird has found a rest
More calm than its mother's downy breast.

O restless heart, learn thou to trust
In God, so tender, strong and just;
In whose love and mercy everywhere
His humblest children have a share.

If in love He numbers ev'ry hair,
Whether the strands be dark or fair,
Shall we not learn to calmly rest,
Like children, on our Father's breast?
                    —FRANCES E. W. HARPER.

THE SEEDLING *

As a quiet little seedling,
 Lay within its darksome bed,
To itself it fell a-talking,
And this is what it said:

"I am not so very robust,
 But I'll do the best I can,"
And the seedling from that moment,
 Its work of life began.

So it pushed a little leaflet,
 Up into the light of day,
To examine the surroundings,
 And show the rest the way.

The leaflet liked the prospect,
 So it called its brother, Stem,
Then two other leaflets heard it,
 And quickly followed them.

To be sure, the haste and hurry,
 Made the seedling sweat an
But almost before it knew it,
 It found itself a plant.

The sunshine poured upon it,
 And the clouds, they gave a shower;
And the little plant kept growing,
 Till it found itself a flower.

Little folks, be like the seedling,
 Always do the best you can,

* Permission, Dodd, Mead & Co.

Every child must share life's labor,
    Just as well as every man.

And the sun and showers will help you,
    Through the lonesome, struggling hours,
Till you raise to light and beauty,
    Virtue's fair, unfading flowers.

                                —PAUL LAURENCE DUNBAR.

WHILE APRIL BREEZES BLOW

A SONG FOR ARBOR DAY

COME, let us plant a tree today—
    Forsake your book, forsake your play,
    Bring out the spade and hie away
While April breezes blow.

Your life is young, and it should be
As full of vigor as this tree,
As fair, as upright and as free,
    While April breezes blow.

Come, let us plant a tree to stand
Both fair and useful in the land,
Supremely tall and nobly grand—
    A strong and trusty oak.

Dig deep and let the long roots hold
A firm embrace within the mold—
And may your life in truth unfold
    A strong and trusty oak.

Come, let us plant a supple ash,*
A tree to bend when others crash,
And stand when vivid lightnings flash,
    And clouds pour down the rain:

So while we plant we'll learn to bend
And hold our ground, tho' storms descend
Throughout our life, and lightnings rend,
    And clouds pour down the rain.

Then let us plant these trees between
A graceful spruce in living green,
That e'en in winter days is seen
    Like changeless springtime still:

And so may you as years go by,
And winter comes and snowflakes fly,
Be yet in heart, and mind and eye,
    Like changeless springtime still.

Bring out the spade and hie away,
And let us plant a tree today
While skies are bright and hearts are gay,
    And April breezes blow.

In other days 'neath April skies,
Around this tree may joyful cries,
And happy children's songs arise,
    While April breezes blow.

                —D. T. WILLIAMSON.

*It is said that lightning never strikes an ash tree.

THANKSGIVING

MY heart gives thanks for many things—
    For strength to labor day by day,
    For sleep that comes when darkness wings
With evening up the eastern way.
I give deep thanks that I'm at peace
    With kith and kin and neighbors, too;
Dear Lord, for all last year's increase,
    That helped me strive and hope and do.

My heart gives thanks for many things;
    I know not how to name them all.
My soul is free from frets and stings,
    My mind from creed and doctrine's thrall.
For sun and stars, for flowers and streams,
    For work and hope and rest and play,
For empty moments given to dreams—
    For these my heart gives thanks today.

WILLIAM STANLEY BRATHWAITE.

From Lyrics of Love and Life, Small, Maynard & Co.

THE CUCUYA OR FIREFLY

THE firefly is heedlessly wandering about,
Through field and through forest is winging his
route,
As free as the butterfly sporting in air,
From flower to flower it flits here and there:
Now glowing with beautiful phosphoric light,
Then paling its lustre and waning in night:
It bears no effulgence in rivalry near,
But shrouds ev'ry gleam as the dawn doth appear.

It sparkles alone in the soft summer's eve,
Itself, though unseen, by the track it doth leave,
The youth of the village at nightfall pursue
O'er hill and o'er dale as it comes into view;
Now shining before them, now lost to their eyes,
The sparkle they catch at, just twinkles and dies;
And the mead is one moment all spangled with fire,
And the next, every sparklet is sure to expire.

On the leaf of the orange awhile it disports,
When the blossom is there to its cup it resorts,
And still the more brightly and dazzling it shines,
It baffles its tiny pursuer's designs.
But see the sweet maiden, the innocent child,
The pride of the village—as fair as the wild
And beautiful flowers she twines in her hair—
How light is her step, and how joyous her air!

And oft as one looks on such brightness and bloom,
On such beauty as hers, one might envy the doom

Of a captive "Cucuya," that's destined like this,
To be touched by her hand and revived by her kiss;
Imprisoned itself by a mistress so kind,
It hardly can seem to be closely confined,
And a prisoner thus tenderly treated, in fine,
By a keeper so gentle might cease to repine.

In the cage which her delicate hands have prepared,
The captive "Cucuya" is shining unscared,
Suspended before her, with others as bright,
In beauty's own bondage revealing their light.
But this amongst all is her favorite one,
And she bears it at dusk, to her alcove alone,
'Tis fed by her hand on the cane that's most choice,
And in secret it gleams at the sound of her voice.

Thus cherished, the honey of Hybla would now
Scarce tempt the "Cucuya" her care to forego;
And daily it seems to grow brighter and gain
Increasing effulgence, forgetting its pain.
O beautiful maiden! may heaven accord
Thy care of the captive its fitting reward;
And never may fortune the fetters remove,
Of a heart that is thine in the bondage of love.

Written by a slave in Cuba, 1838. His father and mother lived and died in slavery in Cuba, but he escaped to Havana. Translated into English by Doctor Madden from the Spanish.

THE CLOCK THAT GAINS

THE clock's too fast they say;
But what matter how it gains!
Time will not pass away
Any faster for its pains.

The tiny hands may race
Round the circle, they may range,
The sun has but one pace,
And his course he cannot change.

The beams that daily shine
On the dial, err not so,
For they're ruled by laws divine,
And they vary not, we know.

But though the clock is fast,
Yet the moments, I must say,
More slowly never passed,
Than they seemed to pass today.

—THE CUBAN SLAVE.

A JUNE SONG

WE would sing a song to the fair young June,
  To the rare and radiant June,
  The lovely, laughing, fragrant June
How shall her praise be sung or said?
Her cheek has caught the roses' hue,
Her eye the heavens' serenest blue.

And the gold of sunset crowns her head,
And her smile—ah! there's never a sweeter, I ween,
Than the smile of this fair young summer queen.
What life, what hope, her coming brings!
What joy anew in the sad heart springs
As her robe of beauty o'er all she flings!

Old earth grows young in her presence sweet,
And thrills at the touch of her gentle feet,
As the flowers spring forth her face to greet.
Hark! how the birds are singing her praise,
In their gladdest, sweetest, roundelays!

The trees on the hillside have caught the glow,
And the heaven smiles down on the earth below,
And our radiant June,
Our lovely, joyous June,
Our summer queen,
Smiles, too, as she stands
With folded hands,
And brow serene.

How shall we crown her bright young head?
Crown it with roses, rare and red;

Crown it with roses, creamy white,
As the lotus bloom that sweetens the night.
Crown it with roses as pink as shell
In which the voices of ocean dwell.
And a fairer queen
Shall ne'er be seen
Than our lovely, laughing June.

We have crowned her now, but she will not stay,
The vision of beauty will steal away
And fade, as faded the fair young May.
Ah, loveliest maiden, linger a while!
Pour into our hearts the warmth of thy smile,
The gloom of the winter will come too soon.
Stay with us, gladden us, beautiful June!
Thou glidest away from our eager clasp.
They will hold thee fast; and the days to be
Will be brighter and sweeter for thoughts of thee.
Our song shall not be a song of farewell,
As with words of love the chorus we swell.
In praise of the fair young June,
Of the rare and radiant June,
The lovely, laughing, fragrant June.

—CHARLOTTE FORTEN GRIMKE.

A CITY GARDEN

HID in a close and lowly nook,
　　In a city yard where no grass grows—
　　Wherein nor sun, nor stars may look
Full faced—are planted three short rows
Of pansies, geraniums, and a rose.

A little girl with quiet, wide eyes,
　　Slender figured, in tattered gown,
Whose pallored face no country skies
　　Have quickened to a healthy brown,
　　Made this garden in the barren town.

Poor little flowers, your life is hard;
　　No sun, nor wind, nor evening dew.
Poor little maid, whose city yard
　　Is a world of happy dreams to you—
　　God grant some day your dreams come true.

　　　　　　　　　—WILLIAM STANLEY BRAITHWAITE.

From Lyrics of Life and Love, Small, Maynard & Co.

DE LIL' BLACK SHEEP

POOR lil' black sheep dat strayed away
Don' los' in de win' an' de rain.
An' de Shepherd He said: "O hirelin',
Go find my sheep again!"—
But de hirelin' frown—"O Shepherd,
Dat lil' black sheep am bad!"
But de Shepherd—He smile—
Seems de lil' black sheep
Was the onliest lamb He had!

An' He says, "O hirelin', hasten,
For de win' an' de rain am col',
An' dat lil' black sheep am lonesome
Out dar so far from the fol'"—
But de hirelin' frown—"O Shepherd,
Dat sheep am ol' an' grey!"
But de Shepherd—He smile—
Seems de lil' black sheep
Was as fair as de break ob day!

An' He says: "O hirelin', hasten,
Lo, here am de ninety an' nine—
But lon' way off from de sheep fol'
Is dat lil' black sheep of Mine!"
An' de hirelin' frown—"O Shepherd,
De rest ob de sheep am here!"
But de Shepherd—He smile—
Seems de lil' black sheep
He hol' it de mostest dear!

An' de Shepherd go out in de darkness
Wher' de night was col' and bleak—
An' lay it again' His cheek.
An' de hirelin' frown—"O Shepherd,
Don' bring dat sheep to me!"
But de Shepherd—He smile—an'
He hol' it close,
An'—dat lil' black sheep was—me!

                    —*Ballarat* (Australia) *Chronicle.*

BOOK II.
Selections in Dialect
(Humorous)

An Evening Prayer

IN THE MORNING *

'LIAS! 'Lias! Bress de Lawd,
　Don' you know de day's erbroad?
　Ef you don't get up, you scamp,
Dey'll be trouble in dis camp.
T'ink I's gwine to let you sleep
W'ile I meks yo' boa'd an' keep?
Dat's a purty howdy-do—
Don' you hyeah me, 'Lias, you!

Bet ef I come crost dis flo'
You won't fin' no time to sno'.
Daylight all a shinin' in
W'ile's you sleep, w'y hit's a sin!
Ain't de can'le light enuff
To bu'n out widout a snuff,
But you go de mo'nin' thoo
Bu'nin' up de daylight, too?

'Lias, don' you hyeah me call?
No use tu'nin' to'ds de wall;
I kin hyeah dat mattuss squeak!
Don' you hyeah me w'en I speak?
Dis hyeah clock done struck off six!
Ca'line, bring me dem ah sticks!
Oh, you's down, suh, huh! you's down?
Look hyeah, don't you daih to frown.

Ma'ch you'se'f an' wash yo' face,
Don' you splattah all de place;

---
* Permission, Dodd, Mead & Co.
3

I got somep'n else to do,
'Sides jes' cleanin' aftah you.
Tek dat com' an' fix yo' haid—
Looks des' lak a feddah baid.
Look hyeah, boy, I let you see,
You cain't roll yo' eyes at me.

Come hyuh! Bring me dat ah strap!
Boy, Ah'll whup you twell you drap;
You done felt yo'se'f too strong,
An' you sholy got me wrong.
Set down at dat table thaih,
Jes' you whimpah ef you daih!
Evah mo'nin' on dis place,
Seems lak I mus' lose my grace.

Fol' yo' han's an' bow yo' haid—
Wait ontwell de blessin's said;
Lawd have mussy on our souls—
Don' you daih to tech dem rolls!—
Bless de food we's gwine to eat—
You set still, I see yo' feet,
Jes' you try dat trick again—
Gin us peace an' joy—AMEN!

—Paul Laurence Dunbar.

HON. FREDERICK DOUGLASS.

DAT OL' MARE O' MINE *

WANT to trade me, do you, mistah? Oh, well,
       now I reckon not,
    Why you couldn' buy my Sukey fu' a thousan'
on de spot,
       Dat ol' mare o' mine!
Yes, huh coat ah long an' shaggy, an' she ain't no shakes
   to see;
Dat's a ring-bone, yes, you right, suh, an' she got a
   on'ry knee;
But dey ain't no use in talkin', she de only hoss fu' me,
       Dat ol' mare o' mine.

Co'se I knows dat Suke's contra'y, an' she moughty ap'
   to vex;
But you got to mek erlowance fu' de nature o' huh sex,
       Dat ol' mare o' mine.
Ef you pull huh on' de lef' han', she plum' 'termined
   to go right,
A cannon couldn' skeer huh, but she boun' to tek a
   fright
At a piece o' common paper, er anyt'ing whut's white,
       Dat ol' mare o' mine.

W'en my eyes commence to fail me, dough, I trus'es to
   huh sight,
An' she'll tote me safe an' hones' on de ve'y da'kes'
   night,
       Dat ol' mare o' mine.
Ef I whup huh, she jes' switch huh tail, and settle to
   a walk,

·* Permission, Dodd, Mead & Co.

Ef I whup huh mo' she shek huh haid, an' lak ez not
    she balk,
But huh sense ain't no ways lackin', she do evaht'ing
    but talk,
        Dat ol' mare o' mine.

But she gentle ez a lady when she know huh beau kin
    see,
An' she sholy got mo' gumption any day den you an' me,
        Dat ol' mare o' mine.
She's a leetle slow a-goin', an' she moughty ha'd to start,
But we's gittin' ol' togeddah, an' she's closah to my
    heart,
An' I doesn't reckon, mistah, dat she'd sca'cely keer
    to part,
        Dat ol' mare o' mine.

W'y I knows de time dat cidah's kin' o' muddled up
    my haid,
Ef it hadn't been fu' Sukey heah, I reckon I'd been daid,
        Dat ol' mare o' mine.
But she got me in de middle o' de road an' tuk me home,
An' she wouldn' let me wandah, ner she wouldn' let
    me roam,
Dat's de kin' o' hoss to tie to, w'en you's seed de cidah's
    foam,
        Dat ol' mare o' mine.

You kin talk erbout yo' heaven, you kin talk erbout yo'
    hell,
Dey is people, dey is hosses, dey is cattle, den dey's—
    well—
        Dat ol' mare o' mine.

She's de beatenes' t'ing dat evah struck de medders
    o' de town,
An' aldough huh haid ain't fitten fu' to weah no golden
    crown,
D'ain't a blessed way fu' Petah fu' to tu'n my Sukey
    down,
      Dat ol' mare o' mine.

                    —PAUL LAURENCE DUNBAR.

THE CASE OF CA'LINE *

A KITCHEN MONOLOGUE

THE man of the house is about to go into the dining-room when he hears voices that tell him his
wife has gone down stairs to give the "hired help"
a threatened going over. He quietly withdraws, closes
the door noiselessly behind him and listens from a safe
point of vantage.

One voice is timid and hesitating; that is his wife's.
The other is fearlessly raised; that is her majesty's, the
queen, who rules the kitchen, and from it the rest of
the house.

This is what he overhears:

"Well, Mis' Ma'tin, hit do seem lak you bent an'
boun' to be a-fin'in' fault wid me, w'en de Lawd knows
I's doin' de ve'y bes' I kin. What 'bout de brekfus'?
De steak too done an' de 'taters ain't done enough!
Now, Mis' Ma'tin, I jes' want to show you I cooked dat
steak an' dem 'taters de same leng't o' time. Seems
to me dey ought to be done de same. Dat uz a thick
steak, too, an' I jes' got it browned thoo nice. What
mo'd you want?

---

* By permission, Dodd, Mead & Co.

"You didn't want it fried at all? Now, Mis' Ma'tin, 'clah to goodness! Who evah hyeah de beat o' dat? Don't you know dat fried meat is de bes' kin' in de worl'? W'y de las' fambly dat I lived wid—dat uz ol' Jedge Johnson—he said dat I beat anybody fryin' he evah seen; said I fried evaht'ing in sight, an' he said my fried food stayed by him longah den anyt'ing he evah et. Even w'en he paid me off he said it was 'case he thought somebody else ought to have de benefit of my wunnerful powahs. Huh, ma'am, I's ust to de bes'! De Jedge paid me de highest kin' o' comperments. De las' t'ing he say to me was, 'Ca'line, Ca'line,' he say, 'yo' cookin' is a pa'dox. It is criminal, dey ain't no 'sputin' dat, but it ain't action'ble.' Co'se I didn' un'erstan' his langidge, but I knowed it was comperments, 'case his wife, Mis' Jedge Johnson, got right jealous, an' tol' him to shet his mouf.

"Dah you goes. Now, who'd a' thought dat a lady o' yo' raisin' an' un'erstan'in' would a' brung dat up. De mo'nin' you come an' ketch me settin' down, an' de brekfus' not ready, I was a-steadyin'. I's a moughty han' to steady, Mis' Ma'tin. 'Deed, I steadies mos' all de time. But dat mo'nin' I got to steadyin', an' aftah while I sot down an' all my troubles come to my min'. I sho has a heap o' trouble. I jes' sot thaih a steadyin' 'bout 'em, an' a' steadyin' tell bime-by hyeah you comes.

"No, ma'am, I wasn't 'sleep. I's mighty apt to nod w'en I's thinkin'. It's a kin' o' keepin' time to my idees. But bless yo' soul, I wasn't 'sleep. I shets my eyes so's to see to think bettah. An' aftah all, Mistah Ma'tin wa'nt mo'n a half houah late dat mo'nin' nohow, 'case w'en I did git up, I sholy flew. Ef you jes' 'membahs 'bout my steadyin', we ain't nevah gwine have no trouble long's I stays hyeah.

"You say dat one night I stayed out 'tell one o'clock? W'y—oh—yes. Dat uz Thu'sday night. Why, la! Mis' Ma'tin, dat's de night my s'ciety meets—de Af'Ame'ican Sons and Daughters of Judah. We had to 'nitiniate a new can'date dat night, an', la! I wish you'd a' been thaih, you'd a killed yo'se'f laffin'.

"You nevah did see such ca'in's on in all yo' bo'n days. It was pow'ful funny. Broth' Eph'am Davis, he's ouah Mos' Wusshipful Rabbi, he says it was de mos' s'cessful 'nitination we evah had. Dat can'date pawed de groun' lak a hoss, an' tried to git outen de windah. But I got to be mighty keerful how I talk; I do' know whethah you 'longs to any secut s'cieties er not. I wouldn' been so late, even fu' dat, but Mistah Hi'am Smif, he gallanted me home, an' you know a lady boun' to stan' at de gate an' talk to huh comp'ny a little w'ile. You know how it is, Mis' Ma'tin?

"I been en'tainin' my comp'ny in de pa'lor? Co'se I has; you wasn' usin' it. What you s'pose my frien's 'ud think ef I'd ax 'em in de kitchin, w'en dey wasn't no one in de front room? Co'se I ax 'em in de pa'lor. I do' wan't my frien's to think I's wo'kin' fu' no low down people. W'y Mis' 'Liza Harris set down an' played mos' splendid on you pianna, an' she compermented you mos' high. S'pose I'd a tuk huh in de kitchin, whaih'd de comperments come in?

"Yass'm, yass'm, I does tek home little things now an' den, dat I does, an' I ain't gwine to 'ny it. I jes' says to myse'f, I ain't wo'kin' fu' no strainers lak de people nex' do', what goes into tantrums ef de lady what cooks fu' dem teks home a bit o' sugah. I 'lows to myse'f I ain't wo'kin' fu' no sich folks; so sometimes I teks home jes' a weenchy bit o' some'p'n dat nobody couldn' want nohow, an' I knows you ain't gwine to 'ject to dat. Huh! You do 'ject? You do 'ject? Huh!

"I's got to come an' ax you, has I? Look a hyeah, Mis' Ma'tin, I knows I has to wuk in yo' kitchin'. I knows I has to cook fu' you, but I want you to know dat even ef I does, I's a lady. I's a lady, but I see you do' know how to 'preciate a lady w'en you meets one. You kin jes' light in an' git yo' own dinnah. I wouldn' wo'k fu' you ef you was made o' gol'. I never did lak to wuk fu' strainers, nohow.

"No, ma'am, I cain't even stay an' git dinnah. I knows w'en I been insulted. Seems lak ef I stay in dis hyeah kitchin anothah minute I'll bile all over de flo'.

"Who excited? Me excited? No, I ain't excited; I's mad. I do' lak nobody pesterin' 'round my kitchin, nohow, huh, uh, honey. Too many places in dis town waitin' fu' Ca'line Mason.

"No, indeed, you needn' 'pologize to me! Needn' 'pologize to me! I b'lieve in people sayin' jes' what dey means, I does.

"Would I stay ef you 'crease my wages? Well—I reckon I could, but—I—but I do' want no foolishness.

(Sola) "Huh! Did she think she was gwine to come down hyeah an' skeer me, huh, uh? Whaih's dat fryin' pan?"

The man of the house hears the rustle of his wife's skirts as she beats a hasty retreat, and he goes upstairs and into the library whistling, "See, the Conquering Hero Comes."

—Paul Laurence Dunbar.

SAMBO'S RIGHT TO BE KILT

SOME tell us 'tis a burnin' shame
      To make the naygurs fight;
   An' that the thrade of bein' kilt
   Belongs but to the white:
But as for me, upon my sowl!
   So liberal are we here,
I'll let Sambo be murthered instead of myself,
   On every day in the year.

On every day in the year, boys,
   An' in every hour of the day,
The right to be kilt, I'll divide wid him,
   An's divil's a word I'll say.

In battle's wild commotion
   I shouldn't at all object
If Sambo's body should stop a ball
   That was comin' for me direct;
An' the prod of a Southern bagnet,
   So ginerous are we here,
I'll resign an' let Sambo take it
   On every day in the year.

On every day of the year, boys,
   And wid none o' your nasty pride,
All my right in a Southern bagnet prod
   Wid Sambo I'll divide!

The men who object to Sambo
   Should take up his place and fight;
And it's better to have a naygur's hue
   Than a liver that's wake and white.

"The right to be kilt we'll divide with him
And give him the largest half."

Though Sambo's black as the ace of spades,
    His finger a thrigger can pull,
And his eye runs straight on the barrel-sights
    From under its thatch of wool.

So hear me all, boys darlin',
    Don't think I'm tippin' you chaff,
The right to be kilt we'll divide wid him,
    And give him the largest half.

—PRIVATE MILES O'REILLY.

AN EASTER SYMBOL *

A Monologue of the Plantation

Speaker—A black girl. *Time*—Easter morning.

SCUSE me knockin' at yo' do' so early, Miss Bettie, but I'se in trouble. Don't set up in bed. Jes' lay still and lemme talk to yer. I come to ax yer to please, ma'am, loand me a pair o' wings, mistus. No'm, I ain't crazy. I mean what I say.

You see, today's Easter Sunday, Miss Bettie, an' we havin' a high time in our church. An' I'se gwine sing de special Easter carol wid Freckled Frances an' Lame Jake jinin' in de chorus in our choir. Hit's one o' deze hyeah visible choirs sot up nex' to de pulpit in front o' de congergation.

Of co'se me singin' de high solo makes me de principulest figger, so we 'ranged fur me to stan' in de middle wid Frances an' Jake on right an' lef' sides, an' I got a bran' new white tarlton frock wid spangles on it, an' a Easter lily wreaf all ready. Of co'se me bein' de fust singer dat entitles me to wear de highest plumage, an' Frances she knows dat, an' she 'lowed to me she was gwine wear dat white nainsook lawn you gin' 'er, an' des a plain secondary hat, an' at de 'p'in time we all three got to rise and courtesy to de congergation, an' den bu'st into song. Lame Jake gwine wear dat white duck suit o' Marse John's, an' a Easter lily in his button hole.

Well, hit was all fixed dat-away, peaceable an' propah, but you know de trouble is, Freckled Frances

---
* By permission, Harper Brothers.

is jealous-hearted, an' she ain't got no principle. I tell you, Miss Bettie, when niggers gits white ꞓnough to freckle, look out fu' 'em!

An' Frances—? She ain't got no mo' principle den a suck-aig dorg! Evah sence we 'ranged dat Easter program, she been studyin' up some owdacious way to outdo me in de face of eve'ybody!

But I'm jes' one too many fur any yaller, freckled-faced gal. I'm black, but dey's a heap o' trouble come out o' ink-bottles befo' today!

I done had my eye on Frances! An' fu' de las' endurin' week I taken notice ev'ry time we had a choir practicin', Frances she'd fetch in some talk about butterflies bein' a Easter sign o' de resurrection o' de daid, an' all sech as dat. Well, I know Frances don' keer no mo' 'bout de resurrection ob de daid'n nothin'. Frances is too tuk up wid dis life fur dat! So I watched her. An' las' night I ketched up wid 'er.

You know dat great big silk paper butterfly dat you had on yo' pianner lamp, Miss Bettie? She's got it pyerched up on a wire on top o' dat secondary hat, an' she's a-fixin' it to wear to chu'ch today. But she don't know I know it. You see, she knows I kin sing all over her, an' dat's huccome she's a projectin' to ketch de eyes o' de congergation!

But ef you'll he'p me out, Miss Bettie, we'll fix 'er. You know dem yaller, gauzy wings you wo' in de tableaux? Ef you'll loand 'em to me, 'an he'p me on wid dem terreckly when I'm dressed, I'll be a *whole live butterfly,* an' I bet yer when I flutters into dat choir Freckled Frances'll feel like snatchin' dat lamp shade off her hat, sho's yer born! An' fur once I'm proud I'm so black-complected, caze black an' yaller, dey goes togedder fur butterflies!

PRINCIPAL WASHINGTON IN HIS PRIVATE OFFICE, TUSKEGEE INSTITUTE.

Frances 'lowed to kill me out today, but I lay, when she sets eyes on de yaller-winged butterfly, she'll 'preciate de resurrection o' de daid ef she never done it befo' in her life!

—RUTH McENERY STUART.

THE FUNAL OF BRUH TONY SMIFF

OR

DE KNIGHTS OF DE RISIN' STAIAH

DE lage will come to audah, please; bruh Isham, tek yo' seat,
    Les git down to de business fyahs fuh which we's call to meet.
Sis Calaway, you'n sis Jones stop walkin' cross de flo';
Bruh Love, put on yo' galia 'n tek yo' station at de do'.

Pull down de windah shade an' shet de blin', bruh Bass,
Go round de lage, bruh wahden, an' guthah up de pass.

Mos' wuthiful, sis Calaway, sis Monroe'n sis Bird,
Bruh Isham an bruh Debumpote, dey done fuhgit de word.

Dose knights an' ladies kin remain an' 'ceive de pass wid pleagah,
Jes so dey comes up to de des' and puts a quatah in de treagah.

Es we's in soht o' hurry, we'll omit de openin' prayah;
Les ev'ybody stan' an' sing "All hail de risin' staiah."

(Italian Hymn.)

All hail de risin' staiah,
Dat sheds o'er earth afaiah
Its gladd'nin' rays;
Dispellin' gloom an' fyull,
Dispensin' light and chuh,
An' guidin' eveh nyuh
Thoo all ouah ways.*

Sis Secahtery, git yo' book an' fetch it to de light,
An' let us hyuh de minutes of de meeting 'tothah night.

"De lage wus call' to audah'n led in prayah by bruthah
Boad;
De pass was took, de minutes read, and den de openin'
ode.
De dues was den collected, and de fines de membahs
yuhn,
An' den we scuss an move an' fuss ontel de meetin'
juhn."

Membahs, you's got de minutes fum de secahtery's
han's,
Ef dere is no objection, we'll approve 'em as dey stan's.

De minutes bein' approve', hit is my solum tas' to say
Dat deaf have come into de lage an' cyahed bruh Smiff
away.

Dis meetin's call' in audah to mek de pepahration
To give de funal of bruh Smiff a propah cellarbration.
Brothahs an' sistahs, 'member whut we's always done
befo'—
Set still dar, bruh Uriah, sis Malindy have de flo'.

* Rap.

PLEADING

"I moves dat fifty carriage be hiahed fuh de rout,
An' ev'y member foun' a dollah dat 'fuses to tu'n out."
You's hyuhd de motion, membahs, bruh vice, how stan's
    de vote?
"Carried, wuthiful." I recognizes brothah Choate.

"Mos' wuthiful, I meks a move,
In 'sideration of ouah love,
Dat twenty dollahs be propahrate,
Bruh Tony's grave to decorate."

Brothahs an' sistahs, you's hyuhd de move
Fuh twenty dollars' wuth o' love.
Es many's has a simlah min'
Will show it by de reglah sign.

How stan's de vote, bruh wuthy vice?
I could 'a had it counted twice.
"Carried." Hol' on dah, sistah Day,
Sis Voluntime, what you wan' say?

"Mos' wuthiful, you's gwine too fas';
I hails dat motion 'fo it pass.
A 'portant 'quiry you has miss,
An' my onreadiness is dis:"

"A hundud dollahs is de tax
We pays de liv'ry man fuh hacks.
Now, twenty mo' you wants for flowahs,
Dat ain' gwine las' as many houahs."

"Dese hack-parades an' flowahs an' sich,
Does mighty well fuh folks dat's rich;
But all dem purty flowahs gwine die
Before de widdah's tyuhs is dry."

"Ef it was me, I'd ruthah have
A tombstone planted at my grave.
'Twould inacate yo' love mo' strongah,
An' he'p as much an' las' me longah."

"Es fuh de hacks, you hear me talk!
I moves dat ev'y member walk,
An' put dat money in a pus
To pay de doctah an' de nus."

"Dis pyuhs a 'normous 'mount to pay
For sentament an' vain display,
When fohty dollahs ben'fits
Is all de wife an' chillun gits."

Sistah, you's out o' audah, one dollah you is foun'.
Bruh treagah, lec dat money; sis cluk, you put it down.
We gwine spec bruh Tony's mem'ry—come to audah
    dah, bruh Nat,
Dis lage ain' gwine listen to no sich foolishness es dat.

Dese is de lage's audahs: Fifty hacks will fohm de line,
An' ev'y absen' membah pays to de lage a dollah fine.
Twenty dollahs fum the treagah goes to buy a flowah
    bade;
Dis is de spec we gwine to tribute to de mem'ry of
    de dade.

"Mos' wuthiful," sis Voluntime: "I wants to ax a ques-
    tion;
De funal 'rangements has been made, now whut is de
    suhgestion
De lage is gwine to offah 'bout de widah an' de chillun?
She owes de undahtakah an' de nus an' Doctah Dillon."

"You knows de fam'ly's succumstance, how bad dey's
    off fo' close,
An' ef de rent ain' paid de man gwine put 'em out o'
    dohs.
Dough hit ain' much, we magines jes de' mount o' good
    'twould do huh
Ef sistah Smiff could git in hand de fohty dollahs comin'
    to huh."

Sis Voluntime, I foun you once, dis time I fines you wus;
Dat question dat you's talkin' 'bout dis lage wan' call'
    to scuss.
De time have come to close de lage. Dismiss us,
    brothah Boad.
Hol' on! dat sistah come nigh mekin' me fuhgit de
    closin' ode.

(America.)

      Knights of de Risin' Staiah,
      May we be known afaiah
        As frien's indeed;
      Who wipes de widah's eye,
      An' stops de auphan's cry,
      An' succah ne'er deny
        To dose who need.

Sis secahtery, read de minutes of de business we has
    done,
An' den we'll close. 'Tis uhly yit, jes' sebumteen to one.

"De lage was call' to audah wid de mastah in de chair;
We read de minutes, sung de ode, and mit de openin'
    prayah,

We lec de dues an' sess de fines an' make de propahra-
tion
To give de funal of bruh Smiff a propah cellabration."

De minutes pyuhs to be cohrec. Broh Love, blow out
de light.
De lage is now adjuhn to meet agin naks Chusday night.

—JOHN RILEY DUNGEE.

TUNK *

A LECTURE ON MODERN EDUCATION

LOOK heah, Tunk!—now ain't it awful! T'ought I
sont you off to school.
Don't you know dat you is growin' up to be a
reglah fool?
Whah's dem books dat I's done bought you? Look
heah, boy, you tell me quick,
Whah's dat Webster blue-back spellah an' dat bran'
new 'rifmatic?
W'ile I'm t'inkin' you is lahnin' in de school, why bless
ma soul!
You off in de woods a-playin'. Can't you do like you
is tole?
Boy, I tell you, it's jes' scan'lous d'way dat you is
goin' on;
An' you sholy go'n be sorry, jes' as true as you is bo'n.
Heah I'm tryin' hard to raise you as a credit to dis race,
An' you tryin' heap much harder fu' to come up in
disgrace.
Dese de days w'en men don't git up to de top by hooks
an' crooks,

* Reprinted from the New York *Independent,* by permission of J.
W. Johnson.

"Tunk."

Tell you now, dey's got to git der standin' on a pile
o' books.

W'en you sees a dahky goin' to de fiel as soon as light,
Followin' a mule across it f'om de mawnin' tel de night,
Wukin' all his life fu' vittles, hoein' 'tween de cott'n
rows,
W'en he knocks off ole an' tiah'd, ownin' nut'n but his
clo'es,
You kin put it down to ignunce, aftah all what's done
an' said,

You kin bet dat dat same dahky ain't got nut'n' in his
  head.
Ain't you seed dem w'ite men set'n' in der awfice?
  Don't you know
Dey goes dere 'bout nine each mawnin'? Bless yo' soul,
  dey's out by fo'.
Dey jes' does a little writin'; does dat by some easy
  means;
Gals jes' set an' play pianah on dem printin'-press
  muchines.
Chile, dem men knows how to figgah, how to use dat
  little pen,
An' dey knows dat blue-back spellah f'om beginnin' to
  de en'.
Dat's de 'fect of education; dat's de t'ing what's gwine
  to rule;
Git dem books, you lazy rascal! Git back to yo' place
  in school.

—JAMES WELDON JOHNSON.

UNCLE IKE'S ROOSTERS

A Story with a Moral

L AS' Sunday while I'se settin' on de bench beside de
do,'
An' feelin' sort o' chilly 'case de sun was gettin'
low,
An' wishin' dat de winter time wa'nt comin' on so fas',
Fo' I pint'ly hates de cuttin' ob a Janewary blas';
I knows de one what's comin', too, is gwine to be
stingin' col',
'Kase de 'simmon trees is hangin' jes' as full as dey
kin hol'.
De pigs is 'gun dey squealin' when de keen win' cut
'em so,
An' de wil' geese, lak dey betters, all is flyin' "Westward
ho!"
I was studyin' 'bout dem ar signs, as 'pon de bench I sot;
When I see my two young roosters come a-struttin' crost
de lot;
Dey was showin' off der elegance, an' dandyfyin' ways,
Jus' lak me an' my ol' mars'r used to do in co'tin' days;
De maskelines is all alike, whareeber dey is foun',
Dey all will strut an' show deyse'f, w'en hens is knockin'
'roun.
One rooster, he was black like, wid some red erpon
he wing;
Rare ol' Virginny game stock, dat kin beat mos' any-
thing.
T'other one was game, too, ob de bery selfsame breed,
Dey was bofe de same hen's chickens, an' was raised
erpon one feed.

De las' one was de han'somest, he had a golden bre's',
An' he nake an' back was yaller, lak Melindy's Sun-
day dress.
I know jes' f'om de minute dem two roosters come in
sight,
Dat bofe of 'em was longin' an a-spilin' fer a fight.
Dey crowed at one ernudder, an' dey wall up bofe dey
eyes,
Jes' de same ez politicians, w'en de 'citement 'gin to rise.
Dey was bristlin' an' a-sparrin' out dar in de open
space,
W'en a big ol' 'baccer-worrum come a trabblin' by in
haste,
Like he had a heap o' business for de public on he's
min',
Or was runnin' for an office, wid his 'ponent clost behin'.
No matter what he business was, dem roosters spied
him out,
An' bofe pounce down erpon him wid a crowin' sort
o' shout;
Der bills hit up tergedder 'pon de 'baccer-worrum's
back,
An' dey butt 'gin one ernudder wid a mighty yearnest
whack.
Bofe let go de worrum in dey anger an' surprise,
An' stared at one ernudder wid der fury-flashin' eyes.
Den dey buckled to de business lak der min' was set
at res',
Dey was fightin' fer a "principle" an' boun' to do der
bes'.
Each knowed der worrum was his'n, an' de odder was
a thief,
An' greedy, an' rapacious, too, an' mean beyon' belief:

Each thought der odder's sassiness was pas' all stan'in',
too;
(An' den de hens was watchin' fer to see der fightin'
fru.)
Dey fit an' fit ontwill der blood was runnin' f'om der
head,
An' I thought I'd had to pa't 'em, 'fo' dey kill one
nudder dead.
I had jes' got up to do it when I seed de big black hen
Jes' a gobblin' up de worrum dat had made de fuss
begin.
I bus' right out a-larfin' as I grab dem chickens' leg,
An' tu'n two boxes ober dem to cool 'em down a peg;
Hit seem so awful foolish lak fo' dem to fight an'
squirm,
An' dat ol' hen come walkin' 'long an' gobble up der
worrum.

—ANONYMOUS.

BOOK III.
Selections in Dialect
(Serious)

A LITTLE CHRISTMAS BASKET *

DE win's hollerin' "Daih you!" to de shuttahs an'
      de fiah,
      De snow's a sayin' "Got you!" to de groun';
Fu' de wintah weddah's comin' widout a-askin' ouah
      desiah,
      An' he's laughin' in his sleeve at whut he foun';
Fu' dey ain't nobody ready wid dey fuel er dey food,
      An' de money-bag look timid lak fu' sho',
So we want ouah Christmas sermon, but we'd lak it
      ef you could
      Leave a little Christmas basket at de do'.
Whut's de use o' tellin' chillen 'bout a Santy er a Nick,
      An' de sto'ies dat a body allus tol'?
W'en de harf is gray wid ashes, an' you hasn't got a
      stick
      Fu' to wa'm dey little toes w'en dey is col'?
Whut's de use o' preachin' ligion to a man dat's sta'ved
      to def,
      An' a tellin' him de Mastah will pu'vide?
Ef you want to tech his feelin's, save yo' sermons an'
      yo' bref,
      Take a little Christmas basket by youah side.
                                   —PAUL LAURENCE DUNBAR.

* Permission, Dodd, Mead & Co.

W'EN DEY 'LISTED COLORED SOLDIERS *

DEY was talkin' in de cabin, dey was talkin' in de hall,
But I listened kind o' keerless, not a-t'inkin' 'bout it all,
An' on Sunday, too, I noticed, dey was whisperin' mighty much,
Stan'in' all erroun' de roadside, w'en dey let us out o' chu'ch.
But I didn't t'ink erbout it, 'twell de middle of de week,
An' my 'Lias come to see me, an' somehow he couldn' speak,
Den I seed all in a minute whut he'd come to see me fu',
Dey had 'listed colored soldiers, an' my 'Lias gwine to wah.

Oh, I hugged him an' I kissed him, an' I baiged him not to go,
But he tol' me dat his conscience it was callin' to him so,
An' he couldn't baih to lingah w'en he had a chanst to fight,
Fu' de freedom dey had gin him, an' de glory of de right.
So he kissed me, an' he lef' me, w'en I'd p'omised to be true,
An' dey put a knapsack on him, an' a coat all colo'ed blue,
So I gin him Pap's ol' Bible f'om de bottom of de draw—
W'en dey 'listed colo'ed sojers an' my 'Lias went to wah.

But I t'ought of all de weary miles dat he would have to tramp,

* Permission, Dodd, Mead & Co.

"W'en Dey 'Listed Colored Soldiers."

An' I couldn' be contented w'en dey tuk him to de camp.
W'y my hea't nigh broke wid grievin' 'twell I seed him
    on de street,
Den I felt lak I could go an' th'ow my body at his feet.
Fu' his buttons was a shinin' an' his face was shinin' too,
An' he looked so strong an' mighty in his coat of sojer
    blue,
Dat I hollahed, "Step up, manny!" do' my tho'at was
    so' an' raw,
W'en dey 'listed colo'ed sojers an' my 'Lias went to wah.

Ol' mis' cried w'en Mastah lef' heh, young Miss mou'ned
her brothah Ned,
An' I didn't know dey feelin's is de ve'y wo'ds dey said
W'en I tol' 'em I was so'y. Dey had done gin up dey all;
But dey only seemed mo' proudah dat dey men had
hyeahed de call.
Bofe my mastahs went in gray suits, but I loved de
Yankee blue,
But I t'ought dat I could sorrer fu' de losin' of 'em too;
But I couldn' fu' I didn' know de half of whut I saw,
Twell dey 'listed colo'ed sojers an' my 'Lias went to
wah.

Mastah Jack come home all sickly; he was broke fu'
life, dey said,
An' dey lef' my po' young mastah some'r's on de road-
side—dead.
W'en de women cried an' mou'ned 'em, I could feel it
thoo an' thoo,
Fu' I had a loved one fightin' in de way o' dangah, too.
Den dey tol' me dey had laid him some'r's way down
souf to res',
Wid de flag dat he had fit fu' shinin' daih acrost his
breast.
Well, I cried, but den, I reckon, dat's whut God had
called him fu',
W'en dey 'listed colo'ed sojers an' my 'Lias went to wah.

—Paul Laurence Dunbar.

SUPPLICATION

THE PRALINE WOMAN

THE praline woman sits by the side of the archbishop's quaint, little old chapel on Royal Street in New Orleans, and slowly waves her latanier fan over her pink and brown wares.

"Pralines? Pralines? Ah, ma'amzelle, you buy? S'il vous plait, ma'amzelle, dey be fine, ver' fresh. Sho chile, ma bébé, she put dese up hissef. He's han's so small, ma'amzelle, lak you's, mais brune. She put dese up dis morn. You tak none? No husband fo' you den.

"Ah, ma petite, you tak? Cinq sous, bébé, may le bon dieu keep you good!

"Mais oui, madame, I know you étranger. You don' look lak dese New Orleans peop'. You lak dose Yankee come down 'fo' de war.

"Praline, madame? You buy lak dat? Dix sous, madame, an' one li'l piece fo' lagniappe, fo' madame's li'l bebe. Ah, c'est bon!

"Pralines? Pralines? So fresh, so fine! M'sieu would lak some fo' he's li'l gal at home? Mais non, what's dat you say? She's daid? Ah, m'sieu, 'tis my li'l gal what died long time ago. Misere, misere!

"Her' come dat lazy Indian squaw. What she good fo' anyhow? She jes' sit lak dat in de French market an' sell her filé, an' sleep, sleep, sleep, lak so in he's blanket. Hey, dere, Tonita! How goes yo' lazy beezness?

"Pralines? Pralines? Holy Father, you give me dat blessin' sho'? Tak' one, I know you lak dat white one. It tas' good, I know, bien.

5

"Pralines, madame? I lak yo' face. What fo' you wear black? You' li'l boy daid? You tak' one, jes' see how it tas'. I had one li'l boy once, he jes' grow twel he's big lak dis, den one day he tek sick an' die. Oh, madame, it mos' brek my po' heart. I bu'n candle in St. Rocque, I say my beads, I sprinkle holy water roun' he's bed; he jes' lay so; he's eyes tu'n up, he say 'Maman! Maman!' den he die! Madame, you tek one, no l'argent. You tek one fo' my li'l boy's sake.

"Praline, pralines, m'sieu? Who mek dese? My li'l gal, Didele, o' cose. Non, non, I don' mek no mo'. Po' Tante Marie get too ol'. She's one li'l gal, I 'dopt. I see her one day in de strit. He walk so; hit col', she shiver, an' I say, 'Wher' you gone, li'l gal?' an' he can' tell. He jes' crip close to me an' cry so! Den I tek her home wid me, an' she say he's name Didele. You see, dey wa'nt nobody dere. My li'l gal, she's daid o' de yellow fever; my li'l boy he's daid; po' Tante Marie all alone. Didele, she grow fine; she keep house, she mek praline. Den, w'en night come, she sit wid he's guitar an' sing:

'Tu l'aime ces trois jours,
Tu l'aime ces trois jours,
　Ma coeur à toi,
　Ma coeur à toi,
Tu l'aime ces trois jours!'

"Ah, he's fine gal, is Didele!

"Pralines? Pralines? Dat li'l cloud, hit look lak rain. I hope no.

"Here come dat lazy l'ishman down de strit. I don' lak l'ishman, me non. Dey so fonny. One day one l'ishman he say to me, 'Auntie, what fo' you talk so?' An' I jes' say back, 'What fo' you say faith an bejabers?' Non, I don' lak l'ishman, me!

"Here come de rain. Now I got fo' to go. Didele,
she be wait fo' me. Down hit come. Hit fall in de
Meesesip an' fill up—up—so, clean to de levee, den we
have big crivasse, an' po' Tante Marie float away. Bon
jour, madame. You come again. Pralines? Pralines?"

—ALICE RUTH MOORE.

MAMMY CLARISSA'S VENGEANCE *

WAL, Mi's Is'bel, I come heah fo' call tu yo' 'membrance de days long back in de fore time.
Yas'm, fust come de days when we war gals.
Yo' 'membah dat time yo' paw sol' me to mars'r gen'l's
gran'paw, an' took he's fambly an' my maw off to de
saouf islands whar he come f'om—Mexico or New
Awleans, some'ers daoun dat-a-way? I min' how I
cried an' took on fo' my maw. I min' how you push
me off'n her 'nd say, "G'long, yo' niggah, dis yers my
mammy," 'nd clim' on her knee 'nd mars stan'nin' by
an' laughin'. I min' how she sail off in de boat 'long
o' yo'n, yo' paw an' maw a-leanin' ova' dat side railin'
an' callin' fo' me an' yo' a pullin' on her dress; I
min' dat. Dat ar' de las' time I evah see my maw.

Dat fambly yo' paw done sol' me to, dat war de ol'
Ma'shall fambly. Ol' Mis' Ma'shall fotch me up right
smaht tu du de fine stitchin' 'nd clar sta'chin,' 'nd i'nin',
an' ova-seein' de linen, an' lookin' aftah de young 'uns,
an' larnin' 'em to wo'k. I nuvva woah nuffin but silk
turb'n dem days, yas'm, 'nd white dress I allus woah
tu.

* * * * * * *

Yas'm, I war thinkin' on dem days. I mind de time

* From "When the Gates Lift Up Their Heads." By permission,
Little, Brown and Company.

young Mars'r John come dar too; I mind dat. Dey wan' no young man nowhar look like he look, so tall an' straight an' han'some in he's so'ger clo'es w'en he come down to visit he's gran'paw. W'en he git mad hit war lak de sto'm claoud rise out'n de sea; an' w'en he smile, yas'm, hit war lak de sun rise up in de mo'nin'. I min' he had twin brudder, tu. He didn' go fu' tu be no so'ger. He wen' up to de No'f schule some'ers, 'nd he fall in lub an' mahy Yankee gal up yandah. I reckon dey war mad. I heah'd 'em say he lub de Yanks dat bad he mout' stay right dar an' bed an' bo'd wid 'em, an' I nuvva see him no mo'.

I min' de time young Mars'r John's fadah, he took sick an' die, 'nd one yar mo' 'nd he's gran'fadah he die tu, 'nd jes' one week f'om dat time ol' grandmiz, she die tu, lak she couldn' lib widout her ol' man—'nd dar we-all wuz sol'. Young Mars'r John, he in de Wes' Point schule, he didn' know nuffin' 'bouts we being sol'. One o' dese yer trader men come 'long 'n' he tuck me. I war mighty skeered o' him. He nuvva hu't me, naw'm, but all de same I couldn' bide tu see him nigh me noh tech me.

He tuk we-all to moughty gran' place, an' dar he come long one day an' he say, "Cl'issy, yo' right peart gal. What-all fo' clo'es you got in dat bun'l?" An' dar he tuk up fine silk headkercher ol' missus done gib me, an' de gol' beads young Mars'r John done gib me, an' a white dress an' gol' pin—young Mars'r John done gib me dat, tu—an' he say, "Wa'r dese. I want you to look fine an' peart." An' I say "Yas'r." 'N' he say "Put 'em on," an' I say, "Yas'r." An' he holla, "Put' em on!" An' I say "Yas'r." 'N' he holla 'gin, "Put 'em on!" 'N' I say "Yas'r," 'gin, 'n' nuvva stir. Den he holla 'gin, 'nd I say "Yo' take yo'se'f whar you b'long 'n' I'll put 'em on."

Den he lif' he's han' lak he gwine hit ha'd, den he laff 'n' say, 'Yo' done got de debbil in you.'" 'Nd I say "Yes'r, 'nd yo' done put 'im dar, tu."

Den I put on de clo'es an' all de oddah niggahs stan'in' roun' in de drove—men, women an' chillun. But I put 'em on, fo' I knowed I'd be killed ef I didn'. Den he tuk me out to de block an' he say, "Git up dar," he say. An' I git up an' look roun' an' dar I see all de man faces lookin' up at me all ova de squar' an' all ova de sidewalkses, an' dar dey point wid de cane. Den one say, "She got a heap o' temper, I reckon." An' trader man he say, "She mil' as a lam'." Den nurrer man say, "She got de berry debbil in 'er eye." An' he say, "She hab de spi'it ob an angel an' she kin sing yo's to sleep lak she bohned a mocker." Den dey all laff an' I feel lak I gwine fall down off'n dat place. Den all 'er a suddent I see young Mars'r John yandah in de crowd, in he's so'ger clo'es wid he's shinin' face, lak he jes' come down f'om heaben, 'an I hol' out my ahms an' try fu' to call 'im; but I couldn' make no soun'. Naw'm. But I see 'im push he's way t'rough all dem rats dar, nigh head taller'n all on 'em, yas'm, an' I see 'im hol' up he's han' an' I see all de faces swimmin' roun' an' de block slip out f'om under my feet like, an' I didn' see no mo' ontwell I heah 'im sayin', "Wake up, Cl'issy. Dey ain' gwine sell yo' no mo'. I done pay de money fo' yo' an' I gwine tek yo' home wid me. Jes' you folla me." I'd a folla'd 'im ef he'd 'a 'axed me tu walk intu de fiah. I'd 'a folla'd 'im ontwell I couldn' walk no mo', an' jes' fall down daid at he's feet 'fo' 'im, yas'm. Dat ar hu-cum de Mars'r Gen'l buy me an' tuk me home. Ol' miz, she rose me mighty kin' an' sof' like. I nuvva didn' look tu' be sol' like common niggah trash off'n de block, naw'm.

Yas'm, wal'm, hit war dat-a-way he tuk me home, an' I tuk keer on he's maw. She war sof' an' gentle like she wait'n' fo' de angels to come an' fotch her tu heaben. Likely dat all she wait'n' fu'. She lie dar one day an' jes' pass like a bref come an' blow her soul 'way, an' dar dey wan' no one lef' but jes' young Mars'r Gen'l an' me, an' a lot o' young trash niggahs wha' I look aftah an' l'arn fo' tu keep de haouse fo' 'im. Young Mars'r Gen'l he grieve he'se'f, I min' dat. Long while he grieve. He go heah an' he go dar, an' eve'y time he come home 'gin he say, "Cl'issy, dis yer's de bes' place aftah all." Aftah while he brung home de ol' haouse ful o' he's frien's. He jes' say, "Cl'issy, git de rooms ready," an' I du hit, an' cook de chicken pie, an' de hot biscuit, an' dar de happy days begin. Nigh on tu five y'ar he go on dat-away; I war right happy den, yas'm, right happy. One day 'come 'long big crowd f'om Wash'n'ton. I min' yo' 'long dat time. I don' know whar he met up wid yo', but dar yo' come wid yo' maids an' yoah gran' clo'es shinin' wid de silk an' de gol', an' yo' walk de haouse like yo' done bohned dar—yes'm—de same little Miz Is'bel wha' done push me off'n my own maw. I knowed you done come fo' tek young Mars'r Gen'l f'om me, tu. Now jes' yo' bide still dar. I ain' come fo' no hu't. I come heah fo' tu bring yo' min' back tu de 'membrance o' de pas', an' yo' gwine set still dar an' hark.

W'en dat crowd go, Mars'r John he mighty res'less. One day he walk de flo' up an' down, up an' down, den he come out on de po'ch whar I set sewin' an' harkin' tu him pace de room, an' he say, "C'lissy, yo' allus been mighty good; yo' been good tu my maw." An' I say, "Yes, Mars'r John." Den he say, "Hit's time I's marr'd 'nd raise up my fadah's house. I gwine bring home heah a mistus, Cl'issy." An' I say, "Yas, yas, Mars'r John." Den he say, "Yo' gwine to be good to her, Cl'issy?" An' I say, "Yes, Mars'r John, I gwine du all yo' ax me. Ef yo' ax me tu walk intu de fiah, I du hit."

Den he come nigh me an' he put he's han' under my chin an' lif' up my haid an' say, "Cl'issy, I b'lieve yo'." An' he kiss my fo'haid an' go off. Den I go tu my own room an' dar I lie on de flo' an' ax de Lawd tek de ha't out'n me an' leab me die an' go tu ol' mistis, but He didn' du hit, naw'm, he done leab me heah yit. When Mars'r John come back he fotch yo' wid 'im, an' dar come 'long lot o' yo' own folkses, tu—gran' an' fine, an' sof' speakin' like yo' own se'f. I couldn' un'erstan' how dey speak, neider. Hit mighty strange talk dey done use. I reckon yo' 'membahs dat time, tu, Miz Is'bel—yas, I reckon so. Yo' mighty fine fu' awhile, den yo' tek de bit in yo' teef an' dar yo' go. Yo' min' de days Mars'r Gen'l go to Wash'ton? Yo' min' how yo' run de place, Miz Is'bel? Yas, I reckon so. Don' yo' go fo' to git 'sited. I jes' gwine tell yo' de troof, den I gwine quit.

Look-a-heah, yo' min' de time yo' beat me an' sta've me? Yo' min' de time yo' git ol' Pete to lay on de lash tu me? Yo' min' dat? An' w'y fo' yo' done hit? Look-a-heah? Yas'm, hit dar as of ol' time. Dar de blood-stain yit. Yo' 'membah dat time yo' tu'n on me an' cut me wid Mars'r John's hunt'n' knife? Heah's de skyah 'crost my ahm yit, an' at de jedgment day dat skyah gwine shine in yo' eyes. I min' de time yo' cut dat skyah an' push me in dat closet dah an' lock de do'. I min' lyin' dar wid de blood flowin' an' hyar'n' yo' walkin' roun' in de room, singin' sof' an' low like nuffin' didn' trouble yo' none; an' dar yo' lef' me all night 'n' no watah tu drink 'n' nuffin' to eat, 'n' no one tu he'p.

Dar de bloodstain on dat flo' yit. Hit ain' nuvva come off, an' hit nuvva will come off, 'dout fiah bu'n hit.

Set yo'se'f still dar ontwell yo' heah de res'. Nex' day yo' done de same—yo' heah me groan an' call fo' one drap o' watah. You nuvva onlock de do' an' de nex' day yo' go 'way wid de key in yo' pocket, an' I try fo' to call, but didn' hab no strenk. I 'low yo' didn' reckon Mars'r John com'n' home dat day, but he come; yas'm, he come an' call yo' an' Ca'line she tell 'im Miz Is'bel done gone ova tu Miz Cun'l Wells fo' de day. An' he come in heah an' set down, an' I mek out fo' to speak he's name, an' he try de do'. Den he call, "Ca'line, hu-come dis do' lock? Wha's de key?" An' she say, "I do' know, Mars'r Gen'l." Den Mars'r John he know dar some'p'n bad duin's, an' he brek de doah an' tek me up in he's ahms an' tote me tu' my baid an' lay me dar an' brung watah an' keer fu' me de whole day, ontwell night come, an' he say ovah an' ovah, "Cl'issy, she shall pay fo' dis." Yas'm, dat what he say. I kin 'membah dat.

Naw yo' doan move ner speak neider. Yo' set yo'se'f dar an' hark. Ca'line, ol' Alexander's wife, she kin 'member tu, an' mo' I reckon. I do' know what-all Mars'r done say tu yo', but yo' nuvva tech me 'gin. Naw'm. I min' dem days how I done de fine stitchin' fu' you', wha' ol' Miz Ma'shall l'arn me tu du. All de long, sof' fine clo'es fo' yo' baby I done de stitchin' on dem. Yas'm, an' I min' how—wen de day war done, an yo' couldn' task me no mo,' w'ile yo' lay sleepin' 'long side Mars'r John I uset to sit by de can'l' light an' sew de co'se white cloff ontwell de daylight streak de sky in de mawnin'. Yas'm, de time pass slow wid de days a-servin', an' de nights cryin', ontwell yo' 'low I gwine spile my eyes fo' de fine stitchin' an' you gwine sell me off Saouth C'liny way.

I min' de night, tu, yas'm, I min' hit w'en my baby come. Ol' Aunt Betsy, f'om Cun'l Wellses, she war by me troo de bitterness an' de darkness an' de heavy-heartedness, an' fo' daylight she done lef' me dar wid my own li'l chile in my ahms, an' I lie in de dark time an' pray de Lawd tek 'im out 'n' de worl' an' tek me wid 'im; but He didn' nuvva hearn me, naw'm, he lef' me dar an' de chile, tu. W'en de mawnin' come I lif' up de kiver an' look at my chile lyin' dar in my ahms, an' I see a angel f'om heaben. I see w'y de Lawd wouldn' tek 'im long back agin, 'case he jes' been dar wid he's sof' skin an' fa'r ha'r like de sun done tech hit, an' w'en he open he's gret eyes dar dey shine wid de blue in 'em, yas'm, an' I cry out in my h'a't an' kiver 'im up an' hol' 'im clost. O Lawd, O Lawd! I min' dat time. I reckon yo' don' 'membah dat, naw'm.

I min' I lie dar an' shet my eyes 'gin, an' 'long 'bout sun-up de do' open mighty ha'd an' suddent like, an' dar come ol' Mars'r Doctor wid de bun'l in he's ahms, an' he lay hit 'long side me an' he say, "Cl'issy, heah's yo' missus' baby. Yo' tek right smaht keer on hit now." An' he stomp off 'gin an' shet de do' ha'd, an' I hyearn 'im stompin' down de hall. Den I lif' myse'f up an' open de bun'l', an' dar, jes' wrop in a clof like an' roll in de blanket, lie yo' baby. Yas'm, yo' baby, sho 'nuff, wid de dark skin an' de black sof' ha'r, like all yo' folkses wha' come up heah f'om de Saouf Islands, an' like yo'se'f tu, wid de big, dark eyes, like de black coals out'n de fiah, lookin' up at me an' I kiver hit up 'g'in an' hol' my chile clost an' cry out in my h'a't 'g'in, "O Lawd, set my chile free. Tek 'im back, Lawd. Don' leab 'im heah," 'case I knowed yo' chile done come to rob my chile like yo' rob me.

Naw'm, set yo'sel'f still. I has mo' tu tell. By'm

by Ca'line come in an' I lie dar wid my eyes shet an'
she onkiver yo' baby an' she say, "Cl'issy, dis yo' chile?"
an' I lie still. Den she step roun' mighty sof' an' mek
fiah an' wahm de watah an' by'm by she onkiver bof de
chillun an' I lie dar wid my eyes shet an' a mighty
so' h'a't, an' she stan' dar lookin' at de chillun sleepin'
so sof' an' still. Den she reach ovah an' tek my chile
out'n' my ahms an' tek hit 'way by de fiah, an' I didn'
open my eyes noh say nuffin'. I jes' lay dar wid de
heavy-heartness ontwell I done drap off tu sleep, sho
'nuff. A'ter a w'ile I done heah a baby cryin', an' I open
my eyes an' dar stan' Ca'line side de baid wid bun'l
wrop up in de co'se cloff an' she say, "Cl'issy, heah, yo'
tek yo' own chile; he nigh sta'vin', I reckon. Missus'
baby don' need nuffin'. He sleepin' heah all right," an'
she lay de bun'l in my ahms an' I tu'n back de cloff
off'n de haid an' dar I see *yo'* chile; yas'm, yo' chile
dress in de co'se cloff wha' I done sew fo' my own in
de night times w'en yo' war sleepin'. Wid de tears
a-fallin' an' de hea't a-griev'n'. I done sew dose clo'es
an' dar I see 'em on *yo'* chile. Yes'm, set yo'se'f still
dar an' hark. I done tek *yo'* chile in my ahms an' heish
'im tu sleep, an' Ca'line she step roun' sof' an' men'
de fiah an' bresh de hyarth an' go off. Den I rose up
an' look at my own li'l baby, an' dar he lie in de sof'
white clo'es wid de lace an' de fine wo'k wid de needle
wha' I done sew, an' I say, "De Lawd done do de
choosin'." I done sew de clo'es, bof de co'se an' de
fine, an' de Lawd done guide de han' wha' put 'em on
de chile. Ef hit ain't nuffin' but de clo'es wha' gib a
chile a place in dis worl', ef dey don't know no dif'unce
'cept'n' dat ar, den de Lawd's name be praise. Ef one
o' dese chillun gwine be mars, an' one gwine be slave,
an' one fadah de fadah o' bofe, den de Lawd's name be

praise an' dey kin do dey own choosin'. By'm by Ca'line come back an' brung my victuals an' she stan' dar lookin' at my boy, an' she says, " 'Pears like he don' look lak her none, but he mighty putty." And I say, "Sholy he ar." An' she say, "Missus done axed fu' 'im," an' she cahy 'im out."

Da's right, Miz Is'bel. Set yo'se'f dar. I ain' come heah fu' no hu't. I come heah to git shet o' dis yer wha' I done ca'y on my hea't like a stone o' lead all dese yeahs. I come heah fu' to tell yo' de troof, how yo' done raised my boy to be de mars'r, an' to be yo' son, an' yo' boy done bin de slave. Dey ain' nuvva been anybody on dis yearth wha' knowed dis, on'y me, an' now I done tole yo' I reckon de Lawd gwine 'low me tu die some time an' go to ol' missus.

I min' de time yo' mek me ma'y ol' Brudder Thomas Ma'shall. Yo' done dat 'case yo' hate me, make me mahy de brackes' niggah on de place. Da's all right. He war mighty good man. He done tol' me to lub dem wha' hate me. Du good to dem dat spitefully uses me, an' I done hit. I done l'arn dat ar. I forgib yo' long w'ile 'go, but yo' wan' heah, an' I couldn' tell yo' de troof ontwell yo' come home 'gin. Mars'r Gen'l he lie dar in de grabeya'd wha' dey done tuk 'im, an' he's soul waitin' de day o' jedgmen', an' fo' long yo' gwine lie dar, tu, I reckon, an' now I done tol' yo' de troof, I 'low I kin be let tu pass f'om dis low worl' an' go home one o' dese days—Lawd, he'p my soul! An' we-all stan' dar 'fo' de gret w'ite t'rone, may de good Lawd he'p yo' soul, tu. I 'low I done sin a gret sin, but I done 'fess hit 'fo' yo', an' 'fo' de God ob heaben, an' He wha' sit on de t'rone, He kin look intu de hea't, an' He kin jedge twixt us an' Mars'r Gen'l, tu. Oh, good Lawd, Mars'r Gen'l done sin, tu! Ef you mus' strike 'im, Lawd, let me b'ar de blow! —PAYNE ERSKINE.

THE FOUR TRAVELERS

THEY were telling their experience—just a small
band of that race
Whose religion oft illumines e'en the darkness of
the face;
Whose true fancy passes limits that cold reason cannot
reach;
Whose expressions are more accurate for the rudeness
of their speech.
And they drew their illustrations—not from ancient
lore profound—
But from nineteenth century wonders that are scattered
all around.

And one said, "I'm goin' to hebben in de row-boat of
God's grace;
An' I'm pullin' mighty lively fer to win de hebbenly
race."
But the leader said, "Be keerful, for de arm of flesh
may fail,
An' de oars may break—or danger may come ridin' on
de gale;
An' be sure you make dat boat large, for no Christian
ken affo'd
To say 'NO' to any helpah who desires to step abo'd."

And one said, "I'm goin' to hebben in de sail-boat ob
de word;
An' my faith, it stitched de canvas, an' my breeze is
from de Lord;
An' my craft it foam de watahs as I speed upon my
way,

"And I think perhaps I'm makin'
Maybe half a mile a day."

Till it seems like I was makin' 'bout a hundred miles
a day."
But the leader said, "Be watchful, work an' struggle
more an' more;
Look for lots o' calms a-comin'—look for breakers on
de shore!"

And one rose and said, "I'm trabelin' in de steamboat
ob God's powah,
An' it seems like I was makin' 'bout a hundred knots
an hour!
An' my berth is all done paid for—an' my d'rection all
is known,

Till our gospel steamer whistles fer her landin' near
de throne!"
And the leader said, "Be earnest: You jus' watch en'
toil an' pray,
Les yer engine bu'st its boiler an' you shipwreck on
de way."

Then a poor old woman rose up—bent and haggard,
worn and weak—
And she leaned upon her crutches and her tongue was
slow to speak;
And she said, "I up an' started moah dan fifty yeahs
ago—
Started off *afoot* fer hebben—an' de journey's mighty
slow!
Dere was streams dat had no bridges—dere was stone
hills fer to clim',
Dere was swamps an' stubs an' briers waitin' for me
all de time;

Dere was clouds ob persecution, full ob thunder an'
cold rain—
Dere was any 'mount ob wanderin', dere was woes I
can't explain;
Dere was folks dat 'fore I asked 'em, my poor waverin'
footsteps showed
Into country dat was pleasant, but dat didn't contain
de road;
But de Lawd, He fin'lly tol' me, when I'm boun' to have
de way,
An' I think perhaps I'm makin' maybe half a mile
a day."

Then the leader said, "Dere's nothin' 'gainst de rapid
transit plan—

Jus' you git to hebben, my brethren, any honest way
    you can!
Ef you folks kin sail to glory, I don't know but dat's
    all right!
But I cannot help believin'—if we all should die to-
    night—
When you boatmen land in Canaan wid some narrer
    'scapes to tell,
You'd fin' dat ol' sister waitin' wid her feet all washed
    and well.

               —WILL CARLETON.

FEAR

BOOK IV.
Dramatic

THE BAND OF GIDEON *

THE band of Gideon roam the sky,
The howling wind is their war-cry,
The thunder's roll is their trump's peal,
And the lightning's flash their vengeful steel.
Each black cloud
Is a fiery steed,
And they cry aloud
With each strong deed,
"The sword of the Lord and Gideon."

And men below rear temples high,
And mock their God with reasons why,
And live in arrogance, sin and shame,
And rape their souls for the world's good name.
Each black cloud
Is a fiery steed,
And they cry aloud
With each strong deed,
"The sword of the Lord and Gideon."

The band of Gideon roam the sky
And view the earth with baleful eye;
In holy wrath they scourge the land
With earthquake, storm and burning brand.
Each black cloud
Is a fiery steed,
And they cry aloud
With each strong deed,
"The sword of the Lord and Gideon."

* From "The Band of Gideon and Other Lyrics." The Cornhill Company.

The lightnings flash and the thunders roll,
And "Lord have mercy on my soul"
Cry men as they fall on the stricken sod
In agony, searching for their God.
        Each black cloud
           Is a fiery steed,
        And they cry aloud
           With each strong deed,
"The sword of the Lord and Gideon."

And men repent and then forget
That heavenly wrath they ever met,
The band of Gideon yet will come
And strike their tongues with blasphemy dumb.
        Each black cloud
           Is a fiery steed,
        And they cry aloud
           With each strong deed,
"The sword of the Lord and Gideon."

                —JOSEPH S. COTTER, JR.

THE WHITE WITCH *

O BROTHERS mine, take care, take care!
    The great white witch rides out tonight,
    Trust not your prowess nor your strength;
  Your only safety lies in flight;
For in her glance there is a snare,
    And in her smile there is a blight.

The great white witch you have not seen?
    Then, younger brothers mine, forsooth,
Like nursery children you have looked
    For ancient hag and snaggled tooth;
But no, not so; the witch appears
    In all the glowing charms of youth.

Her lips are like carnations red,
    Her face like new-born lilies fair,
Her eyes like ocean waters blue,
    She moves with subtle grace and air,
And all about her head there floats
    The golden glory of her hair.

But though she always thus appears
    In form of youth and mood of mirth,
Unnumbered centuries are hers,
    The infant planets saw her birth;
The child of throbbing Life is she,
    Twin sisters to the greedy earth.

----

* The Crisis.

And back behind those smiling lips,
   And down within those laughing eyes,
And underneath the soft caress
   Of hand and voice and purring sighs,
The shadow of the panther lurks,
   The spirit of the vampire lies.

For I have seen the great white witch,
   And she has led me to her lair,
And I have kissed her red, red lips,
   And cruel face as white and fair;
Around me she has twined her arms,
   And bound me with her yellow hair.

I felt those red lips burn and sear
   My body like a living coal;
Obeyed the power of those eyes
   As the needle trembles to the pole;
And did not care, although I felt
   The strength go ebbing from my soul.

Oh! she has seen your strong young limbs,
   And heard your laughter loud and gay,
And in your voices she has caught
   The echo of a far-off day,
When man was closer to the earth;
   And she has marked you for her prey.

She feels the old Antaean strength
   In you, the great dynamic beat
Of primal passions, and she sees
   In you the last besieged retreat
Of love relentless, lusty, fierce,
   Love pain-ecstatic, cruel, sweet.

O brothers mine, take care, take care!
  The great white witch rides out tonight!
O younger brothers mine, beware!
  Look not upon her beauty's snare,
For in her glance there is a snare,
  And in her smile there is a blight.
          —JAMES WELDON JOHNSON.

THE UNSUNG HEROES *

A SONG for the unsung heroes who rose in the
    country's need,
    When the life of the land was threatened by the
slaver's cruel greed,
For the men who came from the cornfield, who came
  from the plow and the flail,
Who rallied round when they heard the sound of the
  mighty man of the rail.

They laid them down in the valleys, they laid them
  down in the wood,
And the world looked on at the work they did, and
  whispered "It is good!"
They fought their way on the hillside, they fought their
  way in the glen,
And God looked down on their sinews brown and said,
  "I have made them men!"

They went to the blue lines gladly, and the blue lines
  took them in,
And the men who saw their muskets' fire thought not
  of their dusky skin.

—————
* Permission, Dodd, Mead & Co.

The gray lines rose and melted beneath their scattering
   showers,
And they said, " 'Tis true, they have force to do, these
   old slave boys of ours."

Ah, Wagner saw their glory, and Pillow knew their
   blood,
That poured on a nation's altar a sacrificial flood.
Port Hudson heard their war-cry that smote its smoke-
   filled air,
And the old free fires of their savage sires again were
   kindled there.

They laid them down where the rivers the greening
   valleys gem,
And the sound of the thunderous cannon was their sole
   requiem,
And the great smoke wreath that mingled its hue with
   the dusky cloud
Was the flag that furled o'er a saddened world and
   the sheet that made their shroud.

O mighty God of Battles, who held them in thy hand,
Who gave them strength through the whole day's length
   to fight for their native land,
They are lying dead on the hillsides, they are lying
   dead on the plain,
And we have not fire to smite the lyre and sing them
   one brief strain.

Give thou some Seer the power to sing them in their
   might,
The men who feared the master's whip, but did not fear
   the fight;

That he may tell of their virtues as minstrels did of old,
Till the pride of face and the hate of race grows
    obsolete and cold.

A song for the unsung heroes who stood the awful test,
When the humblest host that the land could boast went
    forth to meet the best;
A song for the unsung heroes who fell on the bloody
    sod,
Who fought their way from night to day and struggled
    up to God!
                                —Paul Laurence Dunbar.

BLACK SAMSON OF BRANDYWINE *

GRAY are the pages of record,
    Dim are the volumes of eld,
    Else had old Delaware told us,
More than her history held;
Told us with pride in the story,
    Honest and noble and fine,
More of the tale of my hero,
    Black Samson of Brandywine.

Sing of your chiefs and your nobles,
    Saxon and Celt and Gaul,
Breath of mine ever shall join you,
    Highly I honor them all.
Give to them all of their glory,
    But for this noble of mine,
Lend him a tithe of your tribute,
    Black Samson of Brandywine.

---

* Permission, Dodd, Mead & Co.

There in the heat of the battle,
　　There in the stir of the fight,
Loomed he, an ebony giant,
　　Black as the pinions of night.
Swinging his scythe like a mower,
　　Over a field of grain,
Needless the care of the gleaners,
　　Where he had passed amain.

Straight through the human harvest,
　　Cutting a bloody swath,
Woe to you, soldier of Briton!
　　Death is abroad in his path.
Flee from the scythe of the reaper,
　　Flee while the moment is thine,
None may with safety withstand him,
　　Black Samson of Brandywine.

Was he a freeman, a bondman?
　　Was he a man or a thing?
What does it matter? His bravery
　　Renders him royal—a king.
If he were only a chattel,
　　Honor the ransom may pay,
Of the royal, the loyal black giant,
　　Who fought for his country that day.

Noble and bright is the story,
　　Worthy the touch of the lyre,
Sculptor or poet should find it,
　　Full of the stuff to inspire.
Beat it in brass and in copper,
　　Tell it in storied line,
So that the world may remember,
　　Black Samson of Brandywine.
　　　　　　　　—Paul Laurence Dunbar.

THE HAUNTED OAK *

P RAY, why are you so bare, so bare,
    O bough of the old oak tree?
    And why, when I go through the shade you throw
Runs a shudder over me?

My leaves were as green as the best I trow,
    And the sap ran free in my veins,
But I saw in the moonlight dim and weird,
    A guiltless victim's pains.

I bent me down to hear his sigh,
    And I shook with his gurgling moan,
And I trembled sore when they rode away,
    And left him here alone.

They'd charged him with the old, old crime,
    And set him fast in jail;
O why does the dog howl all night long?
    And why does the night wind wail?

He prayed his prayer, and he swore his oath,
    And he raised his hands to the sky;
But the beat of hoofs smote on his ear,
    And the steady tread drew nigh.

Who is it rides by night, by night,
    Over the moonlit road?
What is the spur that keeps the pace?
    What is the galling goad?

And now they beat at the prison door,
    "Ho, keeper, do not stay!

* Permission, Dodd, Mead & Co.

We are friends of him whom you hold within,
    And we fain would take him away

"From those who ride fast on our heels,
    With mind to do him wrong;
They have no care for his innocence,
    And the rope they bear is strong."

"I am burned with dread, I am dried and dead,
From the curse of a guiltless man."

They have fooled the jailer with lying words,
    They have fooled the man with lies;
The bolts unbar, the locks are drawn,
    And the great door open flies.

And now they have taken him from the jail,
  And hard and fast they ride;
And the leader laughs low down in his throat,
  As they halt my trunk beside.

O, the judge he wore a mask of black,
  And the doctor one of white,
And the minister, with his oldest son,
  Was curiously bedight.

O foolish man, why weep you now?
  'Tis but a little space,
And the time will come when these shall dread
  The memory of your face.

I feel the rope against my bark,
  And the weight of him in my grain;
I feel in the throe of his final woe,
  The touch of my own last pain.

And never more shall leaves come forth
  On a bough that bears the ban;
I am burned with dread, I am dried and dead,
  From the curse of a guiltless man.

And ever the judge rides by, rides by,
  And goes to hunt the deer,
And ever another rides his soul,
  In the guise of a mortal fear.

And ever the man, he rides me hard,
  And never a night stays he;
For I feel his curse as a haunted bough,
  On the trunk of a haunted tree.

                    —PAUL LAURENCE DUNBAR.

ODE TO ETHIOPIA *

O MOTHER RACE, to thee I bring
The pledge of faith unwavering,
    This tribute to thy glory.
I know the pangs which thou didst feel,
When slavery crushed thee with its heel,
    With thy dear blood all gory.

Sad days were those, ah, sad indeed!
But through the land the fruitful seed
    Of better times was growing.
The plant of freedom upward sprung
And spread its leaves so fresh and young—
    Its blossoms now are blowing.

On every hand in this fair land,
Proud Ethiope's swarthy children stand
    Beside their fairer neighbor.
The forests flee before their stroke,
Their hammers ring, their forges smoke—
    They stir in honest labor.

They tread the fields where honor calls;
Their voices sound through senate halls
    In majesty and power.
To right they cling; the hymns they sing
Up to the skies in beauty ring,
    And bolder grown each hour.

Be proud, my race, in mind and soul;
Thy name is writ on glory's scroll
    In characters of fire.

---

* Permission, Dodd, Mead & Co.

High 'mid the clouds of Fame's bright sky
Thy banners' blazoned folds now fly,
   And truth shall lift them higher.

Thou hast the right to noble pride,
Whose spotless robes were purified
   By blood's severe baptism.
Upon thy brow the cross was laid,
And labor's painful sweat-beads made
   A consecrating chrism.

No other race or white or black,
When bound, as thou wert, to the rack,
   So seldom stooped to grieving;
No other race, when free again,
Forgot the past and proved them men
   So noble in forgiving.

Go on and up! Our souls and eyes
Shall follow thy continuous rise,
   Our ears shall list thy story
From bards who from thy roots shall spring
And proudly tune their lyres to sing
   Of Ethiopia's glory.

          —Paul Laurence Dunbar.

From THE FINISH OF PATSY BARNES *

(To give this selection effectively, it should be preceded by a brief sketch of the story.)

WHEN the bell sounded and Patsy went out to warm up, he felt as if he were riding on air. Some of the jockeys laughed at his get-up, but there was something in him—or under him, maybe—that made him scorn their derision. He saw a sea of faces about him; then saw no more. Only a shining white track loomed ahead of him, and a restless steed was cantering around the curve. Then the bell called him back to the stand.

They did not get away at first, and back they trooped. A second trial was a failure. But at the third they were off in a line as straight as a chalk mark. There were Essex and Firefly, Queen Bess and Mosquito, galloping away side by side, and Black Boy a neck ahead. Patsy knew the family reputation of his horse for endurance as well as fire, and began riding the race from the first. Black Boy came of blood that would not be passed, and to this his rider trusted. At the eighth the line was hardly broken, but as the quarter was reached Black Boy had forged a length ahead, and Mosquito was at his flank. Then like a flash Essex shot ahead under whip and spur, his jockey standing straight in his stirrups.

The crowd in the stand screamed, but Patsy smiled as he lay low over his horse's neck. He saw that Essex had made her best spurt. His only fear was for Mosquito, who hugged and hugged his flank. They were nearing the three-quarter post and he was tightening his grip on the black. Essex fell back; his spurt was

---

* Permission, Dodd, Mead & Co.

To A Wild Rose

over. The whip fell unheeded on his sides. The spurs dug him in vain.

Black Boy's breath touches the leader's ear. They are neck and neck; nose and nose. The black stallion passes him.

Another cheer from the stand and again Patsy smiles as they turn into the stretch. Mosquito has gained a head. The colored boy flashes one glance at the horse and rider who are so surely gaining upon him, and his lips close in a grim line. They are half way down the stretch, and Mosquito's head is at the stallion's neck.

For a single moment Patsy thinks of the sick woman at home and what that race will mean to her, and then his knees close against the horse's sides with a firmer dig. The spurs shoot deeper into the steaming flanks. Black Boy shall win; he must win. The horse that has taken away his father shall give him back his mother. The stallion leaps away like a flash and goes under the wire—a length ahead!

Then the band thundered and Patsy was off his horse, very warm and very happy, following his mount to the stable. There a little later Brackett found him. He rushed to him and flung his arms around him.

"You little devil!" he cried. "You rode like you was kin to that hoss! We've won! We've won!" and he began sticking banknotes at the boy. At first Patsy's eyes bulged, and then he seized the money and got into his clothes.

"Goin' out to spend it?" asked Brackett.

"I'm goin' fu' a doctah fu' my mothah," said Patsy. "She's sick."

An hour later he walked into his mother's room with a very big doctor, the greatest the druggist could direct

7

him to. The doctor left his medicine and his orders, but when Patsy told his story it was Eliza's pride that started her on the road to recovery.

Pasty did not tell his horse's name.

—PAUL LAURENCE DUNBAR.

From "The Strength of Gideon and Other Stories."

PROPHECY *

I HEAR the pattering footsteps of twenty million
　　dusky children yet unborn,
Echoing down the corridors of time,
A generation hence they will be here barring wide the
　　gates of life.
I hear them muttering the dumb and inarticulate aspira-
　　tions of a race so long restrained.
I hear the firm and steady footfalls of their tread march-
　　ing everywhere resistless in the paths of men—
I hear no voice of yielding, compromise or fear,
But the full voiced notes of free men rising high above
　　the graves of caste.
I see dark visioned countenances everywhere walking
　　in the paths of men erect and unafraid.
I see unwavering eyes look forth from ebony faces no
　　longer mantled with an age long grin,
But with a look of stern determination and resolve.
I see a day of God, and not a day of color or race
In which men trace with pardonable pride the rays
　　of oriental sunshine in their veins.
I see, now near at hand, the opening day of the darker
　　races of mankind in which
Americans of African descent stand forth
Among the first Americans.　　—REVERDY C. RANSOM.

* From the A. M. E. Church Review.

HEAR, O CHURCH

O HALLOWED Church, whose cause for being is
The need of all men for the Word of God,
Today art thou, His living Rock, on trial!
A million souls, thy wards, of ebon hue,
Expectantly in solemn silence wait
The stand that thou shalt take. Think well, O Church!
'Tis whether race or breed or birth shall count
With thee. Does just Jehovah judge of men
To make them benefactors of His grace
By color or by race? O Church, do right!
Remember now the stand thy fathers took
'Midst times that tried men's souls. They held no court
With Hierarchies of Hate. With single eye
Their duty stern beheld, nor faltered they
To follow where it led. Their creed: the world
Was God's, and all men brethren—no North
Nor South, no East nor West, no black nor white,
To Him who all men made of common blood;
Their offering; the sacrifice of old—
An humble and a contrite heart—no more,
No less to them the measure of a man.
O Church, be just! when Methodism speaks
The world gives eager ear. O may they find
Her judgments always true and righteous.

E. A. Long in *Southwestern Christian Advocate.*

DESSALINES

AY, I am here—Monsieur Dessalines, the freedman; made so by his own hand and proclamation. If it suit thy quaking spirit better I am thy master's escaped slave. Take me if thou darest! Hiding place my castle is on the mountains, where dwells no will save mine, and no slave dare breathe the air and refuse to be a man.

Good Dessalines, you say? Good slave! I remember when first I was sent to the master to receive from his lips my first instruction in the art of making self, in all things, subservient to the master's will. On entrance to his presence, in meek and humble tones I showed my aptitude for the first lesson in slavish servitude. This must have pleased the good man, for next he tried to instill in me that God expected of the slave obedience to the master's will. From sundry books he had at hand he read to me; and all he read impressed me with the thought that the gods from the beginning had ordained one race to serve, the other to rule. My people were of the race to serve; his people of the race to rule. Desiring to see how far this mockery went I asked to be taught a prayer whereby I could free my soul from guilt of insolence and hatred to the whites. He directed me to say a prayer, which after him I repeated, and called on all the saints and angels of his faith to witness I was an obdurate, worthless sinner. Again did he seek to impress me with the thought I must learn to love my masters. Then threw I the mask aside. I told him I hated the masters and their gods! I told him the African's gods taught revenge for wrongs, hatred for hatred, and death for death. On this he threatened me with chastisement, torment and the church's most fruitful curses. He dared to call me a pagan dog! Dost know what then I did? I plucked him by his unholy beard, threw him to the ground and spurned him as I would some snarling, fangless cur.

God have mercy on me? Thou, too, art a doler out of superstitious cant—an humble worshipper of thy master's household gods. I have none, I know none, and owe allegiance only to my kind. A race enslaved 'tis true, but not all of us are only fit to be in spirit as thy master hath made thee. Teach the slave if he disobey he receives the lash. 'Tis in reason, for thy corporal frame is captive; but to command the mind to worship at an altar where the sacrifice of liberty and manhood occur each day is as tyrannical as useless. Minds are not made captive with slavery chains, nor are men's souls made for barter and trade.

What has made me master here? What will make ye masters here? Look upon us! I am as black as the shadows of night, with muscles of iron and a will that was never enslaved! What has he that I have not save the arrogance of the accursed Caucasian blood? What have these Franks that we are their household chattels—that we are their beasts? They suffer from the heat more than we, their sight is less keen, the evening dews hasten them to their graves and the noonday's sun finds them under cover. The very fibres of their frames are weak and puny, and, as the gods allotted labor for the part of man, they must depend on us to carry out the law. What fetich have they that sustains their power to rule and ours to serve? We are ten to one their number now in Haiti—perhaps an hundred it may be. Then is it the strong who rules, or is it the natural sequence of our own inward weakness? Have ye mothers, sisters or laughing babes that ye can call your own?

Were ye always slaves and your sires, too? And must it follow that ye must always be?

Listen! When but a stripling in my native land I was wont to hunt the great king of the jungles whose roar is like the distant thunder, and whose bite is death. One day, with five companions, armed with spears and shields, I penetrated a dense undergrowth and suddenly confronted a lioness and her mate. On seeing us they gave forth terrific roars in defiance of our arms and numbers. All unprepared for the meeting, my companions were affrighted and would have fled had I not called on them to halt—as flight meant a fearful death—and to charge upon the foe. We charged upon them, and though they were wounded, they were not disabled, and only made more fierce and desperate. Then there ensued such a battle! The spears were torn from our hand. Three of my companions with their entrails protruding from their tortured abdomens were still in death upon the ground. The brutes' terrific roar and fearful carnage drove terror to our hearts, and routed, we ran ingloriously from the scene. What would I teach thee from this tale? The same lesson I have learned: That wavering is cowardly and desperation makes men brave; that the arms of the oppressors, however great in number, cannot prevail with the desperation of the lion at bay. The masters are wavering like the tall palmetto in the storm's angry blast. Let us but be brave and the shackles now upon your limbs will be turned to anklets of gold and precious stones taken from the bodies of these Frankish dogs. If you will be brutes be lions!

From "Dessalines."   —WILLIAM EDGAR EASTON.

THE SISTERS *

MILLER'S door bell rang loudly, insistently, as though demanding a response. Absorbed in his own grief, into which he had relapsed upon Carteret's departure, the sound was an unwelcome intrusion. Surely the man could not be coming back! If it were someone else— What else might happen to the doomed town concerned him not. His child was dead—his distracted wife could not be left alone.

The door bell rang—clamorously, appealingly. Through the long hall and the closed door of the room where he sat he could hear some one knocking and a faint voice calling,

"Open, for God's sake, open!"

It was a woman's voice—the voice of a woman in distress. Slowly Miller rose and went to the door, which he opened mechanically.

A woman stood there, so near the image of his own wife, whom he had just left, that for a moment he was well nigh startled. A little older, perhaps, a little fairer of complexion, but with the same form, the same features, marked by the same wild grief. She wore a loose wrapper, which clothed her like the drapery of a statue. Her long, dark hair, the counterpart of his wife's, had fallen down and hung disheveled about her shoulders. There was blood upon her knuckles where she had beaten with them upon the door.

"Doctor Miller," she panted, breathless from her flight and laying her hand upon his arm appealingly—

---

* By permission, Houghton, Mifflin and Company. From "The Marrow of Tradition."

when he shrank from the contact she still held it there—
"Doctor Miller, you will come and save my child? You
know what it is to lose a child! I am so sorry about
your little boy! You will come to mine!"

"Your sorrow comes too late, madam," he said
harshly. "My child is dead. I charged your husband
with his murder, and he could not deny it. Why should
I save your husband's child?"

"Ah, Doctor Miller," she cried with his wife's voice—
she never knew how much, in that dark hour, she
owed to that resemblance—"it is *my* child, and I have
never injured you. It is my child, Doctor Miller, my

only child. I brought it into the world at the risk of my own life! I have nursed it, I have watched over it, I have prayed for it—and now it lies dying! Oh, Doctor Miller, dear Doctor Miller, if you have a heart come and save my child!"

"Madam," he answered more gently, moved in spite of himself, "my heart is broken. My people lie dead upon the streets at the hands of your people. The work of my life is in ashes—and yonder, stretched out in death, lies my own child! God! woman, you ask too much of human nature. Love, duty, sorrow, *justice,* call me here. I cannot go."

She rose to her full height. "Then you are a murderer!" she cried wildly. "His blood be on your head, and a mother's curse beside!"

The next moment, with a sudden revulsion of feeling, she had thrown herself at his feet—at the feet of a Negro, this proud, white woman—and was clasping his knees wildly.

"O God!" she prayed, in tones which quivered with anguish, "pardon my husband's sins and my own, and move this man's hard heart by the blood of thy Son who died to save us all!"

It was the last appeal of poor humanity. When the pride of intellect and caste is broken; when we grovel in the dust of humiliation; when sickness and sorrow come and the shadow of death falls upon us and there is no hope elsewhere—we turn to God, who sometimes swallows the insult and answers the appeal.

Miller raised the lady to her feet. He had been deeply moved—but he had been more deeply injured. This was his wife's sister—ah, yes! but a sister who had scorned and slighted and ignored the existence of his wife all of her life. Only Miller of all the world could have guessed what this had meant to Janet, and he had merely divined it through the clairvoyant sympathy of love. This woman could have no claim upon him because of this unacknowledged relationship. Yet, after all, she *was* his wife's sister, his child's kinswoman. She was a fellow creature, too, and in distress.

"Rise, madam," he said with a sudden inspiration, lifting her gently. "I will listen to you on one condition. My child lies dead in the adjoining room, his mother by his side. Go in there and make your request of her. I will abide by the decision.

*　*　*　*　*　*　*

The two women stood confronting each other across the body of the dead child, mute witness of this first meeting between two children of the same father. Standing thus, face to face, each under the stress of the deepest emotions, the resemblance between them was even more striking than it had seemed to Miller when he had admitted Mrs. Carteret to the house. But Death, the great leveler, striking upon the one hand and threatening upon the other, had wrought a marvelous transformation in the bearing of the two women. The sad-eyed Janet towered erect, with menacing aspect, like an avenging goddess. The other, whose pride had been her life, stood in the attitude of a trembling suppliant.

"*You* have come here," cried Janet, pointing with a tragic gesture to the dead child—"*you* to gloat over your husband's work. All my life you have hated and scorned and despised me. Your presence here insults me and my dead. What are you doing here?"

"Mrs. Miller," returned Mrs. Carteret tremulously,

dazed for a moment by this outburst, and clasping her hands with an imploring gesture, "my child, my only child, is dying, and your husband alone can save his life. Ah, let me have my child," she moaned heart rendingly. "It is my only one—my sweet child—my ewe lamb!"

"This was MY only child!" replied the other mother; "and yours is no better to die than mine!"

"You are young," said Mrs. Carteret, "and yet may have many children—this is my only hope! If you have a human heart, tell your husband to come with me. He leaves it to you; he will do as you command."

"Ah," cried Janet, "I have a human heart and therefore I will not let him go. MY child is dead—O God, —my child, my child!"

She threw herself down by the bedside, sobbing hysterically. The other woman knelt beside her and put her arm about her neck. For a moment Janet, absorbed in her grief, did not repulse her.

"Listen," pleaded Mrs. Carteret. "You will not let my baby die? You are my sister—the child is your own near kin!"

"My child was nearer," returned Janet, rising again to her feet and shaking off the other woman's arm. "He was my son and I have seen him die. I have been your sister for twenty-five years, and you have only now, for the first time, called me so!"

"Listen, sister," returned Mrs. Carteret. Was there no way to move this woman? Her child lay dying, if he were not dead already. She would tell everything and leave the rest to God. If it would save her child she would shrink at no sacrifice. Whether the truth would still further incense Janet, or move her to mercy, she could not tell; she would leave the issue to God.

"Listen, sister!" she said. "I have a confession to make. You *are* my lawful sister. My father was married to your mother. You are entitled to his name and half his estate."

Janet's eyes flashed with bitter scorn.

"And you have robbed me all these years and now tell me that as a reason why I should forgive the murder of my child?"

"No, no!" cried the other wildly, fearing the worst. I have known of it only a few weeks, since my Aunt Polly's death. I had not meant to rob you—I had meant to make restitution. Sister! for our father's sake, who did you no wrong, give me my child's life!"

Janet's eyes slowly filled with tears, bitter tears— burning tears. For a moment, even her grief at her child's loss dropped to second place in her thoughts. This, then, was the recognition for which all her life she had longed in secret. It had come, after many days, and in larger measure than she had dreamed; but it had come, not with frank friendliness and sisterly love, but in a storm of blood and tears; not freely given from an open heart, but extorted from a reluctant conscience by the agony of a mother's fears. Janet had obtained her heart's desire, but now that it was at her lips found it but apples of Sodom, filled with dust and ashes!

"Listen!" she cried, dashing her tears aside. "I have but one word for you—one last word—and then I hope never to see your face again! My mother died of want and I was brought up by the hand of charity. Now, when I have married a man who can supply my needs you offer me back the money which you and your friends robbed me of! You imagine that the shame of being a Negro swallowed up every other ignominy—

and in your eyes I am a Negro, though I am your sister and you are white, and people have taken me for you on the streets—and you, therefore, left me nameless all my life! Now, when an honest man has given me a name of which I can be proud, you offer me the one of which you robbed me and of which I can make no use. For twenty-five years I, poor, despicable fool, would have kissed your feet for a word, a nod, a smile. Now, when this tardy recognition comes, for which I have waited so long, it is tainted with fraud and crime and blood, and I must pay for it with my child's life!"

"And I must forfeit that of mine, it seems, for withholding it so long," sobbed the other as tottering she turned to go. "It is but just."

"Stay—do not go yet!" commanded Janet imperiously, her pride still keeping back her tears. "I have not done. I throw you back your father's name, your father's wealth, your sisterly recognition. I want none of them—they are bought too dear! Ah, God, they are bought too dear! But that you may know that a woman may be foully wronged, and yet may have a heart to feel, even for one who has injured her, you may have your child's life if my husband can save it! Will," she said, throwing open the door into the next room, "go with her!"

"God will bless you for a noble woman!" exclaimed Mrs. Carteret, "You do not mean all the cruel things you have said—ah, no! I will see you again and make you take them back; I cannot thank you now! Oh, Doctor, let us go! I pray God we may not be too late!"

Together they went out into the night. Mrs. Carteret tottered under the stress of her emotions and would have fallen had not Miller caught and sustained her with his arm until they reached the house, where he turned over her fainting form to Carteret at the door.

"Is the child still alive?" asked Miller.

"Yes, thank God," answered the father, "but nearly gone."

"Come on up, Doctor Miller," called Evans from the head of the stairs. "There's time enough, but none to spare."

—CHARLES W. CHESNUTT.

MODERN CHRISTMAS ON THE PLANTATION *

IT was Christmas—not the Christmas-tide of the North and West—but Christmas of the Southern South. It was not the festival of the Christ-child, but a time of noise and frolic and license, the great payday of the year, when black men lifted their heads from a year's toiling in the earth and, hat in hand, asked anxiously: "Master, what have I earned? Have I paid my old debts to you? Have I made my clothes and food? Have I got a little of the year's wage coming to me?" Or, more carelessly and cringingly: "Master, gimme a Christmas gift."

The lords of the soil stood around, gauging their cotton, measuring their men. Their stores were crowded, their scales groaned, their gin sang. In the long run public opinion determines all wage, but in more primitive times and places private opinion, personal judgment of some man in power, determines. The Black Belt is primitive and the landlord wields the power.

* By permission, W. E. B. DuBois. From ''The Quest of the Silver Fleece.''

Venus of the Roadside.

"What about Johnson?" calls the head clerk.

"Well, he's a faithful nigger and needs encouragement; cancel his debt and give him ten dollars for Christmas." Colonel Cresswell glowed as if he were full of the season's spirit.

"And Sanders?"

"How's his cotton?"

"Good, and a lot of it."

"He's trying to get away. Keep him in debt, but let him draw what he wants."

"Aunt Rachel?"

"H'm, they're way behind, aren't they? Give her a couple of dollars—not a cent more."

"Jim Sykes?"

" Say, Harry, how about that darky Sykes?" called out the Colonel.

Excusing himself from his guests, Harry Cresswell came into the office.

To them this peculiar spectacle of the market place was of unusual interest. They saw its humor and its crowding, its bizarre effects and unwonted pageantry. Black giants and pygmies were there; kerchiefed aunties, giggling black girls, saffron beauties and loafing white men. There were mules and horses and oxen, wagons and buggies and carts; but above all and in all, rushing through, piled and flying, bound and baled —was cotton. Cotton was currency; cotton was merchandise; cotton was conversation.

All this was "beautiful" to Mrs. Grey and "unusually interesting" to Mrs. Vanderpool. To Mary Taylor, it had the fascination of a puzzle whose other side she had already been partially studying. She was particularly impressed with the joy and abandon of the scene—light laughter, huge guffaws, handshakes and gossipings.

"At all events," she concluded, "this is no oppressed people." And sauntering away from the rest she noted the smiles of an undersized, smirking yellow man who hurried by with a handful of dollar bills. At a side entrance liquor was evidently on sale—men were drinking, and women, too; some were staggering, others cursing, and yet others singing. Then suddenly a man swung around the corner, swearing in bitter rage.

"The damned thieves, they'se stole a year's work— the white—" But someone called, "Hush up, Sanders!

COQUETRY

There's a white woman." He threw a startled look at Mary and hurried by. She was perplexed and upset, and stood hesitating a moment when she heard a well-known voice.

"Why, Miss Taylor, I was alarmed for you; you really must be careful about trusting yourself with these half-drunken Negroes."

"Wouldn't it be better not to give them drink, Mr. Cresswell?"

"And let your neighbor sell them poison at all hours? No, Miss Taylor." They joined the others and all were turning toward the carriage when a figure coming down the road attracted them.

"Quite picturesque," observed Mrs. Vanderpool, looking at the tall, slim girl swaying toward them with a piled basket of white cotton poised lightly on her head. "Why," in abrupt recognition, "it is our Venus of the roadside, is it not?"

* * * * * * *

Colonel Cresswell stood by the door, his hat on, his hand in his pockets.

"Well, Zora, what have you there?" he asked.

"Cotton, sir."

Harry Cresswell bent over it.

"Great heavens! Look at this cotton!" he ejaculated. His father approached. The cotton lay in silken handfuls, clean and shimmering, with threads full two inches long. The idlers, black and white, clustered round, gazing at it and fingering it with repeated exclamations of astonishment.

"Where did this come from?" asked the Colonel sharply. He and Harry were both eyeing the girl intently.

"I raised it in the swamp," Zora replied quietly.

₈

There was no pride of achievement in her manner, no gladness; all that had flown.

"Is that all?"

"No, sir; I think there's two bales."

"Two bales! Where is it? How the dev—" the Colonel was forgetting his guests, but Harry intervened.

"You'll need to get it picked right off," he suggested.

"It's all picked, sir."

"But where is it?"

"If you'll send a wagon, sir—"

But the Colonel hardly waited.

"Here you, Jim, take the big mules and drive like—where's that wench?"

But Zora was already striding on ahead, and was far up the red road when the great mules galloped into sight and the long whip snapped above their backs. The Colonel was still excited.

"That cotton must be ours, Harry, all of it. And see that none is stolen. We've got no contract with the wench, so don't dally with her." But Harry said firmly, quietly:

"It's fine cotton, and she raised it; she must be paid well for it." Colonel Cresswell glanced at him with something between contempt and astonishment on his face.

"You go along with the ladies," Harry added. "I'll see to this cotton." Mary Taylor's smile had rewarded him; now he must get rid of his company—before Zora returned.

It was dark when the cotton came; such a load as Cresswell's store had never seen before. Zora watched it weighed, received the cotton checks and entered the store. Only the clerk was there, and he was closing. He pointed her carelessly to the office in the back part.

She went into the small, dim room and, laying the cotton check on the desk, stood waiting. . . . She dropped her hands listlessly, wearily, and stood, but half conscious as the door opened and Harry Cresswell entered the dimly lighted room. She opened her eyes. She had expected his father. Something way down in the depths of her nature, the primal tiger, woke and snarled. She was suddenly alive from hair to finger tip. Harry Cresswell paused a second and swept her full length with his eye—her profile, the long supple line of bosom and hip, the little foot. Then he closed the door softly and walked slowly toward her. She stood like stone, without a quiver, only her eye followed the crooked line of the Cresswell blue blood on his marble forehead as she looked down from her greater height; her hand closed almost caressingly on a rusty poker lying on the stove near by; and as she sensed the hot breath of him she felt herself purring in a half heard whisper:

"I should not like—to kill you."

He looked at her long and steadily as he passed to his desk. Slowly he lighted a cigarette, opened the great ledger and compared the cotton check with it.

"Three thousand pounds," he announced in a careless tone. "Yes, that will make about two bales of lint. It's extra cotton—say fifteen cents a pound—one hundred fifty dollars—seven'y-five dollars to you—h'm." He took a note-book out of his pocket, pushed his hat back on his head and paused to relight his cigarette.

"Let's see—your rent and rations—"

"Elspeth pays no rent," she said slowly, but he did not seem to hear.

"Your rent and rations, with the five years' back debt"—he made a hasty calculation—"will be one hundred dollars. That leaves you twenty-five in our debt. Here's your receipt."

The blow had fallen. She did not wince nor cry out. She took the receipt calmly and walked out into the darkness.

They had stolen her Silver Fleece.

—WILLIAM E. BURGHARDT DuBois.

THE FAREWELL

OF A VIRGINIA SLAVE MOTHER TO HER DAUGHTERS SOLD
INTO SOUTHERN BONDAGE

GONE, gone—sold and gone,
    To the rice-swamp dank and lone,
    Where the slave whip ceaseless swings,
Where the noisome insect stings,
Where the fever demon strews
Poison with the falling dews,
Where the sickly sunbeams glare
Through the hot and misty air—
    Gone, gone—sold and gone,
    To the rice-swamp dank and lone,
    From Virginia's hills and waters—
    Woe is me, my stolen daughters!

    Gone, gone—sold and gone,
    To the rice-swamp dank and lone.
There no mother's eye is near them,
There no mother's ear can hear them;
Never when the torturing lash
Seams their back with many a gash,

Shall a mother's kindness bless them,
Or a mother's arm caress them.
  Gone, gone—sold and gone,
  To the rice-swamp dank and lone,
  From Virginia's hills and waters—
  Woe is me, my stolen daughters!

  Gone, gone—sold and gone,
  To the rice-swamp dank and lone.
Oh, when weary, sad and slow,
From the fields at night they go,
Faint with toil and racked with pain,
To their cheerless homes again.
There no brother's voice shall greet them—
There no father's welcome greet them.
  Gone, gone—sold and gone,
  To the rice-swamp dank and lone,
  From Virginia's hills and waters—
  Woe is me, my stolen daughters!

  Gone, gone—sold and gone,
  To the rice-swamp dank and lone.
From the tree whose shadow lay
On their childhood place of play—
From the cool spring where they drank—
Rock, and hill, and rivulet bank—
From the solemn house of prayer,
And the holy counsels there—
  Gone, gone—sold and gone,
  To the rice-swamp dank and lone,
  From Virginia's hills and waters—
  Woe is me, my stolen daughters!

  Gone, gone—sold and gone,
  To the rice-swamp dank and lone,

Toiling through the weary day,
And at night the spoiler's prey.
O that they had earlier died,
Sleeping calmly side by side,
Where the tyrant's power is o'er,
And the fetter galls no more!
      Gone, gone—sold and gone,
      To the rice-swamp dank and lone,
      From Virginia's hills and waters—
      Woe is me, my stolen daughters!

      Gone, gone—sold and gone,
      To the rice-swamp dank and lone.
By the holy love he beareth—
By the bruised reed he spareth—
O may He to whom alone
All their cruel wrongs are known,
Still their hope and refuge prove,
With a more than mother's love!
      Gone, gone—sold and gone,
      To the rice-swamp dank and lone,
      From Virginia's hills and waters—
      Woe is me, my stolen daughters!

                    —John G. Whittier.

HOW HE SAVED ST. MICHAELS

SO you beg for a story, my darling—my brown-eyed
     Leopold—
    And you, Alice, with face like morning and curling
locks of gold;
Then come, if you will, and listen—stand close beside
    my knee—
To a tale of a Southern city, proud Charleston by
    the sea.

It was long ago, my children, ere ever the signal gun
That blazed above Fort Sumter had wakened the North
    as one;
Long ere the wondrous pillar of battle-cloud and fire
Had marked where the unchained millions marched
    on to their heart's desire.

On the roofs and the glittering turrets that night as
    the sun went down,
The mellow glow of the twilight shone like a jew-
    eled crown,
And, bathed in the living glory, as the people lifted
    their eyes,
They saw the pride of the city, the spire of St. Michaels,
    rise.

High over the lesser steeples, tipped with a golden ball,
That hung like a radiant planet caught in its earth-
    ward fall;
First glimpse of home to the sailor who made their
    harbor round,
The last slow fading vision dear to the outward bound.

The gently gathering shadows shut out the waning light;
The children prayed at their bedsides as you will pray
    tonight;
The noise of buyer and seller from the busy mart was
    gone,
And in dreams of a peaceful morrow the city slum-
    bered on.

But another light than sunrise aroused the sleeping
    street,
For a cry was heard at midnight and the rush of
    trampling feet;
Men stared in each other's faces through mingled fire
    and smoke,
While the frantic bells went clashing clamorous stroke
    on stroke!

By the glare of her blazing roof-tree the houseless
    mother fled,
With the babe she pressed to her bosom shrieking in
    nameless dread,
While the fire king's wild battalions scaled wall and
    capstone high,
And planted their flaring banners against an inky sky.

From the death that raged behind them and the crash
    of ruin loud,
To the great square of the city were driven the surging
    crowd,
Where yet firm in all the tumult, unscathed by the
    fiery flood,
With its heavenward pointing finger the church of St.
    Michael's stood.

But e'en as they gazed upon it there rose a sudden wail,
A cry of horror blended with the roaring of the gale,
On whose scorching wings undriven a single flaming
brand
Aloft on the towering steeple clung like a bloody hand.

"Will it fade?" The whisper trembled from a thousand
whitening lips;
Far out on the lurid harbor they watched it from the
ships—
A baleful gleam that brighter and ever brighter shone,
Like a flickering, trembling will-o'-wisp to a steady
beacon grown.

"Uncounted gold shall be given to the man whose brave
right hand,
For the love of the periled city plucks down yon burning brand!"
So cried the mayor of Charleston, that all the people
heard,
But they looked each one at his fellow and no man
spoke a word.

Who is it leans from the belfry with face upturned to
the sky?
Clings to a column and measures the dizzy spire with
his eye?
Will he dare it, the hero undaunted, that terrible sicken-
ing height?
Or will the hot blood of his courage freeze in his veins
at the sight?

But see! he has stepped on the railing, he climbs with
his feet and his hands,

And firm on a narrow projection with the belfry beneath him he stands;
Now once, and once only, they cheer him—a single tempestuous breath—
And there falls on the multitude gazing a hush like the stillness of death.

Slow, steadily mounting, unheeding aught save the goal of the fire,
Still higher and higher an atom he moves on the face of the spire;
He stops! Will he fall? Lo! for answer a gleam, like a meteor's track,
And hurled on the stones of the pavement the red brand lies shattered and black.

Once more the shouts of the people have rent the quivering air,
At the church door mayor and council wait with their feet on the stair,
And the eager throng behind them press for a touch of his hand—
The unknown savior whose daring could compass a deed so grand.

But why does a sudden tremor seize on them while they gaze?
And what means that stifled murmur of wonder and amaze?
He stood in the gate of the temple he had periled his life to save,
And the face of the hero, my children, was the sable face of a slave!

With folded arms he was speaking, in tones that were
   clear, not loud,
And his eyes ablaze in their sockets burnt into the eyes
   of the crowd:
"You may keep your gold, I scorn it!—but answer me,
   ye who can,
If the deed I have done before you be not the deed
   of a MAN?"

He stepped but a short pace backward, and from all
   the women and men
There were only sobs for answer, and the mayor called
   for a pen
And the great seal of the city that he might read who
   ran;
And the slave who saved St. Michaels went out from
   the door—a man.

—Mary Anna Phinney Stansbury.

THE FUGITIVE SLAVE'S APOSTROPHE
TO THE NORTH STAR

STAR of the North! Though night winds drift
The fleecy drapery of the sky
Between thy lamp and me, I lift,
Yes, lift with hope my sleepless eye
To the blue heights wherein thou dwellest,
And of a land of freedom tellest.

Star of the North! While blazing day
Pours round me its full tide of light,
And hides thy pale but faithful ray,
I, too, lie hid and long for night:
For night—I dare not walk at noon,
Nor dare I trust the faithless moon—

Nor faithless man, whose burning lust
For gold hath riveted my chain;
Nor other leader can I trust
But thee, of even the starry train;
For all the host around thee burning,
Like faithless man keep turning, turning.

I may not follow where they go:
Star of the North, I look to thee
While on I press; for well I know
Thy light and truth shall set me free—
Thy light that no poor slave deceiveth;
Thy truth that all my soul believeth.

They of the East beheld the star
That over Bethlehem's manger glowed:

With joy they hailed it from afar,
    And followed where it marked the road,
Till where its rays directly fell,
They found the Hope of Israel.

Wise were the men who followed thus
    The star that sets man free from sin!
Star of the North! thou art to us—
    Who're slaves because we wear a skin
Dark as is night's protecting wing—
Thou art to us a holy thing.

And we are wise to follow thee!
    I trust thy steady light alone:
Star of the North! thou seem'st to me
    To burn before the Almighty's throne,
To guide me through these forests dim
And vast to liberty and HIM.

Thy beam is on the glassy breast
    Of the still spring upon whose brink
I lay my weary limbs to rest,
    And bow my parching lips to drink.
Guide of the friendless Negro's way,
I bless thee for this quiet ray!

In the dark top of southern pines
    I nestled when the driver's horn
Called to the field in lengthening lines,
    My fellows at the break of morn.
And there I lay till thy sweet face
Looked in upon my "hiding place."

The tangled cane-brake—where I crept
    For shelter from the heat of noon,

And where, while others toiled, I slept
　　Till wakened by the rising moon—
As its stalks felt the night wind free,
Gave me to catch a glimpse of thee.

Star of the North! in bright array
　　The constellations round thee sweep,
Each holding on its nightly way,
　　Rising or sinking in the deep,
And as it hangs in mid heaven flaming,
The homage of some nation claiming.

This nation to the eagle cowers;
　　Fit ensign; she's a bird of spoil;
Like worships like! for each devours
　　The earnings of another's toil.
I've felt her talons and her beak,
And now the gentler lion seek.

The lion at the virgin's feet
　　Crouches and lays his mighty paw
Into her lap!—an emblem meet
　　Of England's queen and English law—
Queen that hath made her islands free!
Law that holds out its shield to me!

Star of the North! upon that shield
　　Thou shinest—O forever shine!
The Negro from the cotton field
　　Shall then beneath its orb recline,
And feed the lion crouched before it,
Nor heed the eagle screaming o'er it!

　　　　　　　　　　　　—JOHN PIERPONT.

ETHIOPIA SALUTING THE COLORS

WHO are you, dusky woman, so ancient, hardly
    human,
    With your woolly white and turban'd head and
bare, bony feet?
Why, rising by the roadside here, do you the colors
    greet?

('Tis while our army lines, Carolina's sands and pines,
Forth from thy hovel door thou Ethiopia com'st to me,
As under doughty Sherman I march toward the sea.)

Me master years a hundred since from my parents
    sunder'd
A little child they caught me as the savage beast is
    caught,
Then hither me across the sea the cruel slaver brought.

No further does she say, but lingering all the day,
Her high borne turban'd head she wags and rolls her
    darkling eye,
And courtesies to the regiments the guidons moving by.

What is it, fateful woman, so blear, hardly human?
Why wag your head with turban bound yellow, red
    and green?
Are the things so strange and marvelous you see or
    have seen?

                —WALT WHITMAN.

THE AFRICAN CHIEF

CHAINED in the market-place he stood,
  A man of giant frame,
  Amid the gathering multitude
That shrunk to hear his name—
All stern of look and strong of limb,
  His dark eye on the ground—
And silently they gazed on him,
  As on a lion bound.

Vainly but well that chief had fought,
  He was a captive now,
Yet pride, that fortune humbles not,
  Was written on his brow.
The scars his dark, broad bosom wore
  Show warrior true and brave;
A prince among his tribe before,
  He could not be a slave.

Then to his conqueror he spake—
  "My brother is a king;
Undo this necklace from my neck,
  And take this bracelet ring,
And send me where my brother reigns,
  And I will fill thy hands
With store of ivory from the plains,
  And gold dust from the sands."

"Not for thy ivory or thy gold
  Will I unbind thy chain;
That bloody hand shall never hold
  The battle spear again.

A price thy nation never gave,
   Shall yet be paid for thee;
For thou shalt be the Christian's slave,
   In lands beyond the sea."

Then wept the warrior chief and bade
   To shred his locks away;
And one by one each heavy braid
   Before the victor lay.
Thick were the platted locks and long,
   And deftly hidden there
Shone many a wedge of gold among
   The dark and crispéd hair.

"Look, feast thy greedy eye with gold
   Long kept for sorest need;
Take it—thou askest sums untold,
   And say that I am freed.
Take it—my wife, the livelong day
   Weeps by the cocoa-tree,
And my young children leave their play,
   And ask in vain for me."

"I take thy gold, but I have made
   Thy fetters fast and strong,
And ween that by the cocoa shade
   Thy wife will wait thee long."
Strong was the agony that shook
   The captive's frame to hear,
And the proud meaning of his look
   Was changed to mortal fear.

His heart was broken—crazed his brain:
   At once his eye grew wild;

9

He struggled fiercely with his chain,
  Whispered and wept and smiled;
Yet wore not long those fatal bands,
  And once at shut of day,
They drew him forth upon the sands,
  The foul hyena's prey.

—WILLIAM CULLEN BRYANT.

THE BLACK MAN'S BURDEN

TAKE up the black man's burden!
  Not his across the seas,
  But his who grows your cotton,
  And sets your heart at ease.
When to the sodden rice fields,
  Your children dare not go,
Nor brave the heat that singes,
  Like the foundry's fiery glow.

Take up the black man's burden!
  He helped to share your own,
On many a scene by battle clouds,
  Portentously o'erblown;
On Wagner's awful parapet,
  As late, when Shafter's plan
Was for the "boys" to take the lead,
  He showed himself a man.

Take up the black man's burden!
  'Tis heavy with the weight
Of old ancestral taint, the curse
  Of new engendered hate;

The scorn of those who throw to him
    Their table's meanest crust—
Children of these who made him serve
    Their idleness and lust.

Take up the black man's burden!
    When you were out for votes,
His geese—they were all swans to you,
    And sheep were all his goats.
'Twas "Pompey this" and "Pompey that,"
    And "Pompey, bless your heart!"
But it's "Devil take you, Pompey!"
    Now you play the lion's part.

Take up the black man's burden!
    If you have got a brief
For all the suffering of the earth,
    To give them swift relief.
Don't let the millions here at home,
    Whose bonds you struck away,
Learn from your heedlessness to cry,
    "Give back the evil day!"

Take up the black man's burden!
    O black men, unto you
The summons is, when those forget
    Who should be kind and true!
Put not your trust in such a boast,
    Straight hair and paler skin;
The duty calls them otherwhere,
    Fight your own fight—and win!

Take up the black man's burden!
    Poor patient folk and tame—

The heritage of cursing,
  Of foolishness and blame.
Your task, the task of earning,
  By many an evil pressed,
Warm, touched with human pity,
  The friendship of the best.

—JOHN WHITE CHADWICK.

THE LIGHTS AT CARNEY'S POINT *

O WHITE little lights at Carney's Point,
    You shine so clear o'er the Delaware;
  When the moon rides high in the silver sky,
    Then you gleam, white gems on the Delaware.
Diamond circlet on a full white throat,
    You laugh your rays on a questing boat;
Is it peace you dream in your flashing gleam,
    O'er the quiet flow of the Delaware?

And the lights grew dim at the water's brim,
    For the smoke of the mills shredded slow between;
And the smoke was red, as is new bloodshed,
    And the lights went lurid 'neath the livid screen.

O red little lights at Carney's Point,
    You glower so grim o'er the Delaware;
When the moon hides low sombrous clouds below,
    Then you glow like coals o'er the Delaware.
Blood red rubies on a throat of fire,
    You flash through the dusk of a funeral pyre;
Are there hearth fires red whom you fear and dread
    O'er the turgid flow of the Delaware?

---

* The lights of the great powder mills at Carney's Point can be seen
for miles across and down the river.

And the lights gleamed gold o'er the river cold,
   For the murk of the furnace shed a copper veil;
And the veil was grim at the great cloud's brim,
   And the lights went molten, now hot, now pale.

O gold little lights at Carney's Point,
   You gleam so proud o'er the Delaware;
When the moon grows wan in the eastering dawn,
   Then you sparkle gold points o'er the Delaware.
Aureate filagree on a Croesus' brow,
   You hasten the dawn on a gray ship's prow.
Light you streams of gold in the grim ship's hold
   O'er the sullen flow of the Delaware?

And the lights went gray in the ash of day,
   For a quiet Aurora brought a halcyon balm;
And the sun laughed high in the infinite sky,
   And the lights were forgot in the sweet, sane calm.

                —ALICE DUNBAR-NELSON.

IT'S ME, O LORD!*

THEY stood in an immaculate row across the stage, their dignity saved from seriousness and a certain friendliness established with the audience by little pleasant touches of African foolishness that one of them understood so well how to supply.

Usually we got folding chairs from the big pile and sat a little way back from the tent, under the moon and stars, where we could hear a cricket or two, and sometimes see off over a park or a valley or a hillside.

They sang the quaint, deep old spirituals simply, earnestly and well. Strange music that, from the hearts of a race bowed down; shot through, too, in some of its minors, with eerie, barbaric glints of who knows what echoes of jungles and voodooism. There is a strain in it that is surely far older than America. Its weary patience, its childlike freedom from malice in the face of crushing injustice, its sweet, unaffected humility—these are home grown and jab into your heart if you are Southern, and feel your share of the blame lying heavy upon you.

We sat there sometimes and wanted to hear the white race line up with them and sing, with the same plangent, haunting inescapable sincerity:

> It's *me*, it's *me*, it's *me*, O Lord,
> Standing in the need of prayer!
> Not my sister, not my brother,
> But it's *me*, O Lord,

---

* From a story of the Jubilee Singers in Collier's Weekly. By permission of Collier's Weekly.

> Standing in the need of prayer!
> Not my father, not my mother,
> But it's *me*, O Lord;
> It's *me*, it's *me*, it's *me*, O Lord,
> Standing in the need of prayer!

How the spirit of the old, humble, heavy laden days lives in these cadences and hurts you as you listen! Heaven is a place where the black man may

> Sing and shout,
> Nobody there to turn me out!

very different from the big house on the plantation in the old days, where the white folks lived. Only parts of that were open to him and his barefooted fellows. So he sings of the time when he can say:

> I got shoes, you got shoes,
> *All* God's chillun got shoes;
> When I git to heaven go'n' put on my shoes
> And walk *all over* God's heaven!

And in the meantime he says explicitly in one song and implicitly in many, "live a-humble," and means it, and accepts it with a marvelous sweetness that must have come, we Christians say, from Christ.

The places to which they might not go! The things they should not do! The pleasantnesses of the world that were not for them! They suffered long and silently and left this little barb forever in their music to prick us on moonlit nights as we sit outside the Chautauqua tents and listen to their humble millions speaking through their representatives of today, who, like the rest of us, are trying somehow to scramble up and on to something better, if that may be.

—Alma and Paul Ellerbe.

HOW FRANCE RECEIVED THE NEGRO SOLDIERS *

A PEACEFUL town, far from the front. A beautiful June day full of perfume of roses; resplendent summer freely bursting into blooms, indifferent to human plaints, frets and agitations. A boy of ten years, head like the urchin of the year one, runs through the streets crying "The Americans are coming to B——; the inhabitants are invited to greet them!"

The Americans! For months they had been discussed; they had been expected, and there was great curiosity; groups of people go down to the public square of the town where they see upon our white streets the first ranks of the Allied troops. But what a surprise! They are black soldiers! Black soldiers? There is great astonishment, a little fear. The rural population, not well informed, knows well the Negro of Africa, but those from America's soil, the country of the classical type, characterized by the cold, smooth, white face; that from America could come this dark troupe—none could believe it with his own eyes.

They dispute among themselves; they are a little irritated; some of the women become afraid; one of them confides to me that she feels the symptoms of an attack of indigestion. Smiling, reassurably, "Lady, with the all too emotional stomach, quiet yourself! They do not eat human flesh; two or three days from now you will be perfectly used to them." I said two or three days, but from that very evening the ice is

* From "The American Negro in the World War," by Emmett J. Scott.

broken. Natives and foreigners smile at each other and try to understand each other. The next day we see the little children in the arms of the huge Negroes, confidently pressing their rosy cheeks to the cheeks of ebony, while their mothers look on with approbation.

A deep sympathy is in store for those men, which yesterday was not surmised. Very quickly it is seen that they have nothing of the savage in them, but on the other hand one could not find a soldier more faultless in his bearing and in his manners more affable or more delicate than these children of the sun, whose ancestors dreamed under the wonderful nights along murmuring streams. We admire their forms—handsome, vigorous and athletic; their intelligent and loyal faces with their large, gleaming eyes, at times dreamy, and with a bit of sadness in them.

Far removed is the time when their inauspicious influence was felt upon the digestive organs of the affrighted lady. Now one honors himself to have them at his table. He spends hours in long talks with them; with a great supply of dictionaries and manuals of conversation. The white mothers of France weep to see the photographs of the colored mothers, and display the portrait of their soldier sons. The fiancées of our own "Poilus" become interested in the fiancées across the sea, in their dress, in their head-dress, and in everything which makes woman resemble woman in every clime. Late at night the workers of the field forget their fatigue as they hear arise in the peaceful night the melancholy voices which call up to the memory of the exile his distant country, America. In the lanes, along the flowery hedges, more than one group of colored American soldiers fraternize with our people, while the setting sun makes blue the neighboring hills and gently the song of night is awakened.

And then these soldiers, who had become our friends, depart. One evening sad adieux are exchanged. Adieu? How we wish they may be only "Au revoirs." Promises to correspond, to return when furloughs are granted, here and there tears fall, and when the next day the heavy trucks roll off in the chilly morning, carrying away to the front our exotic guests, a veritable sadness seizes us.

Soldier friends, our hearts, our wishes, go with you. That destiny may be merciful to you; that the bullets of the enemy may spare you. And, if any of you should never see your native home again, may the soil of France give you sweet repose.

Soldiers, who arrived among us one clear June day, redolent with the scent of roses, you will always live in our hearts.

HOW JIM EUROPE AND HIS JAZZ OUT-FIT BROKE INTO THE WAR *

THEN the war broke out and Europe broke in. If he had been built that way he could have ducked it and stayed in town with his bank deposits, but he couldn't figure it. He told Colonel Hayward that he was ready to follow, or even to go ahead of the flag to the last ounce of jazz, and there were ninety-nine others like him. So the band was signed up and sworn in, and Daniel C. Reid and some others made a pool of enough thousands of dollars to supply instruments that would stand the wear and tear of war and not go bad if dented up with shrapnel and such like.

Among the men who slipped into olive drab with the boss, come weal, come woe, were Sergeant Noble Sissle, who plays the cornet like anything and knows all the tricks of drum majoring, and sings like a lark and writes verses by the yard; Herbert and Steve whistlers, and oh! such drummers; Raphael Hernandez, baritone saxophoner; War Andres, better known as Trombone Andres; Elijah Rigos, clarinetist; and Frank De Bronte, who, next to Europe himself, is called the king of jazz. The rest of the band, the marimbaphones, the double b-flat helicons, the bunch of French horns and all the rest, clear down to the cymbals, were manned by other eminent operators, making what is called a *toot* ensemble, at once hope reviving and awe inspiring.

* From ''Filling France with Jazz''—The World Magazine, March 30, 1919. Reproduced in "The American Negro in the World War," by Emmett J. Scott.

To understand jazz it is well to know that it isn't merely a series of uncontrollable spasms or outbursts of enthusiasm scattered through a composition and discharged on the four winds, first by one wing, then by another of the band. Of course, if a player feels an attack of something which he believes to be a jazz novelty rumbling in his system, it is not the Europe rule to make him choke it back and thus run the risk of cheating the world out of a good thing. Any player can try anything once. If it doesn't come out a fliv on harmony, it can remain as a toot to be used whenever there's a place where it won't crowd regular notes over the bars.

The basic fundamental of jazz, however, is created by means of a variety of cones inserted point down in the bells of the horns. These cones are of two kinds. One is of metal and the other is of leather. The leather cones are usually soaked in water before the band goes out for a blow. The metal cones muffle and modify the natural tones of the instruments and make them come across with new sound values.

When a leather cone is wrung out and fitted into the vestibule of a horn, and the man back of the works contributes the best that is in him, it is somewhat difficult to explain what happens in mere words. You might get it with both ears and almost see it. The cone, being wet, the sound might be called liquefied harmony. It runs and ripples, then has a sort of choking sensation; next it takes on the musical color of Niagara Falls at a distance, and subsides to a trout brook near by. The brassiness of the horn is changed and there is a sort of throbbing nasal effect, half moan, half hallelujah. Get me?

Having set this down, we may now land with the band at Brest, France.

The first thing that Jim Europe's outfit did when it got ashore wasn't to eat. It wanted France to know that it was present, so it blew some plain, ordinary jazz over the town. Twenty minutes before the 369th embarked, Brest wasn't at all la-la, so to speak; but as soon as Europe got to work that part of France could see that hope wasn't entirely dead.

From Brest the Europe outfit went to St. Nazaire, sowing jazz selections over the agricultural terrain, and bunching bits of it in the cantons en route. There was a rest center at St. Nazaire. Europe went to the center of the center, and for two months all he had to do was to help the boys rest by providing a brand of soothing syrup. All the sects in all the sectors round about that had carfare commuted into town and lolled in the rest zone. The city council adopted resolutions and the prefect delivered an eulogium right at Noble Sissle and the backstop of snare drums.

A call for help from Aix-le-Bains took the band to that resort. It arrived just in time to capture the Casino in a night attack. On all fronts at this time soldiers that had been dodging minenwerfers were buoyed by the promise that Jim Europe had enough jazz in stock to last until the war was over over there. Troops suffering with aches were hurried down to Aix—honest, they were, and the band did the rest.

Between concerts, so to express it, the 369th band would get from under the coils of horns, unsling its drums, and load up with machine gune and go into the deep and mussy trenches and practice on the unhappy wretches on the other side of no man's land. Europe himself was the first colored officer to rest elbows against a first line trench in one of the uncomfortable bois countries. He did solo work with a machine gun forty times heavier than a trombone, and actually got it to working in syncopated time. If we ever have another war, and it could be fought exclusively by syncopating, Jim Europe would have a major general's rating.

—CHARLES WELTON.

THE STEVEDORES *

WE are the army stevedores, lusty and virile and
        strong;
    We are given the hardest work of the war, and
the hours are long;
We handle the heavy boxes and shovel the dirty coal;
While the soldiers and sailors work in the light,
We burrow below like a mole.
But somebody has to do this work, or the soldiers
    could not fight;
And whatever work is given a man is good if he does
    it right.
We are the army stevedores, and we are volunteers;
We did not wait for the draft to come and put aside
    our fears.
We flung them away to the winds of fate at the very
    first call of our land,
And each of us offered a willing heart and the strength
    of a brawny hand.
We are the army stevedores and work as we must
    and may,
The Cross of Honor will never be ours to proudly wear
    away.

* From "The American Negro in the World War."

But the men at the front would never be there
And the battles could not be won,
If the stevedores stopped in their dull routine
And left their work undone.
But somebody has to do this work;
Be glad that it isn't you!
We are the the army stevedores; give us our due!

—ELLA WHEELER WILCOX.

SHALL I SAY, "MY SON YOU ARE BRANDED"? *

SHALL I say, "My son, you are branded in this country's pageantry,
Foully tethered, bound forever, and no forum makes you free"?
Shall I mark the young light fading through your soul-enchanneled eye,
As the dusky pall of the shadows screen the highway of your sky?

Or shall I, with love prophetic, bid you dauntlessly arise,
Spurn the handicap that binds you, taking what the world denies?
Bid you storm the sullen fortress built by prejudice and wrong,
With a faith that shall not falter in your heart and on your tongue?

—GEORGIA DOUGLASS JOHNSON.

_____

* From ''The Crisis.''

IN FLANDERS FIELDS

An Echo

IN Flanders fields the poppies blow
  Between the crosses, row on row
    That mark the graves where black men lie;
    Their souls, long wafted to the sky,
Look down upon the earth below.

E'en while we mourn their loss, we see
Their brothers hanged upon a tree
    By whom they saved. Their pain fraught cry
    Mounts up to those who stand on high,
And watch the scarlet flowered sea
    In Flanders fields.

In Flanders fields they shall not sleep!
No! For their murdered kin they keep
    A vigil through the day and night,
    'Til God Himself shall snatch from sight
Such scenes as make our heroes weep
    In Flanders fields.

—ORLANDO C. W. TAYLOR.

Listen

I SIT AND SEW *

I SIT and sew—a useless task it seems,
My hands grown tired, my head weighed down with
dreams—
The panoply of war, the martial tread of men,
Grim faced, stern eyed, gazing beyond the ken
Of lesser souls, whose eyes have not seen Death,
Nor learned to hold their lives but as a breath—
But—I must sit and sew.

I sit and sew—my heart aches with desire—
That pageant terrible, that fiercely pouring fire
On wasted fields, and writhing grotesque things
Once men. My soul in pity flings
Appealing cries, yearning only to go
There in that holocaust of hell, those fields of woe—
But—I must sit and sew

The little useless seam, the idle patch;
Why dream I here beneath my homely thatch,
When there they lie in sodden mud and rain,
Pitifully calling me, the quick ones and the slain?
You need me, Christ. It is no roseate dream
That beckons me—this pretty futile seam
It stifles me—God, *must* I sit and sew?

—ALICE DUNBAR-NELSON.

* From the A. M. E. Church Review.

10

At the moon's down going let it be
On the quarry hill with its one gnarled tree.

THE LYNCHERS

AT the moon's down going let it be
On the quarry hill with its one gnarled tree.

The red rock road of the underbrush,
Where the woman came through the summer hush.

The sumac high and the elder thick,
Where we found the stone and the ragged stick.

The trampled road of the thicket full
Of footprints down to the quarry pool.

The rocks that ooze with the hue of lead,
Where we found her lying stark and dead.

The scraggy wood; the Negro hut,
With its doors and windows locked and shut.

A secret signal, a foot's rough tramp;
A knock at the door, a lifted lamp.

An oath, a scuffle; a ring of masks;
A voice that answers, a voice that asks.

A group of shadows; the moon's red fleck;
A running noose and a man's bared neck.

A word, a curse, and a shape that swings;
The lonely night and a bat's black wings. . . .

At the moon's down going let it be
On the quarry hill with its one gnarled tree.

—Madison Cawein.

KU-KLUX

WE have sent him seeds of the melon's core,
And nailed a warning upon his door;
By the Ku-Klux laws we can do no more.

Down in the hollow, mid crib and stack,
The roof of his low-porched house looms black,
Not a line of light at the door sill's crack.

Yet arm and mount! and mask and ride!
The hounds can sense though the fox may hide!
And for a word too much men oft have died.

The clouds blow heavy towards the moon,
The edge of the storm will reach it soon,
The kildee cries and the lonesome loon.

The clouds shall flush with a wilder glare,
Than the lightning makes with its angled flare,
When the Ku-Klux verdict is given there.

In the pause of the thunder rolling low,
A rifle's answer, who shall know
From the wind's fierce hurl and the rain's black blow?

Only the signature written grim
At the end of the message brought to him—
A hempen rope and a twisted limb.

So arm and mount! and mask! and ride!
The hounds can sense though the fox may hide!
And for a word too much men oft have died!

—MADISON CAWEIN.

THE SECOND LOUISIANA

MAY 27, 1863

D ARK as the clouds of even,
   Ranked in the western heaven,
    Waiting the breath that lifts
All the dread mass, and drifts
Tempest and falling brand
Over a ruined land—
So still and orderly,
Arm to arm, knee to knee,
Waiting the great event,
Stands the black regiment.

Down the long dusky line
Teeth gleam and eyeballs shine;
And the bright bayonet,
Bristling and firmly set,
Flashed with a purpose grand,
Long ere the sharp command
Of the fierce rolling drum
Told them their time had come,
Told them what work was sent
For the black regiment.

"Now," the flag sergeant cried,
"Though death and hell betide,
Let the whole nation see
If we are fit to be
Free in this land; or bound
Down, like the whining hound—

Bound with red stripes of pain
In our old chains again!"
Oh! what a shout there went
From the black regiment!

"Charge!" Trump and drum awoke,
Onward the bondmen broke;
Bayonet and saber stroke
Vainly opposed their rush
Through the wild battle's crush,
With but one thought aflush,
Driving their lords like chaff,
In the guns' mouths they laugh;
Or, at the slippery brands,
Leaping with open hands,
Down they tear man and horse,
Down in their awful course;
Trampling with bloody heel
Over the crashing steel,
All their eyes forward bent,
Rushed the black regiment.

"Freedom!" their battle cry—
"Freedom!" or leave to die!
Ah! and they meant the word,
Not as with us 'tis heard,
Not as a mere party shout:
They gave their spirits out;
Trusted the end to God,
And on the gory sod
Rolled in triumphant blow,
Whether for weal or woe;
Glad to breathe one free breath,
Though on the lips of death;

Praying alas! in vain!—
That they might fall again,
So they could once more see
That burst to liberty!
This was what "freedom" lent
To the black regiment.

Hundreds on hundreds fell;
But they are resting well;
Scourges and shackles strong
Never shall do them wrong.
O to the living few,
Soldiers, be just and true!
Hail them as comrades tried;
Fight with them side by side;
Never in field or tent,
Scorn the black regiment!

—George H. Boker.

TO CANAAN

WHERE are you going, soldiers,
    With banner, gun and sword?
    We're marching south to Can'aan
To battle for the Lord!
What Captain leads your armies
    Along the rebel coasts?
The Mighty One of Israel,
    His name is Lord of Hosts!
        To Canaan, to Canaan,
        The Lord has led us forth,
        To blow before the heathen walls
        The trumpets of the North!

What flag is this you carry
    Along the sea and shore?
The same our grandsires lifted up—
    The same our fathers bore!
In many a battle's tempest
    It shed the crimson rain—
What God has woven in his loom
    Let no man rend in twain!
        To Canaan, to Canaan,
        The Lord has led us forth,
        To plant upon the rebel towers
        The banners of the North!

What troop is this that follows,
    All armed with picks and spades?*
These are the swarthy bondsmen—
    The iron skin brigades!

---

* The captured slaves were at this time organized as pioneers.

They'll pile up Freedom's breastworks,
    They'll scoop out rebel's graves;
Who then will be the owner
    And march them off for slaves?
        To Canaan, to Canaan,
        The Lord has led us forth,
        To strike upon the captive's chain
        The hammers of the North!

What song is this you're singing?
    The same that Israel sung
When Moses led the mighty choir,
    And Miriam's timbrel rung!
To Canaan! To Canaan!
    The priests and maidens cried:
To Canaan! To Canaan!
    The people's voice replied.
        To Canaan, to Canaan,
        The Lord has led us forth,
        To thunder through its adder dens
        The anthems of the North!

When Canaan's hosts are scattered,
    And all her walls lie flat,
What follows next in order?
    The Lord will see to that!
We'll break the tyrant's scepter—
    We'll build the people's throne—
When half the world is Freedom's,
    Then all the world's our own!
        To Canaan, to Canaan,
        The Lord has led us forth,
        To sweep the rebel threshing floors,
        A whirlwind from the North!
                —OLIVER WENDELL HOLMES.

THE HERO OF FORT WAGNER

FORT WAGNER! that is a place for us
　　To remember well, my lad!
　For us, who were under the guns, and know
　　The bloody work we had.

I should not speak to one so young,
　　Perhaps, as I do to you;
But you are a soldier's son, my boy,
　　And you know what soldiers do.

And when peace comes to our land again,
　　And your father sits in his home,
You will hear such tales of war as this,
　　For many a year to come.

We were repulsed from the fort, you know,
　　And saw our heroes fall,
Till the dead were piled in bloody heaps
　　Under the frowning wall.

Yet crushed as we were and beaten back,
　　Our spirits never bowed;
And gallant deeds there were done
　　To make a soldier proud.

Brave men were there for their country's sake,
　　To spend their latest breath;
But the bravest was one who gave his life
　　And his body after death.

No greater words than his dying ones
    Have been spoken under the sun;
Not even his who brought the news
    On the field at Ratisbon.

I was pressing up to try if yet
    Our men might take the place,
And my feet had slipped in his oozing blood
    Before I saw his face.

His face! it was black as the skies o'erhead
    With the smoke of the angry guns;
And a gash in his bosom showed the work
    Of our country's traitor sons.

Your pardon, my poor boy! I said,
    I did not see you here;
But I will not hurt you as I pass;
    I'll have a care; no fear!

He smiled; he had only strength to say
    These words, and that was all:
"I'm done gone, massa; step on me;
    And you can scale the wall!"

                    —PHOEBE CARY.

BURY THEM

WAGNER, JULY 18, 1863

BURY the dragon's teeth!
   Bury them deep and dark!
   The incisors, swart and stark,
The molars, heavy and dark—
And the one white fang underneath!

Bury the hope forlorn!
   Never shudder to fling,
With its fellows, dusky and worn,
   The strong and beautiful thing
(Pallid ivory and pearl!)
   Into the horrible pit—
Hurry it in and hurl
   All the rest over it!

Trample them, clod by clod,
   Stamp them in dust amain!
   The cuspids, cruent and red,
   That the monster, Freedom, shed
On the sacred, strong slave-sod—
   They never shall rise again!

Never?—what hideous growth
   Is sprouting through clod and clay?
   What terror starts to the day?
A crop of steel on our oath!
   How the burnished stamens glance!
Spike and anther and blade,
How they burst from the bloody shade,
   And spindle to spear and lance!

There are tassels of blood-red maize—
   How the horrible harvest grows!
'Tis sabres that glint and daze—
'Tis bayonets all ablaze
   Uprearing in dreadful rows!

For one that we buried there,
A thousand are come to air!
Ever by door stone and hearth,
They break from the angry earth—
   And out of the crimson sand,
Where the cold white fang was laid,
Rises a terrible shade,
   The wraith of a sleepless brand!

And our hearts wax strange and chill,
With an ominous shudder and thrill,
   Even here on the strong slave-sod,
Lest haply we be found
(Ah, dread no brave hath drowned!)
   Fighting against Great God.

          —Henry Howard Brownell.

WHETHER WHITE OR BLACK, A MAN *

FELLOW men, you come to take my life; it is at your disposal if I have forfeited the right to live. But I ask to be heard before you kill me.

(Hear him! Hear him!)

In the first place I ask you to consider what you have already done in striking that old man who gave his lifeblood to uphold your rights and the honor of your state. The empty sleeve that hangs at his side ought to have been his protection. Be it said to your shame that it was not!

The innocent members of yonder household should be held sacred by you, for they are dependent women, too feeble to strike back, and no American should be a Turk, making war upon defenseless women and children!

(No, no, they are safe!)

Then upon me and me alone let your vengeance rest, but first let me tell you why I am willing to die.

I am not the first man who has died for a principle, neither shall I be the last. Human history is written in blood, and the Civil War did not end the struggle of the black man for freedom.

Fellow men, I appeal to you as men—not as brothers, not as fellow citizens—but simply on the plane of a common manhood have I not the right to be? Have I not the right to be what I am?

I confess to you that I am black. In yonder cabin is the old, wrinkled, careworn woman whom I call my grandmother. She is the only mother that I have

---

* From "Whether White or Black, a Man."

ever known. My own mother gave me to her—gave me, a puny, crying, crippled babe—too feeble and crippled to be of any use to anybody in this world.

I had no grandfather. My grandfather did not belong to the black race—therefore he did not belong to me.

Cast off by both father and mother I became the idol of that poor old grandmother. For me she has toiled when her fingers were knotted with pain and her back bent with the burden and heat of the day. For me she has poured out her life blood, drop by drop. Have I not the right to try to be somebody for her sake? Again, in this home is a woman. To you she belongs to that hated class called "nigger teachers"; to me she belongs to that rare, rare class of noble, unselfish women who have left beautiful homes in the North to come here and work like the little coral insects deep down under the surface, while the waves of public sentiment have rolled tumultuously over their heads. She came to build up the character of the black child; God gave mine into her hands, and she moulded it. She gave her time, her strength, her money to me. She sent me to a northern college. She opened homes of culture to me. She made it possible for me to become something of a scholar. She sent me abroad. She watched over me; she prayed for me. Fellow men—I appeal to your manhood—have I not the right, in view of that noble unselfishness, to try to be somebody for her sake?

In this home, too, is the woman that I love, the woman whom I hoped in a few days to call by the sacred name of wife. Her young life has not been free from sorrow, for she, too, belongs to the despised black race; but she has given to me the great wealth of her love. Have I not the right, because of that gift, to try to be somebody for her sake?

Again, in this home are friends, friends whom I have grown to love and trust; in their number are both white and black. There are men who, like that old, white-haired soldier, have defied public sentiment in order to become my friends. They forgot to ask the question whether I was black or whether I was white, but believed in my manhood, in my integrity of purpose, in my honesty of character, in my purity of life. I appeal to you as men, have I not the right to be all that their faith in me calls for me to be? Fellow men, I have the right!

(That's all right; but you ain't got no right to represent us!)

Represent *you!* Could *I* ever do that! But I know what you mean. You mean that I, a black man, have no right to enter congress as the representative of both white and black men. You mean that it is all right for a white man to represent both races, but it is all wrong for a black man. I declare to you, as I expect soon to be judged by a just God, that I cannot see a bit more right in the one case than in the other. It is not a question of whiteness or of blackness that is to be considered, but a question of manhood and of fitness. But I want to tell you now, standing as I do, on the border land between life and death, that I am prouder of one drop of the black blood that flows in my veins from the honest heart of my bent old grandmother than I am of all the white blood that flows there from the corrupt heart of him who in God's sight was my grandfather. Him you made governor of one of your proudest southern states; the old grandmother you will send to the grave of a broken-hearted woman.

I'm So Sleepy

Such has been the history of the struggle between the races. Fellow men, I am ready to die, but remember this, that though you kill the body, you cannot kill the principle for which I have lived and for which I die—the RIGHT OF A BLACK MAN TO BE A FREE MAN.

—EDITH SMITH DAVIS.

ETHIOPIAN MAID *

I MINGLE my goblet with oil of the vine,
And drink to the health of a maid most benign;
No less do I drink to her beauty and youth,
Than to her meek innocence, virtue and truth;
And meekly arrayed in thy modest brocade,
I drink to thy health, Ethiopian maid.

'Mid noon-tide and moon-tide whatever my themes,
Thy vision creeps in the enchantments of dreams;
The pipings of skylarks and trills of the wren
Are mixed in the midst of the melody when
Thy laughter rings out in the vine scented glade,
As I drink to thy health, Ethiopian maid.

When sun of the tropics turns westward and dies,
The magic still lingers in light of thine eyes;
I mingle my goblet with oil of the palm,
Where spices hang over and summer smiles warm,
And there, 'mid the magic of forest and shade,
I drink thy sweet health, Ethiopian maid.

—WALTER EVERETTE HAWKINS.

---

* Reprinted from "The Crisis."
11

MAT

I N the swamp by black gum in a little log hut
    Lived Mat,
  The toughest little cuss in tatters and rags
  At that.
"A reg'lar good-for-nothing," the neighbors all vowed,
Who would rob a hen nest; not a melon he allowed
To remain in the patch, yet we, but for that,
    Liked Mat.

With his tatters all flying and a crownless hat,
    Came Mat
'Cross the hill by the cornfield and "sweet tater" patch,
    And that
Was a sign that "taters" and corn disappeared,
For when Mat was about, why everybody feared,
But then, when you saw him, your sorrow changed that
    For Mat.

For ten or eleven little brothers and sisters
    Had Mat;
And his poor mother labored to feed and clothe them,
    At that.
And work in the country when you wash the whole day,
And receive but a quarter is mighty poor pay,
No wonder he was ragged and would steal at that,
    Poor Mat!

Yet the world often wonders as it speeds its way
    At the Mats,
Who are reared in ignorance, the world's "good-for-
        nothings,"
    But for that,

How many called better, who've never felt the smart,
Of poverty's nettle can boast of a heart
As free from guile and as tender as that
    Of Mat's?

                  —D. WEBSTER DAVIS.

BELGIUM

FOUR years ago
    They took our young chief
      And led him away.
Stalwart he was,
As strong as the water bull,
As beautiful to look upon
As the tampa tree in the first dew of the morning.
Him the Belgians took and led away,
Captive for the rubber crew.

A sickness came upon our tribe,
A sickness laid our men low,
And killed our women;
And there were none to gather rubber.
And when the Belgians came
There was no rubber to give them.
And they grew angry, the Belgians,
And sent back to us Shenzi Khanga,
Him, whom they held as hostage.
He came back, but not he that went forth:

Never more would Shenzi Khanga hunt the fierce water
    bull;
Never more would Shenzi Khanga
Gaze on the fair Askaris maidens.

Back came Shenzi Khanga,
His arms but useless stumps,
And his eyeballs seared with the red hot iron;
Then we saw and were sorry and wept.

Today they tell us of a great fight
In the land of the white men;
They tell us of a curse, a curse fallen
On Belgium, the land of our oppressors;
They tell us of invading armies, ruthless and cruel;
They cry of homes burned, of men and women slaugh-
    tered;
Of women, hunted and ravished and killed.
So we look about us
At the blackened ruins of our huts;
At the thinned numbers of our tribe,
And at Shenzi Khanga;
And we hasten to him and gather about him and tell
    him
The news from the North.
Shenzi Khanga hears,
And raises his face with the useless eyes,
And lifts the useless stumps,
And Shenzi Khanga
Laughs!

—Lester B. Granger.

LAUS DEO

(On hearing the bells ring on the passage of the constitutional amendment abolishing slavery.)

IT is done!
Clang of bell and roar of gun
Send the tidings up and down.
How the belfries rock and reel!
How the great guns peal on peal,
Fling the joy from town to town!

Ring, O bells!
Every stroke exulting tells
Of the burial hour of crime.
Loud and long, that all may hear,
Ring for every listening ear
Of Eternity and Time!

Let us kneel:
God's own voice is in that peal,
And this spot is holy ground.
Lord, forgive us! What are we
That our eyes this glory see,
That our ears have heard the sound!

For the Lord
On the whirlwind is abroad
In the earthquake He has spoken;
He has smitten with His thunder
The iron walls asunder,
And the gates of brass are broken!

Loud and long
Lift the old exulting song;
Sing, with Miriam by the sea,
   "He has cast the mighty down;
   Horse and rider sink and drown;
He hath triumphed gloriously!"

Did we dare,
In our agony of prayer,
Ask for more than he has done?
   When was ever His right hand
   Over any time or land
Stretched as now beneath the sun?

How they pale,
Ancient myth and song and tale,
In this wonder of our days,
   When the cruel rod of war
   Blossoms white with righteous law,
And the wrath of man is praise!

Blotted out!
All within and all without,
Shall a fresher life begin;
   Freer breathe the universe
   As it rolls its heavy curse
On the dead and buried sin!

It is done!
In the circuit of the sun
Shall the sound thereof go forth.
   It shall bid the sad rejoice,
   It shall give the dumb a voice,
It shall belt with joy the earth!

Ring and swing,
Bells of joy! On morning's wing
Send the song of praise abroad!
With a sound of broken chains
Tell the nation that He reigns,
Who alone is Lord and God!

—JOHN GREENLEAF WHITTIER.

O BLACK AND UNKNOWN BARDS *

O BLACK and unknown bards of long ago,
How came your lips to touch the sacred fire?
How in your darkness did you come to know
The power and beauty of the minstrel's lyre?
Who first from midst his bonds lifted his eyes?
Who first from out the still watch, lone and long,
Feeling the ancient faith of prophets rise
Within his dark-kept soul, burst into song?

Heart of what slave poured out such melody
As "Steal away to Jesus"? On its strains
His spirit must have nightly floated free,
Though still about his hands he felt his chains.
Who heard great "Jordan roll"? Whose starward eye
Saw chariot "Swing low"? And who was he
That breathed that comforting, melodic sigh,
"Nobody knows de trouble I see"?

What merely living clod, what captive thing,
Could up toward God through all its darkness grope,

---

* Reprinted from the Century Magazine by permission J. W.
Johnson.

And find within its deadened heart to sing
    These songs of sorrow, love and faith, and hope?
How did it catch that subtle undertone,
    That note in music heard not with the ears?
How sound the elusive reed so seldom blown,
    Which stirs the soul or melts the heart to tears?

Not that great German master in his dream
    Of harmonies that thundered amongst the stars
At the creation, ever heard a theme
    Nobler than "Go down, Moses." Mark its bars,
How like a mighty trumpet call they stir
    The blood. Such are the notes that men have sung
Going to valorous deeds; such tones they were
    That helped make history when Time was young.

There is a wide, wide wonder in it all,
    That from degraded rest and servile toil
The fiery spirit of the seer should call
    These simple children of the sun and soil.
O black slave singers, gone, forgot, unfamed,
    You—you alone, of all the long, long line
Of those who've sung untaught, unknown, unnamed,
    Have stretched out upward, seeking the divine.

You sang not deeds of heroes or of kings;
    No chant of bloody war, no exulting pean
Of arms won triumphs; but your humble strings
    You touched in chord empyrean.
You sang far better than you knew; the songs
    That for your listeners' hungry hearts sufficed
Still live—but more than this to you belongs:
    You sang a race from wood and stone to Christ.

—JAMES WELDON JOHNSON.

THE YOUNG WARRIOR *

TODAY there is being sung in many a hard contested trench in Europe a new battle hymn. Men are being inspired to greater deeds of heroism by its soul stirring melody, and are giving up their lives to the spirit it inspires.

It is called "The Young Warrior," and was written by an American Negro.

Quite a few years ago there lived in Erie, Pennsylvania, a little Negro boy. His father and mother were in the service of a well-to-do family of that town. This family was to entertain a world famous violinist on a certain evening. The music loving heart of the little Negro ached to hear the great master, but how could he manage it? Poor little Negro boys are not welcome guests when the "white folks" entertain famous personages. However, though saying nothing of his wish, the boy formed a plan all his own.

The looked for evening came; deep and white lay the snow on the hard frozen ground. The great mansion was all alight. Softly the little Negro lad stole from his father's cabin. Come what might, he must hear the great master.

Taking up his station outside one of the parlor windows he listened, standing knee deep in the snow. The master drew his bow across his violin and straightway Harry forgot everything, how bitter the cold, how deep the winter snow—forgot time and place. He had found his life's work, the soul of a musician was born.

The next day the little Negro boy lay sick. Inquiry was made. It was learned by questioning the lad of

* Reprinted by permission of E. Stoutenburg.

the long vigil in the snow. Such sacrifice deserved a reward, and after that Harry heard all the concerts at the great house.

By patient and persevering effort—by waiting on the table days and studying nights—the young Negro won first an education, then musical reputation, then fame.

Today the name of Harry Burleigh is known throughout the musical world—and the end is not yet. Only the other day he was awarded the Spingarn medal, the highest award of merit that a Negro can win. If a member of the once despised Negro race can rise so far from such a small beginning, should it not inspire all of us to greater effort?

The young warrior! Need one question how such a man could write a battle hymn? His whole life has been a struggle against terrible odds and he has won.

Surely life is a battle. If life is a battle, your best weapon is your mind. Your mind is to you what a soldier's sword is to him. If you would win with it, see that you know how to use it. Practice with it; keep it keen and bright.

E. Stoutenburg.

MINE EYES HAVE SEEN *

A Play in One Act

CHARACTERS

DAN: *The Cripple.*
CHRIS: *The Younger Brother.*
LUCY: *The Sister.*
MRS. O'NEILL: *An Irish Neighbor.*
JAKE: *A Jewish Boy.*
JULIA: *Chris' Sweetheart.*
BILL HARVEY: *A Muleteer.*
CORNELIA LEWIS: *A Settlement Worker.*
Time—1918.
Place: A manufacturing city in the northern part of the United States.

SCENE

Kitchen of a tenement. All details of furnishing emphasize sordidness—laundry tubs, range, table covered with oilcloth, pine chairs. Curtain discloses DAN *in a rude imitation of a steamer chair, propped by faded pillows, his feet covered with a patch-work quilt. Practicable window at back.*

LUCY *is bustling about the range preparing a meal. During the conversation she moves from range to table, setting latter and making ready the noon-day meal.*

DAN *is about thirty years old; face thin, pinched, bearing traces of suffering. His hair is prematurely gray; nose finely chiseled; eyes wide, as if seeing* BEYOND. *Complexion brown.*

LUCY *is slight, frail, brown skinned, about twenty, with a pathetic face. She walks with a slight limp.*

---

* By Alice Dunbar-Nelson. Reprinted from "The Crisis."

DAN: Isn't it most time for him to come home, Lucy?

LUCY: It's hard to tell, Danny, dear; Chris doesn't come home on time any more. It's half past twelve, and he ought to be here by the clock, but you can't tell any more—you can't tell.

DAN: Where does he go?

LUCY: I know where he doesn't go, Dan, but where he does, I can't say. He's not going to Julia's any more lately. I'm afraid, Dan, I'm afraid!

DAN: Of what, little sister?

LUCY: Of everything; oh, Dan, it's too big, too much for me—the world outside, the street—Chris going out and coming home nights moody-eyed; I don't understand.

DAN: And so you're afraid? That's been the trouble from the beginning of time—we're afraid because we don't understand.

LUCY (*coming down front, with a dish cloth in her hand*): Oh, Dan, wasn't it better in the old days when we were back home—in the little house with the garden, and you and father coming home nights and mother getting supper, and Chris and I studying lessons in the dining-room at the table—we didn't have to eat and live in the kitchen then, and—

DAN (*grimly*): —And the notices posted on the fence for us to leave town because niggers had no business having such a decent home.

LUCY (*unheeding the interruption*): —And Chris and I reading the wonderful books and laying our plans—

DAN: To see them go up in the smoke of our burned home.

LUCY (*continuing, her back to* DAN, *her eyes lifted,*

as if seeing a vision of retrospect) : —And everyone petting me because I had hurt my foot when I was little, and father—

DAN: —Shot down like a dog for daring to defend his home—

LUCY: —Calling me "Little Brown Princess" and telling mother—

DAN: —Dead of pneumonia and heartbreak in this bleak climate.

LUCY: That when you—

DAN: Maimed for life in a factory of hell! Useless—useless—broken on the wheel.

(*His voice breaks in a dry sob.*)

LUCY (*coming out of her trance, throws aside the dish cloth, and running to* DAN, *lays her cheek against his and strokes his hair*): Poor Danny, poor Danny, forgive me, I'm selfish.

DAN: Not selfish, little sister, merely natural.

(*Enter roughly and unceremoniously* CHRIS. *He glances at the two with their arms about each other, shrugs his shoulders, hangs up his rough cap and mackinaw on a nail, then seats himself at the table, his shoulders hunched up; his face dropping on his hand.* LUCY *approaches him timidly.*)

LUCY: Tired, Chris?

CHRIS: No.

LUCY: Ready for dinner?

CHRIS: If it is ready for me.

LUCY (*busies herself bringing dishes to the table*): You're late today.

CHRIS: I have bad news. My number was posted today.

LUCY: Number? Posted? (*Pauses with a plate in her hand.*)

CHRIS: I'm drafted.

LUCY (*drops plate with a crash;* DAN *leans forward tensely, his hands gripping the arms of his chair*): Oh, it can't be! They won't take you from us! And shoot you down, too? What will Dan do?

DAN: Never mind about me, sister. And you're drafted, boy?

CHRIS: Yes—yes—but—(*he rises and strikes the table heavily with his hand*) I'm not going.

DAN: Your duty—

CHRIS: —Is here with you. I owe none elsewhere, I'll pay none.

LUCY: Chris! Treason! I'm afraid!

CHRIS: Yes, of course, you're afraid, little sister, why shouldn't you be? Haven't you had your soul shriveled with fear since we were driven like dogs from our home? And for what? Because we were living like Christians. Must I go and fight for the nation that let my father's murder go unpunished? That killed my mother—that took away my chances for making a man out of myself? Look at us—you—Dan, a shell of a man—

DAN: Useless—useless—

LUCY: Hush, Chris!

CHRIS: And me, with a fragment of an education and no chance—only half a man. And you, poor little sister, there's no chance for you; what is there in life for you? No, if other~ want to fight, let them. I'll claim exemption.

DAN: On what grounds?

CHRIS: You—and sister. I am all you have; I support you.

DAN (*half rising in his chair*): Hush! Have I

come to this, that I should be the excuse, the woman's skirts, for a slacker to hide behind?

CHRIS (*clenching his fists*): You call me that? You, whom I'd lay down my life for? I'm no slacker when I hear the real call of duty. Shall I desert the cause that needs me—you—sister—home—for a fancied glory? Am I to take up the cause of a lot of kings and politicians who play with men's souls, as if they are cards—dealing them out, a hand here, in the Somme—a hand there, in Palestine—a hand there, in the Alps—a hand there, in Russia—and because the cards don't match well, call it a misdeal, gather them up, throw them in the discard, and call for a new deal of a million human, suffering souls? And must I be the Deuce of Spades?

(*During the speech the door opens slowly and* JAKE *lounges in. He is a slight, pale youth, Hebraic, thin lipped, eager eyed. His hands are in his pockets, his narrow shoulders drawn forward. At the end of* CHRIS' *speech he applauds softly.*)

JAKE: Bravo! You've learned the patter well. Talk like the fellows at the Socialist meetings.

DAN and LUCY: Socialist meetings!

CHRIS (*defiantly*): Well?

DAN: Oh, nothing; it explains. All right, go on—any more?

JAKE: Guess he's said all he's got breath for. I'll go; it's too muggy in here. What's the row?

CHRIS: I'm drafted.

JAKE: Get exempt. Easy—if you don't want to go. As for me—

(*Door opens, and* MRS. O'NEILL *bustles in. She is in deep mourning, plump, Irish, shrewd looking, bright eyed.*)

Mrs. O'Neill: Lucy, they do be sayin' as how down by the chain stores they be a raid on the potatoes, an' ef ye're wantin' some ye'd better be after gittin' into yer things an' comin' wid me. I kin kape the crowd off yer game foot—an' what's the matter wid youse all?

Lucy: Oh, Mrs. O'Neill, Chris has got to go to war.

Mrs. O'Neill: An' ef he has, what of it? Ye'll starve, that's all.

Dan: Starve? Never! He'll go, we'll live.

(Lucy *wrings her hands impotently.* Mrs. O'Neill *drops a protecting arm about the girl's shoulder.*)

Mrs. O'Neill: An' it's hard it seems to yer? But they took me man from me year before last, an' he wint afore I came over here, an' it's a widder I am wid me five kiddies, an' I've niver a word to say but—

Chris: He went to fight for his own. What do they do for my people? They don't want us, except in extremity. They treat us like—like—like—

Jake: Like Jews in Russia, eh? (*He slouches forward, then his frame straightens itself electrically.*) Like Jews in Russia, eh? Denied the right of honor in men, eh? Or the right of virtue in women, eh? There isn't a wrong you can name that your race has endured that mine has not suffered, too. But there's a future, Chris—a big one. We younger ones must be in that future—ready for it, ready for it— (*His voice trails off and he sinks despondently into a chair.*)

Chris: Future? Where? Not in this country? Where?

(*The door opens and* Julia *rushes in impulsively. She is small, slightly built, eager eyed, light brown skin, wealth of black hair; full of sudden shyness.*)

Julia: Oh, Chris, someone has just told me—I was

passing by—one of the girls said your number was called. Oh, Chris, will you have to go?

(*She puts her arms up to* CHRIS' *neck; he removes them gently, and makes a slight gesture towards* DAN'S *chair.*)

JULIA: Oh, I forgot. Dan, excuse me. Lucy, it's terrible, isn't it?

CHRIS: I'm not going, Julia.

MRS. O'NEILL: Not going!

DAN: Our men have always gone, Chris. They went in 1776.

CHRIS: Yes, as slaves. Promised a freedom they never got.

DAN: No, gladly, and saved the day, too, many a time. Ours was the first blood shed on the altar of national liberty. We went in 1812 on land and sea. Our men were through the struggles of 1861—

CHRIS: When the nation was afraid not to call them. Didn't want 'em at first.

DAN: Never mind; they helped work out their own salvation. And they were there in 1898—

CHRIS: Only to have their valor disputed.

DAN: —And they were at Carrizal, my boy, and now—

MRS. O'NEILL: An' sure, wid a record like that— ah, 'tis me ould man who said at first 'twasn't his quarrel. His Oireland bled an' the work of thim divils to try to make him a thraitor nearly broke his heart— but he said he'd go to do his bit—an' here I am.

(*There is a sound of noise and bustle without, and with a loud laugh,* BILL HARVEY *enters. He is big, muscular, rough, his voice thunderous. He emits cries of joy at seeing the group, shakes hands and claps* CHRIS *and* DAN *on their backs.*)

12

DAN: And so you weren't torpedoed?

HARVEY: No, I'm here for a while—to get more mules and carry them to the front to kick their bit.

MRS. O'NEILL: You've been—over there?

HARVEY: Yes, over the top, too. Mules, rough-necks, wires, mud, dead bodies, stench, terror!

JULIA (*horror stricken*): Ah—Chris!

CHRIS: Never mind, not for mine.

HARVEY: It's a great life—not. But I'm off again, first chance.

MRS. O'NEILL: They're brutes, eh?

HARVEY: Don't remind me.

MRS. O'NEILL (*whispering*): They maimed my man before he died.

JULIA (*clinging to* CHRIS): Not you, oh, not you!

HARVEY: They crucified children.

DAN: Little children? They crucified little children.

CHRIS: Well, what's that to us? They're little white children. But here our fellow countrymen throw our little black babies in the flames—as did the worshippers of Moloch, only they haven't the excuse of a religious rite.

JAKE (*slouches out of his chair in which he has been sitting brooding*): Say, don't you get tired sitting around grieving because you're colored? I'd be ashamed to be—

DAN: Stop! Who's ashamed of his race? Ours the glorious inheritance; ours the price of achievement. Ashamed! I'm PROUD. And you, too, Chris, smouldering in youthful wrath, you, too, are proud to be numbered with the darker ones, soon to come into their inheritance.

MRS. O'NEILL: Aye, but you've got to fight to keep

yer inheritance. Ye can't lay down when someone else has done the work and expect it to go on. Ye've got to fight.

JAKE: If you're proud, show it. All of your people —well, look at us! Is there a greater race than ours? Have any people had more horrible persecutions—and yet—we're loyal always to the country where we live and serve.

MRS. O'NEILL: And us! Look at us!

DAN (*half tears himself from the chair, the upper part of his body writhing, while the lower part is inert, dead*): Oh, God! If I were but whole and strong! If I could only prove to a doubting world of what stuff my people are made!

JULIA: But why, Dan, it isn't our quarrel? What have we to do with their affairs? These white people, they hate us. Only today I was sneered at when I went to help with some of their relief work. Why should you, my Chris, go to help those who hate you?

(CHRIS *clasps her in his arms and they stand, defying the others.*)

HARVEY: If you could have seen the babies and girls—and old women—if you could have— (*Covers his eyes with his hand.*)

CHRIS: Well, it's good for things to be evened up somewhere.

DAN: Hush, Chris! It is not for us to visit retribution. Nor to wish hatred on others. Let us rather remember the good that has come to us. Love of humanity is above the small considerations of time or place or race or sect. Can't you be big enough to feel pity for the little crucified French children—for the ravished Polish girls, even as their mothers must have felt sorrow, if they had known, for OUR burned and maimed little ones? Oh, Mothers of Europe, we be of one blood, you and I!

(*There is a tense silence.* JULIA *turns from* CHRIS *and drops her hand. He moves slowly to the window and looks out. The door opens quietly and* CORNELIA LEWIS *comes in. She stands still a moment, as if sensing a difficult situation.*)

CORNELIA: I've heard about it, Chris, your country calls you. (CHRIS *turns from the window and waves hopeless hands at* DAN *and* LUCY.) Yes, I understand; they do need you, don't they?

DAN (*fiercely*): No!

LUCY: Yes, we do, Chris, we do need you, but your country needs you more. And, above that, your race is calling you to carry on its good name, and with that the voice of humanity is calling to us all—we can manage without you, Chris.

CHRIS: You? Poor little crippled sister. Poor Dan—

DAN: Don't pity me, pity your poor, weak self.

CHRIS (*clenching his fist*): Brother, you've called me two names today that no man ought to have to take—a slacker and a weakling!

DAN: True. Aren't you both? (*Leans back and looks at* CHRIS *speculatively.*)

CHRIS (*makes an angry lunge towards the chair, then flings his hands above his head in an impotent gesture*): Oh, God! (*Turns back to window.*)

JULIA: Chris, it's wicked for them to taunt you so—but Chris—it IS our country—our race—

(*Outside the strains of music from a passing band are heard. The music comes faintly, gradually growing louder and louder until it reaches a crescendo.*

The tune is "The Battle Hymn of the Republic," played in stirring march time.)

DAN (*singing softly*): "Mine eyes have seen the glory of the coming of the Lord!"

CHRIS (*turns from the window and straightens his shoulders*): And mine!

CORNELIA: "As He died to make men holy, let us die to make them free!"

MRS. O'NEILL: An' ye'll make the sacrifice, me boy, an' ye'll be the happier.

JAKE: Sacrifice! No sacrifice for him, it's those who stay behind. Ah, if they would only call me and call me soon!

LUCY: We'll get on, never fear. I'm proud! PROUD!

(*Her voice breaks a little, but her head is thrown back.*)

(*As the music draws nearer the group breaks up, and the whole roomful rushes to the window and looks out. CHRIS remains in the center of the floor, rigidly at attention, a rapt look on his face. DAN strains at his chair, as if he would rise, then sinks back, his hand feebly beating time to the music, which swells to a martial crash.*)

CURTAIN.

WINTER MORNING

FROST and sun—the day is wondrous;
  Thou still art slumbering; charmed friend,
   'Tis time, O beauty, to awaken;
Ope thine eyes now in sweetness closed,
To meet the Northern Dawn of Morning.
Thyself a North Star do thou appear.

Last night remember the storm scolded,
And the darkness floated in the clouded sky;
Like a yellow, clouded spot
Through the clouds the moon was gleaming—
And melancholy thou wert sitting—
But now, through the window cast a look.

Stretched beneath the heavens blue,
Carpet like magnificent,
In the sun the snow is sparkling;
Dark alone is the wood transparent,
And through the hoar gleams green the fir,
And under the ice the rivulet sparkles.

Entire is lighted with diamond splendor
Thy chamber; with merry crackle
The wood is crackling in the oven.
But know you? In the sleigh not ordered, why
The brownish mare to harness?

Over the morning snow we gliding
Trust we shall, my friend, ourselves
To the speed of impatient steed:
Visit we shall the fields forsaken,
The woods, dense, but recently,
And the banks so dear to me.

—ALEXANDER POUSHKIN.

WINTER EVENING

THE storm the sky with darkness covers,
The snowy whirlings bursting;
Like a beast wild now is howling,
Like an infant now is crying;
Over the aged roof now sudden
In the straw it rustling is;
Like a traveler now belayed
For entrance at our window knocking.

With melancholy and with darkness
Our little aged hut is filled,
Why in silence then thou sittest
By the window, wife old mine?
Or by the howling storms art
Wearied thou, O companion mine?
Or perchance art slumbering
By the rustling spindle soothed?

Let us drink, O kindly friend,
Of my poverty and youth;
Away with grief—where is the cup?
Joy it shall bring to our heart.
A song now sing me, how the bird
Beyond the sea and quiet lived;
A song now sing me, how the maiden
In the morning for water went.

The storm the sky with darkness covers
The snowy whirlings bursting;
Like a beast wild now is howling,
Like an infant now is crying;
Let us drink, O kindly friend,
Of my poverty and youth;
Away with grief—where is the cup?
Joy it shall bring to our heart.

—ALEXANDER POUSHKIN.

FRIENDSHIP

Thus it ever was and ever will be,
Such fold is the world wide:
The learned are many, the sages few,
Acquaintances many, but not a friend.

—ALEXANDER POUSHKIN.

THE BARD

Have ye heard in the woods of the mighty voice
The bard of love, the bard of grief?
When the fields in the morning hours were still,
The flute's sad sound and simple.
    Have ye heard?
Have ye met in the desert darkness of the forest
The bard of love, the bard of grief?
Was it a brack of bears, was it a smile
Of a quiet glance filled with melancholy?
    Have ye met?
Have ye sighed listening to the calm voice
Of the bard of love, the bard of his grief?
When in the woods the youth ye saw,
And met the glance of his dulled eyes.
    Have ye sighed?

—ALEXANDER POUSHKIN.

BOOK V.

FREDERICK DOUGLASS

THE pendulum of time has swerved past the one hundredth anniversary of Frederick Douglass, greatest of all American Negroes; an abolitionist, a statesman, an orator, and so far as the modern epoch is concerned, second only to Toussaint L'Ouverture, the savior of Hayti. Two races, and especially that race for which he made so many sacrifices, bow before his shrine in reverence to his blessed memory.

He was born in a slave hut, amid densest darkness and deepest moral degradation. Yet it was aptly said of him by a friend: "He was a graduate from a peculiar institution, with his diploma written on his back. He lifted himself from the lowest round of life's ladder a slave, and climbed to the sunlit hills of a life of marvelous achievement. And when he died, in the fullness of years and honors, the best of two worlds gathered in homage about his more than royal bier. He arose unaided, save by his genius and character, from the lowest circle of slavery and American caste prejudice."

What picturesque and dramatic contrasts of light and shade, personal degradation and elevation, social heights and depths, illustrate his seventy-eight years among us! Chattel and citizen; slave and orator; fugitive and reformer; preacher and philosopher! Yesterday saw him scrambling and fighting with dogs for bones and crumbs from his master's table; today acclaims him anointed leader and tribune of a race; hero, patriot, philanthropist! He rose from abject poverty to affluence; climbed from a point in the social scale below zero to the lofty table-lands of freedom, and thence to greatness; from the legal status of a mere piece of human property in the American republic to the rank of one of its most illustrious citizens, to immortal deeds and an immortal name.

What amazing obstacles; what amazing progress! Bruised and weary, sad and bleeding, he trod unshod the roughest ways, climbed to dizzy heights, overcame all difficulties when every inch onward and upward wrung his brave soul with agony. But behold a miracle! The slave's agony has turned to sweet music; his sorrows to gladness; his sobs and heart-breaking anguish to rain of wondrous eloquence, which falls in golden showers upon a land of slavery parched and devoured by power and oppression.

The slave boy has now attained the tall stature of a man, and no cry now breaks from his sensitive and indomitable lips. For he is flying with freedom's spark in his breast, beneath a brightening sky, holding fast, as he flies to the long, shining fingers of the North Star.

But while the bright day of freedom brought to the new man joy and deliverance, yet he never forgot to advocate for his people in bondage. His heart swelled with love and pity for them—his brethren in pain—and the tragedy of their terrible condition caused a flame of sacred fervor in his soul. It was not for him amidst his strange environment to sit still with folded arms after he had reached the Northland.

In his new field of labor, tidings reached him of the Liberator, and of its God-anointed editor, thrilling echoes of brave voices from the resounding battlefield where William Lloyd Garrison was leading the anti-slavery host to the moral victory of the age. A something divine stirred and leaped within the breast of the former slave. The hour struck for our hero, Frederick Douglass, to champion the cause of his people.

Douglass' greatness lay in the force that he gave to his convictions, and his keen insight into the future needs of his people. Other men of color fought for the abolition of slavery; other men of African descent were political leaders during the era of reconstruction; but none moulded so successfully his ideals into the American conception of racial justice as did this former Maryland slave. Turner and Vesey were martyrs, but their martyrdom did little to shake the Gibraltar of slavery; Remond and Ward were brilliant agitators, but their agitation, compared to the work of Douglass, was as the dashing of the waves against the rocks. To him, of all men save Charles Sumner and Thaddeus Stevens, is due the credit of the fifteenth amendment, which gave the emancipated Negro the political rights to defend his liberty.

We admire the versatility of Julius Cæesar and Benjamin Disraeli and Theodore Roosevelt, but none of those possessed the range of statesmanship that we must credit to Douglass. He was among the first to conceive the idea of equal rights for all races; he anticipated Booker T. Washington on the subject of industrial education by at least thirty years; he stemmed a Negro exodus that would have been as far reaching as the exodus of today, by his conservative estimate of the best element in the South.

We cannot call him a radical; he was conservative, as conservative as he was eloquent. He believed in and fought for the rights of all men. He saw good in all men, even those who had degraded themselves by holding him in chattel bondage. He was, in addition to being a conservative, a true man. He was of the people, with the people, and for the people. He moved among the lowly with all the dignity and graciousness with which he moved among kings, statesmen and nobility. He was loyal to the ideal that the least on earth shall be first in the ultimate conception of the universe.

—CHARLES H. CHIPMAN.

A NEGRO'S REBUKE

WE have a record to defend, but no treason, thank God, to atone or explain. While in chains we fought to free white men—from Lexington to Carrizal, and returned again to our chains. No Negro has ever insulted the flag. No Negro ever struck down a President of these United States. No Negro ever sold a military map or a secret to a foreign government. No Negro ever ran under fire or lost an opportunity to serve, to fight, to bleed and to die in the republic's cause. Accuse us of what you will—justly or wrongly —no man can point to a single instance of our disloyalty.

We have but one country and one flag, the flag that set us free. Its language is our only tongue and no hyphen bridges or qualifies our loyalty. Today the nation faces danger from a foreign foe, treason stalks and skulks up and down our land, in dark councils intrigue is being hatched. I am a republican, but a Wilson republican. Woodrow Wilson is my leader. What he commands me to do I shall do. Where he commands me to go I shall go. If he calls me to the colors I shall not ask whether my colonel is black or white. I shall be there to pick out no color except the white of an enemy's face. Grievances I have against

the people, against this government. Injustice to me
there is, bad laws there are upon the statute books, but
in this hour of peril I forget—and you must forget—
all the thoughts of self or race or creed of politics
and color. That, boys, is loyalty.

—ROSCOE CONKLING SIMMONS.

ASK OUR CONSTITUTIONAL RIGHTS NOW

IN my opinion this is the proper time for us to make
a special request for our constitutional rights as
American citizens. The ten million Negroes of this
country were never so badly needed as now. They are
not only needed in the business firms and on the farms
to help produce the necessities of life, but they are
needed to help keep the Mexicans quiet, to help sweep
the commerce destroying submarines of the Central
Powers from the ocean, to help crush German mili-
tarism, and they will be needed sooner than some people expect to help prevent the Japanese from landing
on these islands. This then is the time to ask for a
redress of their grievances which have been piling up
for the last few years. As a race we ought to let
our Government know that if it wants us to fight
foreign powers we must first be given assurance of
better treatment at home. Perhaps some people will
say that this is an inopportune time for such talk.
Some may argue that to demand our rights now when
the nation is perhaps facing the greatest crisis in its
history is a lack of loyalty and patriotism. But those
who make such arguments are not acquainted with the
rise and development of races. All history will prove

that most oppressed people have secured their rights when their oppressors were facing a crisis. The Irish people thoroughly understand this philosophy of history, and they are now making a supreme effort. This effort, too, is being made at a time when our English government needs all of its men and all of its resources to fight enemies on land or sea. And everything indicates that the Irish are going to get the independence for which they have been seeking for years because they know how to seek at the proper time.

Four hundred thousand railroad employes received eight hours' work with ten hours' pay because they threatened to walk out at a time when America needed every single car and every railroad man in the country. At a normal time the Americans would not have yielded so readily to their just demands.

For centuries the common people of Russia have been depressed and murdered by plutocracy and absolutism; in vain they have tried to secure their liberties in times of peace, but a few days ago when surrounded by foreign foes they arose en masse and accomplished the complete overthrow of the colossal, rotten superstructure of the Romanoff dynasty. And in twenty-four hours they succeeded in abolishing all racial, social and religious distinctions, and the new government has already assured the entire Russian people of their political equality and freedom before the law.

Why should not the colored Americans make a bloodless demand for the rights they have been trying to receive for the past fifty years, instead of hurrying telegrams and special deliveries to Washington assuring the Government that has persistently stood by with folded arms while we were oppressed and murdered, that the ten million Negroes of the country

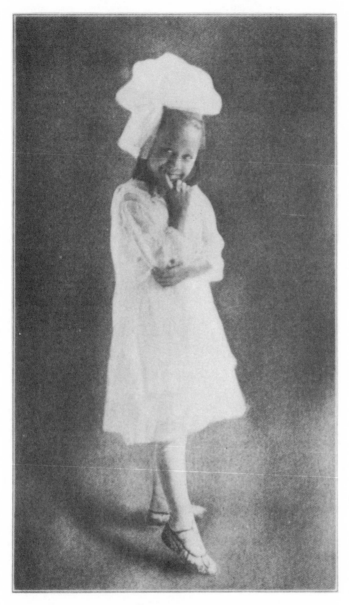

BASHFULNESS

might be used as targets for German bullets and shells? It would cost the President and representatives not one single cent to ask in their speeches and messages for the American people to abolish Jim Crowism, segregation and the awful lynching institution, and give to colored men political equality. But it would mean a new birth of freedom for ten million people who have always stood ready to give their life blood to perpetuate American institutions.

In spite of all this, the big Negro, to the contrary is saying this is a critical moment, and urging all to say to the white Americans from every pulpit and platform and through every newspaper that we are loyal. Yes, we are loyal and patriotic—Boston Common, Bunker Hill, Fort Pillow, San Juan Hill, Appomattox and Carrizal will testify to our loyalty. While we love our flag and country, we do not believe in fighting for the protection of commerce on the high seas until the powers that be give us, at least some verbal assurance that the lives and property of the members of our race will be protected from Maine to Mississippi. Let us have the courage to say to the white Americans, Give us the rights which you enjoy, then will we fight by your side with all of our might for every international right on land and sea.

If this kind of talk is not loyal, then I am disloyal. If this is not patriotism, then I am unpatriotic. If this is treason, then I am a traitor. It is not that I love Cæsar less, but these black Romans more.

It is infinitely more disgraceful and outrageous to hang and burn colored men, boys and women without a trial in the days of peace than it is for Germans in time of war to blow up vessels loaded with mules and molasses.　　　　　—CLAYTON POWELL.

13

THE FOURTH OF JULY *

Fellow Citizens:

Pardon me, and allow me to ask, why am I called upon to speak here today? What have I, or those I represent, to do with your national independence? Are the great principles of political freedom and of natural justice, embodied in that declaration of independence, extended to us? and am I, therefore, called upon to bring our humble offering to the national altar, and to confess the benefits, and express devout gratitude for the blessings resulting from your independence to us?

Would to God, both for your sakes and ours, that an affirmative answer could be truthfully returned to these questions. Then would my talk be light and my burden easy and delightful. For who is there so cold that a nation's sympathy could not warm him? Who so obdurate and dead to the claims of gratitude that would not thankfully acknowledge such priceless benefits? Who so stolid and selfish that would not give his voice to swell the hallelujahs of a nation's jubilees, when the chains of his servitude had been torn from his limbs? I am not that man. In a case like that the dumb might eloquently speak, and the "lame man leap like a hare."

But such is not the state of the case, I say it with a sad sense of disparity, between us. I am not included within the pale of this glorious anniversary! Your high independence only reveals the immeasurable distance between us. The blessings in which you this day rejoice are not enjoyed in common. The rich inheritance of justice, liberty, prosperity and independence bequeathed by your fathers is shared by you, not by me. The sunlight that brought life and healing to you has brought stripes and death to me. This Fourth of July is *yours,* not *mine. You* may rejoice, *I* must mourn. To drag a man in fetters into the grand illuminated temple of liberty, and call upon him to join you in joyous anthems, were inhuman mockery and sacrilegious irony. Do you mean, citizens, to mock me by asking me to speak today? If so, there is a parallel to your conduct. And let me warn you, that it is dangerous to copy the example of a nation whose crimes, towering up to heaven, were thrown down by the breath of the Almighty, burying that nation in irrecoverable ruin. I can, today, take up the lament of a peeled and woe-smitten people.

BY the rivers of Babylon, there we sat down! Yes! We wept when we remembered Zion. We hanged our harps upon the willows in the midst thereof. For there they that carried us away captive required of us a song; and they who wasted us required of us mirth, saying, Sing us one of the songs of Zion. How can we sing the Lord's song in a strange land? If I forget thee, O Jerusalem, let my right hand forget her cunning. If I do not remember thee, let my tongue cleave to the roof of her mouth."

Fellow citizens, above your national, tumultuous joy I hear the mournful wail of millions whose chains, heavy and grievous yesterday, are today rendered more

---

* Abridged from "What to the Slave is the Fourth of July?" From "Masterpieces of Modern Eloquence."

intolerable by the jubilant shouts that reach them. If I forget, if I do not remember those bleeding children of sorrow this day, "May my right hand forget her cunning, and may my tongue cleave to the roof of my mouth!" To forget them, to pass lightly over their wrongs, and to chime in with the popular theme would be treason most scandalous and shocking, and would make me a reproach before God and the world.

My subject, then, fellow citizens, is "American Slavery." I shall see this day and its popular characteristics from the slave's point of view. Standing here, identified with the American bondman, making his wrongs mine, I do not hesitate to declare with all my soul that the character and conduct of this nation never looked blacker to me than on this Fourth of July. Whether we turn to the declarations of the past, or to the professions of the present, the conduct of the nation seems equally hideous and revolting. America is false to the past, false to the present, and solemnly binds herself to be false to the future. Standing with God and the crushed and bleeding slave on this occasion I will, in the name of humanity, which is outraged; in the name of liberty, which is fettered; in the name of the Constitution and the Bible, which are disregarded and trampled upon, dare to call in question and to denounce, with all the emphasis I can command, everything that serves to perpetuate slavery—the great sin and shame of America! "I will not equivocate, I will not excuse;" I will use the severest language that I can command, and yet not one word shall escape my lips that any man, whose judgment is not blinded by prejudice or who is not at heart a slaveholder, shall not confess to be right and just.

Oh! had I the ability and could reach the nation's ear I would today pour out a fiery streak of biting ridicule, blasting reproach, withering sarcasm, and stern rebuke. For it is not light that is needed, but fire; it is not the gentle shower, but thunder. We need the storm, the whirlwind, and the earthquake. The feeling of the nation must be quickened; the conscience of the nation must be roused; the propriety of the nation must be startled; the hypocrisy of the nation must be exposed; and its crimes against God and man must be denounced.

What to the American slave is your Fourth of July? I answer, a day that reveals to him, more than all other days in the year, the gross injustice and cruelty to which he is the constant victim. To him your celebration is a sham; your boasted liberty an unholy license; your national greatness swelling vanity; your sounds of rejoicing are empty and heartless; your denunciations of tyrants brass-fronted impudence; your shouts of liberty and equality hollow mockery; your prayers and hymns, your sermons and thanksgivings, with all your religious parade and solemnity, are to him mere bombast, fraud, deception, impiety and hypocrisy—a thin veil to cover up crimes which would disgrace a nation of savages. There is not a nation on the earth guilty of practices more shocking and bloody than are the people of these United States at this very hour.

Go where you may, search where you will, roam through all the monarchies and despotisms of the Old World, travel through South America, search out every abuse, and when you have found the last, lay your facts by the side of the everyday practices of this nation and you will say with me that for revolting barbarity and shameless hypocrisy, America reigns without a rival.   —FREDERICK DOUGLASS.

LINCOLN AND DOUGLASS *

FREDERICK DOUGLASS once said: "Any many may say things that are true of Abraham Lincoln, but no man can say anything that is new of Abraham Lincoln." If that were true in the past century, in the early seventies, how much more is it true today, when over a century has passed since the hero of America opened his eyes in a log cabin of Kentucky.

It is eminently fitting and proper that we, as Americans, celebrate the birth of the man who, by a single stroke of his pen—albeit, a reluctant stroke—gave the Negro the right to stand with his face to the sun and proclaim to the world, "I am a man!" It is our right and our duty to commemorate his birth, to mourn his death, to revere the twelfth of February as a holiday, to come together to lay laurel wreaths on his tomb. But we Americans of the darker skin have another day as dear to us as the twelfth of February, less well known, perhaps, but which we should acclaim with shouts of joy, even as we acclaim the day which has grown familiar by long usage. That day is the birthday of Frederick Douglass.

* * * * * * *

Lincoln and Douglass; Douglass and Lincoln! Names ever linked in history and in the hearts of a grateful race as the two great emancipators, the two men above all other Americans, fearless, true, brave, strong, the western ideal of manhood. Is it not fitting that their natal days should come within a few hours of

---

* From "The Lives of Douglass and Lincoln."

ABRAHAM LINCOLN

each other? Is it not right that when the Negro child lifts its eyes to the American flag on Lincoln's day he should, at the same time, think of the man whose thunderous voice never ceased in its denunciation of wrong, its acclamation of right, its spurring the immortal Lincoln to be true to his highest ideals; its sorrowful wail when he seemed to fail the nation? Verily, on this day of days we of the darker hued skin have a richer heritage than our white brothers—ours the proud possession of two heroes, theirs of but one.

* * * * * * *

Every school boy in the nation knows Abraham Lincoln—his gaunt figure, his seamed and pain lined face, with its sweetness and patience, are familiar to their eyes. His life, with its romance of poverty and toil, its tragic sorrow and tragic end, are as close to the heart of the nation as the stories of the Bible and the Christ-child. The utterances of Lincoln, the anecdotes of his life, the whimsical stories of his early days and his quaint humor furnish a never ending theme of interest to the American school boy. His sublime speeches; the delicate pathos of his first inaugural address; the splendid, stern, yet tender beauty of the second inaugural address are recited from thousands of school platforms annually, while the Gettysburg speech is as well known in America as the Lord's Prayer and the Beatitudes, and I deem it no sacrilege to say that in point of literary beauty it stands with them. It is graven in bronze in the national cemeteries, on school walls, in the halls of colleges and universities. It is recited semi-annually by the majority of the school boys in the country, and it is right that it should be, for is not Lincoln the nation's idol, the American ideal?

Yet how many Negro youths in the land know as much of the ideal of Negro manhood, Frederick Douglass? If Lincoln is the American idol, so is Douglass the Negro's idol. If Lincoln's was a romance of life, with its toilsome youth culminating in a splendid manhood, attaining the highest gift which the nation could bestow, how much more is Douglass' life a romance? The slave, beaten, starved, stripped, fleeing from slavery at the most deadly peril, to become in his later manhood the guest of nobles and kings, the cynosure of the nation's eyes, the friend of this same Lincoln, the great man of the century? If Lincoln's utterances are inspiring, calling in clarion notes for right and justice and truth, so much more are Douglass' inspiring to us, calling for manhood and strength and power.

For he was no soft-tongued apologist,
    He spoke straightforward, fearlessly, uncowed;
The sunlight of his truth dispelled the mist,
    And set in bold relief each dark-hued cloud;
To sin and crime he gave their proper hue,
And hurled at evil what was evil's due.

The Negro youth of the land recites the Gettysburg speech, and it is right that he should do so; but does he know Douglass' "What to the Slave is the Fourth of July?" The Negro youth of the land admires Lincoln's Second Inaugural address, but does he know Douglass' splendid tribute to the man who wrote the Second Inaugural address, when the freedmen of this country erected the Lincoln monument at Washington? The Negro youth rolls over his tongue the witty epigrams of the mighty Lincoln, but has he been made familiar with some of the pithy aphorisms of his own Douglass?

But, I hear you say, Lincoln's speeches were for all time: Douglass' for the period in which slavery existed; Lincoln addressed an entire nation: Douglass only a limited portion. Not so. What Douglass said was true today, as it was in his own day. If America were guilty in holding slaves, she is no less guilty in her attitude towards the men whose fathers were slaves. If the conscience of the nation needed quickening in 1860, how much more so does it need quickening in this year?

Lincoln reached the zenith of his fame only to be struck down in cold blood by the ruthless hand of an assassin. Douglass lived to an honored age, to die in the fulness of love and fame and admiration. It was the sad duty of Douglass to pay the tribute of a grateful and sorrowing race to the name and fame of the Emancipator. While the nation mourned, aghast, at the heinousness of the crime, while North and South alike agreed in the execrations which were hurled at the assassin, there was the humble, child-like Negro race, whose shackles he had struck off, bowed in dumb misery at the spectacle of his one and only true white friend, cold in death. It seemed a wise dispensation of Providence that one of that race could come forward fearlessly and lay the tributes of his people on the prostrate form.

Hurt was the nation with a mighty wound,
And all her ways were filled with clam'rous sound;
Wailed loud the South with unremitting grief,
And wept the North that could not find relief.

* * * * * * *

Lincoln and Douglass; Douglass and Lincoln! We honor them both today, but more than the mere men, we honor their impress on our own people. We glean from their lives lessons of worth, but more than from their lives we learn from their characters what we need to make our own strong, and of their characters the two lessons which we most need we may take to heart—moral honesty and moral courage.

Abraham Lincoln does not need the tribute we give him today; the world is paying him tributes greater than ours, more glorious and resounding. But the sweeter praise which we pay him is that of a race, profiting by the lesson of a life. Fame has written Lincoln's name with the greatest men of the world— with the statesmen, with the wisest of monarchs, with the prince of republicans—and placed his laurel wreath higher than the rest. But it remains for the descendants of slaves to give him what no man in history has ever had—the divine breath of gratitude, the determination to make the world see, centuries hence, that he was not mistaken in his greatest deed, his life work, his martyrdom.

But Frederick Douglass, whom we honor equally, has not yet had the full meed of his praise, and we celebrate the passing of his natal day with a finer appreciation of what he has done for us, and of what his life will mean, not only to the men who were his contemporaries, nor yet to us of a later generation, but to the race of the future; to the children yet unborn. History has not yet given him his rightful place on its pages, but the history of tomorrow will place him where he should be—with the courageous, the wise, the far-seeing. It remains for us, his own people, to pour out at his altar the incense he deserves, the praise he merits; to let his life be a beacon to light us to that higher, truer patriotism—the fearlessness of real manhood.

My friends, we do well to gather here today to honor the memory of Abraham Lincoln; we do better to remember his great contemporary, Frederick Douglass. The twelfth of February is to us, as Americans, a sacred occasion—the fourteenth of February is to us, as Negroes, a no less holy day. When the race which shares with us this great country lays its laurel wreaths on the tomb of Lincoln, we, of the dark-hued skin and saddened eyes, must lay our palms on the grave of Frederick Douglass. Both heroes are ours to remember, to extol, to revere, to emulate.

Lincoln and Douglass; Douglass and Lincoln! May their names ever be welded into one memory in the hearts of every Negro in the land!

—ALICE DUNBAR-NELSON.

THE BETTER PART

ON an important occasion in the life of the Master, when it fell to Him to pronounce judgment on two courses of action, these memorable words fell from His lips: "And Mary hath chosen the better part." This was the supreme test in the case of an individual. It is the highest test in the case of a race or a nation. Let us apply this test to the American Negro.

In the life of our republic, when he has had the opportunity to choose, has it been the better or worse part? When in the childhood of this nation the Negro was asked to submit to slavery or choose death and extinction, as did the aborigines, he chose the better part, that which perpetuated the race.

When in 1776 the Negro was asked to decide between British oppression and American independence, we find him choosing the better part, and Crispus Attucks, a Negro, was the first to shed his blood on State Street, Boston, that the white American might enjoy liberty forever, though his race remained in slavery.

When in 1814 at New Orleans the test of patriotism came again, we find the Negro choosing the better part, and General Andrew Jackson himself testifying that no heart was more loyal and no arm more strong and useful in defense of righteousness.

When the long and memorable struggle came between union and separation, when he knew that victory on the one hand meant freedom, and defeat on the other his continual enslavement, with a full knowledge of the portentous meaning of it all, when the suggestion and the temptation came to burn the home and massacre wife and children during the absence of the master in battle, and thus insure his liberty, we find him choosing the better part, and for four long years protecting and supporting the helpless, defenseless ones entrusted to his care.

When in 1863 the cause of the Union seemed to quiver in the balance and there was doubt and distrust, the Negro was asked to come to the rescue in arms, and the valor displayed at Fort Wagner and Port Hudson and Fort Pillow testify most eloquently again that the Negro chose the better part.

When a few years ago the safety and honor of the republic were threatened by a foreign foe, when the wail and anguish of the oppressed from a distant isle reached his ears, we find the Negro forgetting his own wrongs, forgetting the laws and customs that discriminate against him in his own country, and again we find our black citizen choosing the better part. And if you would know how he deported himself in the field at Santiago, apply for answer to Shafter and Roosevelt and Wheeler. Let them tell you how the Negro faced death and laid down his life in defense of honor and humanity, and when you have gotten the full story of the heroic conduct of the Negro in the Spanish-American War—heard it from the lips of Northern soldiers and Southern soldiers, from ex-abolitionist and ex-master, then decide within yourselves whether a race that is thus willing to die for its country should not be given the highest opportunity to live for its country.

In the midst of all the complaints of suffering in the camp and field, suffering from fever and hunger, where is the official or citizen that has heard a word of complaint from the lips of a black soldier? The only request that has come from a Negro soldier has been that he might be permitted to replace the white soldier when heat and malaria began to decimate the ranks of the white regiment, and to occupy at the same time the post of greatest danger.

This country has been most fortunate in her victories. She has twice measured arms with England and has won. She has met the spirit of rebellion within her borders and was victorious. She has met the proud Spaniard, and he lies prostrate at her feet. All this is well; it is magnificent. But there remains one other victory for Americans to win—a victory as far-reaching and important as any that has occupied our army and navy. We have succeeded in every conflict, except the effort to conquer ourselves in the blotting out of racial prejudices. We can celebrate the era of peace in no more effectual way than by a firm resolve on the part of Northern men and Southern men, black men and white men, that the trenches which we together dug around Santiago shall be the eternal burial place of all that which separates us in our business and civil relations. Let us be as generous in peace as we have been brave in battle. Until we thus conquer ourselves, I make no empty statement when I say that we shall have, especially in the southern part of our country, a cancer gnawing at the heart of the republic that shall one day prove as dangerous as an attack from an army without or within.

In this presence, and on this auspicious occasion, I want to present the deep gratitude of nearly ten millions of my people to our wise, patient and brave Chief Executive for the generous manner in which my race has been represented in this conflict; a recognition which has done more to blot out sectional and racial lines than any event since the dawn of freedom.

I know how vain and impotent is all abstract talk of this subject. In your efforts to rise on stepping-stones of your dead selves, we of the black race shall not leave you unaided. We shall make the task easier for you by acquiring property, habits of thrift, economy, intelligence and character, by each making himself an individual worth in his community. We shall aid you in this as we did in El Caney and Santiago, when we helped you hasten the peace we here celebrate. You know us; you are not afraid of us. When the crucial test comes you are not ashamed of us. We have never betrayed or deceived you. You know that as it has been, so it will be. Whether in war or in peace, whether in slavery or in freedom, we have always been loyal to the Stars and Stripes.

—BOOKER T. WASHINGTON.

AFTER EMANCIPATION—SUFFRAGE

WE have broken the material shackles from four million slaves. We have unchained them from the stake so as to provide them locomotion, provided they do not walk in paths trod by white men. We have allowed them the unwonted privilege of attending church, if they can do so without offending the sight of their former masters. We have even given them that highest and most agreeable evidence of liberty as defined by the "great plebeian," the "right to work." But in what have we enlarged their liberty of thought? In what have we taught them the science and granted them the privilege of self-government? We have imposed upon them the privilege of fighting our battles, of dying in defense of freedom, and of bearing their equal portion of the taxes; but where have we given them the privilege of even participating in the formation of the laws for the government of their native land? By what civil weapon have we enabled them to defend themselves against oppression and justice? Call you this liberty? Call you this a free republic, where four millions are subjects, not citizens? Then Persia, with her kings and satraps, was free! Then Turkey is free! Their subjects had liberty of motion and labor, but the laws were made without and against their will; but I must declare that in my judgment they were as really free governments as ours is today. Think not I would slander my native land; I would reform it. Twenty years ago I denounced it as a despotism. Then twenty million white men enchained four million black men. I pronounce it no nearer to

MEDITATION

a true republic now, when twenty-five millions of a privileged class exclude five millions from all participation in the rights of government. The freedom of a government does not depend upon the quality of its laws, but upon the power that has the right to create them. During the dictatorship of Pericles his laws were just, but Greece was not free. During the last century Russia has been blest with most remarkable emperors, who have generally decreed wise and just laws, but Russia is not free. No government can be free that does not allow all its citizens to participate in the formation and execution of her laws. These are decrees of tyranny; but every other government is a despotism. It has always been observed that the larger the number of rulers the more cruel the treatment of the subject races. It were better for the black man if he were governed by one king than by twenty million. . . . But it will be said: "This is Negro equality." What is Negro equality about which so much is said by knaves, and some of which is believed by men who are not fools? It means, as understood by honest republicans, just this and no more; every man, no matter what his race or color, has an equal right to justice, honesty and fair play with every other man; and the law should secure him those rights. The same law which condemns or acquits an African should condemn or acquit a white man. The same law which gives a verdict in a white man's favor should give a verdict in a black man's favor on the same state of facts. Such is the law of God, and such ought to be the law of man.

—Thaddeus Stevens.

January 3, 1867.

14

MEMORIAL DAY IN THE SOUTH

AS Decoration Day draws nigh, recollections of the struggle of 1861, which so tried the two sections of our country, become more vivid, and the many years that have passed since then seem less distant. The veteran in his faded coat of blue, his rugged visage and empty sleeve; the militiaman in brilliant uniform; citizens in holiday attire, booming cannon and martial music, give to that particular day a significance which apparently no other day possesses. While in the North we celebrate in gala attire, and bands and drum corps blare out patriotic airs, in the South the observance is in striking contrast; all is funereal, solemn and sedate. With arms reversed, the veteran, with slow and measured tread, follows behind muffled drums and bands play dirges, while choirs sing most solemn and touching music. While the 30th of May is universally observed for the decoration of the graves of Union dead, the Daughters of the Confederacy and other such organizations, in the South, although such a day is observed in every Southern State, do not move in concert. In the far Southern States, where spring puts on her richest attire in early April, Confederate graves are decorated in that month, while in States further North, a day in May is observed. In North Carolina it is the 10th of May; in Virginia it is the 30th. This is an observance of the most intense interest to lovers of the "Lost Cause." An air of profound sadness and thoughtfulness pervades the very atmosphere, and the gray veteran again salutes the "Stars and Bars," which hang in profusion about the speaker's stand and wave above the Confederate dead. Father Ryan's famous poem, "The Conquered Banner," is recited with a pathos that is touching. Old wounds bleed a-fresh as impassioned orators tell of the causes that led up to the struggle; the justness of the Southern side and the bravery of the Southern soldier. Pickett's gallant charge at Gettysburg is rehearsed with fervor; what might have been gained to the South on that gory field had Lee listened to the advice of Longstreet is also regretfully told, together with the story of the foolhardiness of Sidney Johnston at Shiloh, which lost the West to the Confederacy.

But on the 30th of May, when Union soldiers' graves are decorated, a different program is rendered. There, over those grass-covered mounds, other orators—nowadays mostly colored men—tell of the victories of the "Silent Man" at Donaldson, at Shiloh, at Vicksburg, at Chattanooga, at Petersburg and Richmond, and of Sherman's famous March to the Sea. The decoration of these graves is, and has ever been done almost solely by Afro-American women. And when we consider the fact that nearly all of the men who fell in that awful struggle sleep south of Mason's and Dixon's line, we can appreciate the importance of the part the Afro-American woman plays in this work of love. At Richmond, Culpeper, Wilmington, Salisbury, Nashville, Chattanooga, Memphis, and other places lie acres upon acres of grass-covered mounds.

"Asleep are the ranks of the dead"—Union dead. The Government provides only for the placing of a small American flag on that day upon each headstone, no more. But it is the loving hand of black woman and child that places the rose, the jasmine, the lilac and forget-me-not there, with wreaths of cedar and of pine; so that wafted upon the breeze which comes upward from that hallowed ground is the breath of sweet flowers. What shall be done for this obscure Shunammite, who for so many years has faithfully performed this work of love? "Shall we mention her to the king? or shall we ship her to the Philippines?" The Grand Army veteran will doubtless say "No," when he looks backward and thinks of Andersonville, Libby, Florence and Danville, and of the fate that might have been his, had it not been for the devotion of some colored woman or boy, who hid him in kitchen loft or barn or haystack, from the heartless Rebel, and under cover of darkness piloted him safely into Union lines.

"Lord God of hosts, be with us yet,
Lest we forget, lest we forget."

To the Afro-American woman of the South on that day will come vivid recollections of the inexplicable gloom that pervaded the land everywhere when John Brown went to the scaffold, or the excitement attending the bombardment of Fort Sumter, the hastening northward of the soldier in gray, of the constant scudding off of husband, brother or father to break through Rebel lines to fight on "the Lord's side." She will hear again the sad wail of the massacred at Fort Pillow, see those black forms dashing toward the parapets of Fort Wagner, and hear again the thunderings of the awful crater at Petersburg. With this must come the consoling thought that she has done what she could. For among those sleeping heroes her husband, her brother, her father is lying, having given up their lives that "a nation of the people, by the people, and for the people, shall not perish from the earth."

—"Jack Thorne" (David B. Fulton).

TOUSSAINT L'OUVERTURE

IF I stood here to tell you the story of Napoleon I should take it from the lips of Frenchmen, who find no language rich enough to paint the great captain of the nineteenth century. Were I to tell you the story of Washington I should take it from your hearts—you who think no marble white enough on which to carve the name of the Father of his country. But I am to tell you the story of a Negro, who has left hardly one written line. I am to glean it from the reluctant testimony of Britons, Frenchmen, Spaniards—men who despised him as a Negro and a slave, and hated him because he had beaten them in battle. All the materials for his biography are from the lips of his enemies. Let us pause a moment and find something to measure him by. You remember Macaulay says, comparing Cromwell with Napoleon, that Cromwell showed the greater military genius, if we consider that he never saw an army until he was forty; while Napoleon was educated from a boy in the best military schools in Europe. Cromwell manufactured his own army; Napoleon at the age of twenty-seven was placed at the head of the best troops Europe ever saw. They were both successful; but, says Macaulay, with such disadvantages the Englishman showed the greater genius. Whether you allow the inference or not, you will at least grant that it is a fair mode of measurement. Apply it to this Negro. Cromwell never saw an army until he was forty; this man never saw a soldier until he was fifty. Cromwell manufactured his own army—out of what? Englishmen—the best blood in Europe. Out of the middle class of Englishmen—the best blood of the island. And with it he conquered what? Englishmen—their equals. This man manufactured his army out of what? Out of what you call the despicable race of Negroes, debased, demoralized by two hundred years of slavery, one hundred thousand of them imported into the island within four years, unable to speak a dialect intelligible even to each other. Yet out of this mixed, and as you say despicable, mass, he forged a thunderbolt and hurled it at what? At the proudest blood in Europe, the Spaniard, and sent him home conquered; at the most warlike blood in Europe, the French, and put them under his feet; at the pluckiest blood in Europe, the English, and they skulked home to Jamaica. Now, if Cromwell was a general, at least this man was a soldier.

Now, blue-eyed Saxon, proud of your race, go back with me to the commencement of the century and select what statesman you please. Let him be either American or European; let him have a brain the result of six generations of culture; let him have the ripest training of university routine; let him add to it the better education of practical life; crown his temples with the silver locks of seventy years, and show me the man of Saxon lineage for whom his most sanguine admirer will wreathe a laurel rich as embittered foes have placed on the name of this Negro—rare military skill, profound knowledge of human nature, content to blot out all party distinctions and trust a state to the blood of its sons—anticipating Sir Robert Peel fifty years, and taking his station by the side of Roger Williams, before any Englishman or American had won the right; and yet this is the record which the history of rival states makes up for this inspired black of St. Domingo.

Some doubt the courage of the Negro. Go to Hayti and stand on those fifty thousand graves of the best soldiers France ever had, and ask them what they think of the Negro's sword.

I would call him Napoleon, but Napoleon made his way to empire over broken oaths and through a sea of blood. This man never broke his word. I would call him Cromwell, but Cromwell was only a soldier, and the state he founded went down with him into his grave. I would call him Washington, but the great Virginian held slaves. This man risked his empire rather than permit the slave trade in the humblest village of his dominions.

You think me a fanatic, for you read history, not with your eyes, but with your prejudices. But fifty years hence, when Truth gets a hearing, the Muse of history will put Phocion for the Greek, Brutus for the Roman, Hampden for England, Fayette for France, choose Washington as the bright consummate flower of our earlier civilization, then dipping her pen in the clear blue, above them all, write the name of the soldier, the statesman, the martyr, TOUSSAINT L'OUVERTURE.

—Wendell Phillips.

ABRAHAM LINCOLN *

FRIENDS and Fellow Citizens: The story of our presence here is soon and easily told. We are here to express, as best we may, by appropriate forms and ceremonies, our grateful sense of the vast, high and pre-eminent services rendered to ourselves, to our race, to our country, and to the whole world by Abraham Lincoln.

The sentiment that brings us here today is one of the noblest that can stir and thrill the human heart. It has crowned and made glorious the high places of all civilized nations with the grandest and most enduring works of art, designed to illustrate the characters and perpetuate the memories of great public men. It is the sentiment which, from year to year, adorns with fragrant and beautiful flowers the graves of our loyal, brave and patriotic soldiers who fell in defense of the Union and Liberty. It is the sentiment of gratitude and appreciation which often in the presence of many who hear me has filled yonder heights of Arlington with the eloquence of eulogy and the sublime enthusiasm of poetry and song; a sentiment which can never die while the republic lives.

*   *   *   *   *   *   *

Fellow citizens, ours is no new-born zeal and devotion—merely a thing of the moment. The name of Abraham Lincoln was near and dear to our hearts in the darkest and most perilous hours of the republic.

---

* Abridged from Speech on Unveiling of the Freedmen's Monument to Abraham Lincoln.

We were no more ashamed of him when shrouded in clouds of darkness, or doubt and defeat, than when we saw him crowned with victory, honor and glory. Our faith in him was often taxed and strained to the uttermost, but it never failed. When he tarried long in the mountains; when he strangely told us that we were the cause of the war; when he still more strangely told us to leave the land in which we were born; when he refused to employ our arms in defense of the Union; when, after accepting our services as colored soldiers, he refused to retaliate our murder and torture as colored prisoners; when he told us he would save the Union, if he could, with slavery; when he revoked the Proclamation of Emancipation of General Fremont; when he refused to remove the popular commander of the army of the Potomac in the days of its inaction and defeat, who was more zealous in his efforts to protect slavery than to suppress rebellion; when we saw all this and more, we were at times grieved, stunned and greatly bewildered, but our hearts believed while they ached and bled. Nor was this, at that time, a blind and unreasoning superstition. Despite the mist and hate that surrounded him; despite the tumult, the hurry and confusion of the hour, we were able to take a comprehensive view of Abraham Lincoln, and to make reasonable allowance for the circumstances of his position. We saw him, measured him, and estimated him; not by stray utterances to injudicious and tedious delegations, who often tried his patience; not by isolated facts torn from their connection; not by partial and imperfect glimpses caught at inopportune moments; but by a broad survey in the light of the stern logic of great events, and in view of that divinity which "shapes our ends, rough hew them as we will," we came to the conclusion that the hour and the man of our redemption had somehow met in the person of Abraham Lincoln. It mattered little to us what language he might employ on special occasions; it mattered little to us when we fully knew him whether he was swift or slow in his movements; it was enough for us that Abraham Lincoln was at the head of a great movement, and was in living and earnest sympathy with that movement, which, in the nature of things, must go on until slavery should be utterly and forever abolished in the United States.

When, therefore, it shall be asked what we have to do with the memory of Abraham Lincoln, or what Abraham Lincoln had to do with us, the answer is ready, full and complete. Though he loved Cæsar less than Rome, though the Union was more to him than our freedom or our future, under his wise and beneficent rule, and by measures approved and vigorously pressed by him, we saw that the handwriting of ages, in the form of prejudice and proscription, was rapidly fading away from the face of our whole country; under his rule and in due time, about as soon, after all, as the country could tolerate the strange spectacle, we saw our brave sons and brothers laying off the rags of bondage and being clothed all over in the blue uniforms of the soldiers of the United States; under his rule we saw two hundred thousand of our dark and dusky people responding to the call of Abraham Lincoln, and with muskets on their shoulders and eagles on their buttons, timing their high footsteps to liberty and union under the national flag; under his rule we saw the independence of the black republic of Hayti, the special object of slave holding aversion and horror fully recognized, and her minister, a colored gentleman, duly received here in the city of Washington; under his rule we saw the internal slave trade, which so long disgraced the nation, abolished, and slavery abolished in the District of Columbia; under his rule we saw, for the first time, the law enforced against the foreign slave trade and the first slave trader hanged like any other pirate or murderer; under his rule, assisted by the greatest captain of our age, we saw the Confederate States, based upon the idea that our race must be slaves and slaves forever, battered to pieces and scattered to the four winds; under his rule, and in the fullness of time, we saw Abraham Lincoln, after giving the slaveholders three months' grace in which to save their hateful slave system, penning the immortal paper which, though special in its language, was general in its principles and effect, making slavery forever impossible in the United States. Though we waited long, we saw all this and more.

* * * * * * *

Fellow citizens, whatever else in the world may be partial, unjust and uncertain, time—time—is impartial, just and certain in its action. In the realm of mind, as well as in the realm of matter, it is a great worker, and often works wonders. The honest and comprehensive statesman, clearly discerning the needs of his country and earnestly endeavoring to do his whole duty, though covered and blistered with reproaches, may safely leave his course to the silent judgment of time. Few great public men have ever been the victims of fiercer denunciations than Abraham Lincoln was during his administration. He was often wounded in the house of his friends. Reproaches came thick and fast from within and from without, and from opposite quarters. He was assailed by abolitionists; he was assailed by slaveholders; he was assailed by slave-holders who were for peace at any price; he was assailed by those who were for a more vigorous prosecution of the war; he was assailed for not making the war an abolition war; and he was most bitterly assailed for making the war an abolition war.

But now, behold the change; the judgment of the present hour is, that taking him for all in all, measuring the tremendous magnitude of the work before him, considering the necessary means to ends, and surveying the end from the beginning, infinite wisdom has seldom sent any man into the world better fitted for his mission than Abraham Lincoln. His birth, his training and his natural endowments, both mental and physical, were strongly in his favor. Born and reared among the lowly, a stranger to wealth and luxury, compelled to grapple single handed with the flintiest hardships of life, from tender youth to sturdy manhood, he grew strong in the manly and heroic qualities demanded by the great mission to which he was called by the votes of his countrymen. The hard condition of his early life, which would have depressed and broken down weaker men, only gave greater life, vigor and buoyancy to the heroic spirit of Abraham Lincoln. He was ready for any kind and quality of work. What other young men dreaded in the shape of toil he took hold of with the utmost cheerfulness.

> A spade, a rake, a hoe,
>   A pick-axe or a bill,
> A hook to reap, a scythe to mow,
>   A flail, or what you will.

All day long he could split heavy rails in the woods, and half the night long he could study his English grammar by the uncertain flare and glare of the light made by a pine knot. He was at home on the land with his axe, with his maul, with gluts and his wedges; and he was equally at home on water, with his oars, with his poles, with his planks, and with his boat hooks. And whether in his flat boat on the Mississippi River or on the fireside of his frontier cabin, he was a man of work. A son of toil himself, he was linked in brotherly sympathy with the sons of toil in every loyal part of the republic. This very fact gave him tremendous power with the American people, and materially contributed not only to selecting him to the Presidency, but in sustaining his administration of the Government.

Upon his inauguration as President of the United States, an office, even where assumed under the most favorable conditions, fitted to tax and strain the largest abilities, Abraham Lincoln was met by a tremendous crisis. He was called upon not merely to administer the government, but to decide in the face of terrible odds the fate of the republic.

* * * * * * *

He calmly and bravely heard the voice of doubt and fear all around him; but he had an oath in heaven, and there was not power enough on earth to make this honest boatman, backwoodsman and broad handed rail splitter evade or violate that sacred oath. He had not been schooled in the ethics of slavery; his plain life had favored his love of truth. He had not been taught that treason and perjury were the proofs of honor and honesty. His moral training was against his saying one thing when he meant another. The trust which Abraham Lincoln had in himself and in the people was surprising and grand, but it was also enlightened and well founded. He knew the American people better than they knew themselves, and his truth was based upon this knowledge.

*　*　*　*　*　*　*

Had Abraham Lincoln died from any of the numerous ills to which flesh is heir; had he reached that good old age of which his vigorous constitution and his temperate habits gave promise; had he been permitted to see the end of his work; had the solemn curtain of death come down but gradually—we should still have been smitten with a heavy grief and treasured his name lovingly. But dying as he did die, by the red hand of violence, killed, assassinated, taken off without warning, not because of personal hate, for no man who knew Abraham Lincoln could hate him—but because of his fidelity to union and liberty, he is doubly dear to us, and his memory will be precious forever.

Fellow citizens, I end as I began, with congratulations. We have done a good work for our race today. In doing honor to the memory of our friend and liberator, we have been doing highest honors to ourselves and those who come after us; we have been fastening ourselves to a name and fame imperishable and immortal; we have also been defending ourselves from a blighting scandal. When now it shall be said that the colored man is soulless, that he has no appreciation of benefits or benefactors, when the foul reproach of ingratitude is hurled at us, and it is attempted to scourge us beyond the range of human brotherhood, we may calmly point to the monument we have this day erected to the memory of Abraham Lincoln.

—FREDERICK DOUGLASS.

FORT WAGNER

THROUGH the whole afternoon there had been a tremendous cannonading of the fort from the gunboats and land forces. About six o'clock there came moving up the island, over the burning sands and under the burning sky, a stalwart, splendid appearing set of men who looked equal to any daring and capable of any heroism. Weary, travel stained with the mire and the rain of a two-days' tramp; weakened by the incessant strain and lack of food, with gaps in their ranks made by the death of comrades who had fallen in battle but a little time before, it was plain to be seen of what stuff these men were made, and for what work they were ready.

As this regiment, the famous Fifty-fourth, came up the island to take its place at the head of the storming party, it was cheered from all side by the white soldiers.

The day was lurid and sultry. Great masses of clouds, heavy and black, were piled in the western sky, fringed here and there by an angry red, and torn by vivid streams of lightning. Not a breath of wind shook the leaves or stirred the high rank grass by the water side; a portentous and awful stillness filled the air.

Quiet, with the like awful and portentous calm, the black regiment, headed by its young, fair haired, knightly colonel, marched to its destined place and action. A slightly rising ground, raked by a murderous fire; a ditch holding three feet of water; a straight lift of parapet thirty feet high—an impregnable position, held by a desperate and invincible foe. Here the word of command was given.

"We are ordered and expected to take Battery Wagner at the point of the bayonet. Are you ready?"

"Ay, ay, sir, ready!" was the answer.

And the order went pealing down the line: "Ready! Close ranks! Charge bayonets! Forward! Double-quick, march!"

And away they went under a scattering fire in one compact line, till within one hundred feet of the fort, when the storm of death broke upon them. Every gun belched forth its great shot and shell; every rifle whizzed out its sharp stinging, death-freighted messenger. The men wavered not for an instant—forward, forward they went. They plunged into the ditch; waded through the deep water, no longer of muddy hue, but stained crimson with their blood, and commenced to climb the parapet. The foremost line fell, and then the next, and the next, On, over the piled up mounds of dead and dying, of wounded and slain, to the mouth of the battery; seizing the guns; bayoneting the guns at their posts; planting their flag and struggling around it; their leader on the walls, sword in hand, his blue eyes blazing, his fair face aflame, his clear voice calling out: "Forward, my brave boys!" then plunging into the hell of battle before him.

As the men were clambering up the parapet their color sergeant was shot dead. A nameless hero, who was just behind, sprang forward, seized the staff from his dying hand, and with it mounted upward. A ball struck his right arm, but before it could fall shattered by his side, his left hand caught the flag and carried it onward. Though faint from loss of blood and wrung with agony, he kept his place—the colors flying—up the slippery steep; up to the walls of the fort; on the wall itself, planting the flag where the men made that

HOPE

brief, splendid stand, and melted away like snow before furnace heat. Here a bayonet thrust met him and brought him down, a great wound in his brave breast, but he did not yield; dropping to his knees, pressing his unbroken arm upon the gaping wound—the colors still flew, an inspiration to the men about him, a defiance to the foe.

At last, when the shattered ranks fell back, sullenly and slowly retreating, he was seen painfully working his way downward, still holding aloft the flag, bent evidently on saving it, and saving it, as flag had rarely, if ever, been saved before.

Slowly, painfully he dragged himself onward—step by step down the hill, inch by inch across the ground—to the door of the hospital; and then, while dying eyes brightened, while dying men held back their souls from the eternities to cheer him, gasped out: "I did—but do—my duty, boys—and the dear—old flag—never once—touched the ground." And then, away from the reach and sight of its foes, in the midst of its defenders who loved and were dying for it, the flag at last fell.

The next day a flag of truce went up to beg the body of the heroic young chief who had so gallantly led that marvelous assault. It came back without him. A ditch, deep and wide, had been dug; his body and those of twenty-two of his men, found dead upon and about him, flung into it in one common heap; and the word sent back was, "We have buried him with his niggers."

It was well done. Slavery buried these men, black and white together—black and white in a common grave. Let Liberty see to it, then, that black and white be raised together in a life better than the old.

—ANNA E. DICKINSON.

15

THE BOYS OF HOWARD SCHOOL *

MADAM PRINCIPAL: It was not my purpose to make a speech today; I know too well my limitations as an orator, but I find myself constrained to arise and say a few words, and those words on behalf of the boys of Howard School.

Madam Principal, the complaint has been made that the boys of your school do not measure up to the standard of the girls; that they are indifferent to the welfare of the institution which honors them by admitting them. You have not said so, for you know us better, you understand and love us and we are conceited enough to believe that we hold the first place in your heart. So I rise today to make a plea, not to you, for you know, but to the ones who have found us wanting—a plea for the boys of Howard School.

For fifty years or more the boys of Wilmington have passed through the beloved halls of Howard School. Some have stayed to graduate, others, alas, too many, have been forced by the pinch of poverty to go forth into the world before they could claim the coveted diploma. But whether graduated or not, whether high school boys or not, no matter how brief the connection with the school, the world has never complained of the boys of Howard School. They may not have carried off many honors; they may not be high in the councils of the nation; they may not be millionaires; they may not have forged ahead as captains of industry—but, Madam Principal, neither you nor our school has ever had occasion to be ashamed of the boys of Howard School.

---

* Applicable to any boys of any school.

I might give you dull statistics and remind you how many of our number, who have graduated from here, have graduated from colleges or professional schools; how many of us are doctors, teachers, government employees, business men—but I am not speaking for the graduates alone. I might call your attention to the fact that some of your boys who did not stay to graduate have become successful men, have achieved some distinction in the world, but I am not speaking for those who have left the school alone—I am speaking for those who have gone and those who are here. Perhaps we do not carry off the honors of the school always, but the success of the world is not always bestowed upon the men and women who were the brightest in their classes in school. Perhaps we do not measure up to the standard set us by you and our teachers, but that is not because we are idle, disloyal, or indifferent. Perhaps it is because we are JUST BOYS, and Nature made us so.

But, Madam Principal, when it comes to loyalty to you and to our beloved school, there can be no complaint of us. Whether grammar school boys or high school boys, whether boys who were not fortunate enough to graduate, or boys who proudly claim this school as their ALMA MATER, there are no boys who are more loyal or more devoted on the face of the earth to their school than the boys of Howard School. You know it, for go where they will, wander as they may, your boys always come back to visit their school when their footsteps turn homeward to Wilmington. You have called upon us as boys, you have called upon us as men, and we have never failed you, nor will we ever fail you, when there is a man's work to be done. And those lessons of unswerving loyalty and devotion learned here we shall never forget, and in the days when our race or our country needs us, when the call shall come for the loyal boys and men of the race, high above all in the answer to the clarion call to duty will rise the "We're ready!" of THE BOYS OF HOWARD SCHOOL."

THE MULATTO TO HIS CRITICS *

ASHAMED of my race?
    And of what race am I?
        I am many in one.
Through my veins there flows the blood
Of red man, black man, Briton, Celt and Scot,
In warring clash and tumultuous riot.
I welcome all,
But love the blood of the kindly race
That swarthes my skin, crinkles my hair,
And puts sweet music in my soul.

JOSEPH S. COTTER, JR.

---

* From "The Band of Gideon and Other Lyrics." The Cornhill Company.

NEGRO MUSIC *

SINCE "the morning stars sang together" in scriptural narrative, music has exerted a profound influence upon mankind, be it in peace or in war, in gladness or in sorrow, or in the tender sentiment that makes for love of country, affection for kindred, or the divine passion for "ye ladye fayre." Music knows no land or clime, no season or circumstance, and no race, creed or clan. It speaks the language universal, and appeals to all peoples with a force irresistible, and no training in ethics or science is necessary to reach the common ground that its philosophy instinctively creates in the human understanding.

The War Department was conscious of this and gave practical application to its theory that music makes a soldier "fit to fight." . . . . It was the belief that every man became a better warrior for freedom when his mind could be diverted from the dull routine of camp life by arousing his higher nature by song, and that he fared forth to battle with a stouter heart when his steps were attuned to the march by bands that drove out all fear of bodily danger and robbed "grim visaged war" of its terrors. . . . .

The emotional nature of the Negro fitted him for this musical program. The colored American was a "close-up" in every picture from the start to the finish, and was a conspicuous figure in every scenario, playing with credit and distinction alike in melody or with the musket.

No instrumentality was more potent than music in offsetting the propaganda of the wily German agents,

---

* From "The American Negro in the World War."

who sought to break down the loyalty of the Negro. The music he knew was intensely American—in sentiment and rhythm. It saturated his being—and all the blandishments of the enemy were powerless to sway him from the flag he loved. His grievances were overshadowed by the realization that the welfare of the nation was menaced and that his help was needed. American music harmonized with the innate patriotism of the race, and the majestic sweep of "The Star Spangled Banner," or the sympathetic appeal of "My Country, 'Tis of Thee," were sufficient to counteract the sinister efforts of the missionaries of the Hohenzollerns to move him from his moorings.

No labor is ever so onerous that it can bar music from the soul of black folk. This race sings at work, at play, and in every mood. Visitors to any army camp found the Negro doing musical "stunts" of some kind from reveille to taps—every hour, every minute of the day. All the time the trumpeters were not blowing out actual routine bugle calls, they were somewhere practicing them. Mouth organs were going, concertinas were being drawn back and forth, and guitars, banjos, mandolins and what not were in use—playing all varieties of music, from the classic, like "Lucia," "Poet and Peasant," and "Il Trovatore," to the folk songs and the rollicking "jazz." Music is indeed the chiefest outlet of the Negro's emotions, and the state of his soul can best be determined by the type of melody he pours forth.

Some writer has said that a handful of pipers at the head of a Scotch regiment could lead that regiment down to the mouth of a cannon. It is not doubted that a Negro regiment could be made to duplicate the "Charge of the Light Brigade" at Balaklava—"into the mouth of hell," as Tennyson puts it, if one of their regimental bands should play—as none but a colored band *can* play—the vivacious strains of "There'll be a Hot Time in the Old Town Tonight."

—EMMETT J. SCOTT.

CRISPUS ATTUCKS *

(Extract from an address delivered before the Banneker Literary Club of Boston, Mass., on the occasion of the commemoration of the "Boston Massacre," March 7, 1776).

THE 5th of March, 1770, had been a cold day, and a slight fall of snow had covered the ground, but at nine o'clock at night it was clear and cold, not a cloud to be seen in the sky and the moon was shining brightly. A British guard was patroling the streets with clanking sword and overbearing swagger. A sentry was stationed in Dock Square. A party of young men, four in number, came out of a house in Cornhill. One of the soldiers was whirling his sword about his head, striking fire with it; the sentry challenged one of the four young men; there was no good blood between them, and it took but little to start a disturbance. An apprentice boy cried to one of the guards, "You haven't paid my master for dressing your hair!" A soldier said, "Where are the d—d Yankee boogers; I'll kill them!" A boy's head was split; there was more quarreling between the young men and guard, great noise and confusion; a vast concourse of excited people soon collected. Cries of "Kill them!" "Drive them out!" "They have no business here!" were heard. Some citizens were knocked down, as were also some

* From "The Masterpieces of Negro Eloquence."

soldiers. Generally speaking, the soldiers got the worst of it. They were reinforced, but steadily the infuriated citizens drove them back until they were forced to take refuge in the Custom House, upon the steps of which they were pelted with snowballs and pieces of ice.

By this time the whole town was aroused; exaggerated accounts of the events in Dock Square flew like wildfire all over the settlement. The people turned out *en masse* in the streets, and to add to the general din the bells of the town were rung. The regiment which held the town at that time was the Twenty-ninth; Captain Preston seemed to have been in command. He was sent for, went to the Custom House, learned what had occurred, and at once put troops in motion. On they came, up King Street, now State Street, with fixed bayonets, clearing everything before them as they came. They had nearly reached the head of King Street when they met with opposition. A body of citizens had been formed near by, and came pushing violently through the street, then called Cornhill, around into King Street. They were armed only with clubs, sticks and pieces of ice, but on they came. Nothing daunted, they went up to the points of the soldiers' bayonets. The long pent up feeling of resentment against a foreign soldiery was finding a vent. This was the time and the opportunity to teach tyrants that freemen can at least strike back, though for the time they strike in vain.

At the head of this body of citizens was a stalwart colored man, Crispus Attucks. He was the leading spirit of their body, and their spokesman. They pressed the British sorely on all sides, making the best use of their rude arms, crying, "They dare not strike!" "Let us drive them out!" The soldiers stood firm; the reach of their long bayonets protected them from any serious injury for a while.

From time to time Attucks' voice could be heard urging his companions on. Said he, "The way to get rid of these soldiers is to attack the main guard! Strike at the root! This is the nest!" At that time someone gave the order to fire. Captain Preston said he did not; at any rate, the order was given. The soldiers fired. It was a death dealing volley. Of the citizens three lay dead, two mortally wounded, and a number more or less injured. Crispus Attucks, James Caldwell and Samuel Gray were killed outright. Attucks fell, his face to the foe, with two bullets in his breast.

That night closed an eventful day. The first martyr blood had reddened the streets of Boston, and the commencement of the downfall of British rule in America had set in. Said Daniel Webster, "From that moment we may date the severance of the British Empire. The patriotic fires kindled in the breasts of those earnest and true men, upon whose necks the British yoke never sat easily, never were quenched after that massacre, until the invader had been driven from the land and independence achieved. The sight of the blood of their comrades in King Street quickened their impulses and hastened the day for a more general outbreak, which we now call the Revolutionary War."

This was no mob, as some were disposed to call it. They had not the low and groveling spirit which usually incites mobs. This was resistance to tyranny; this was striking for homes and firesides; this was the noblest work which a patriot can perform. As well call Lexington a mob, and Bunker Hill a mob. I prefer to call this skirmish in King Street on the 5th of March, 1770, as Anson Burlingame called it, "The dawn of the Revolution."

—GEORGE L. RUFFIN.

BOOK VI.
Commemorative

EMANCIPATION PROCLAMATION BY PRESIDENT LINCOLN, JANUARY 1, 1863

WHEREAS, On the twenty-second day of September, in the year of our Lord one thousand eight hundred and sixty-two, a proclamation was issued by the President of the United States, containing among other things the following, to-wit: "That on the first day of January, in the year of our Lord one thousand eight hundred and sixty-three, all persons held as slaves within any state or designated part of the state, the people whereof shall be in rebellion against the United States, shall be then, thenceforward, and forever free; and the executive government of the United States, including the military and naval authority thereof, will recognize and maintain the freedom of such persons, and will do no act or acts to repress such persons or any of them in any efforts they may make for their actual freedom; that the executive will, on the first day of January aforesaid, by proclamation, designate the states, and parts of the states, if any, in which the people thereof, respectively, shall then be in rebellion against the United States; and the fact that any state, or the people thereof, shall on that day be in good faith represented in the Congress of the United States by the members chosen thereto at elections wherein a majority of the qualified voters of such states shall have participated, shall, in the absence of strong countervailing testimony, be deemed conclusive evidence that such state, and the people thereof, be not then in rebellion against the United States."

Now, therefore, I, Abraham Lincoln, President of the United States, by the virtue of the power in me vested as commander-in-chief of the army and navy of the United States in the time of actual armed rebellion against the authority and government of the United States, and as a fit and necessary war-measure for suppressing said rebellion, do, on this first day of January, in the year of our Lord one thousand eight hundred and sixty-three, and in accordance with my purpose so to do, publicly proclaimed for the full period of one hundred days from the day first above mentioned, order and designate as the states and part of states, wherein the people thereof, respectively, are this day in rebellion against the United States, the following, to-wit: Arkansas, Texas, Louisiana (except the parishes of St. Bernard, Plaquemines, Jefferson, St. John, St. Charles, St. James, Ascension, Assumption, Terre-Bonne, Lafourche, Ste. Marie, St. Martin, and Orleans, including the city of New Orleans), Mississippi, Alabama, Florida, Georgia, South Carolina, North Carolina, and Virginia (except the forty-eight counties designated as West Virginia, and also the counties of Berkley, Accomac, Northampton, Elizabeth City, York, Princess Anna, and Norfolk, including the cities of Norfolk and Portsmouth), and which excepted parts are, for the present, left precisely as if this proclamation were not issued. And by virtue of the power, and for the purpose aforesaid, I do order and declare, that all persons held as slaves within said designated states and parts of states are, and henceforth shall be, free; and that the executive government of the United States, including the military and naval authorities thereof, will recognize and maintain the freedom of said persons. And I hereby enjoin upon the people so declared to be free to abstain from all violence, unless in necessary self-defense; and I recommend to them, that in all cases, when allowed, they labor faithfully for reasonable wages. And I further declare and make known, that such persons, of suitable condition, will be received into the armed service of the United States, to garrison forts, positions, stations, and other places, and to man vessels of all sorts in said service. And upon this act, sincerely believed to be an act of justice, warranted by the Constitution upon military necessity, I invoke the considerate judgment of mankind and the gracious favor of Almighty God.

In testimony whereof I have hereunto set my name, and caused the seal of the United States to be affixed. Done at the City of Washington this first day of January, in the year of our Lord one thousand eight hundred and sixty-three, and of the independence of the United States the eighty-seventh.

By the President. ABRAHAM LINCOLN.

William H. Steward,
     Secretary of State.

TO THE NEGRO FARMERS OF THE UNITED STATES

GOD washes clean the souls and hearts of you,
His favored ones, whose backs bend o'er the soil,
Which grudging gives to them requite for toil
In sober graces and in vision true.
God places in your hands the pow'r to do
A service sweet. Your gift supreme to foil
The bare-fanged wolves of hunger in the moil
Of Life's activities. Yet all too few
Your glorious band, clean sprung from Nature's heart;
The hope of hungry thousands, in whose breast
Dwells fear that you should fail. God placed no dart
Of war within your hands, but pow'r to start
Tears, praise, love, joy, enwoven in a crest
To crown you glorious, brave ones of the soil.

—ALICE DUNBAR-NELSON.

A Secret (Silence)

TOUSSAINT L'OUVERTURE

TOUSSAINT, the most unhappy of men!
  Whether the whistling rustic tend his plough,
  Within thy hearing, or thou liest now
Buried in some deep dungeon's earless den—
O miserable chieftain! where and when
Wilt thou find patience? Yet die not; do then
Wear rather in thy bonds a cheerful brow.
Though fallen thyself never to rise again,
Live and take comfort, thou hast left behind
Powers that will work for thee—air, earth and sky;
There's not a breathing of the common wind
That will forget thee—thou hast great allies;
Thy friends are exultations, agonies,
And love, and man's unconquerable mind.

—WILLIAM WORDSWORTH.

TOUISSAINT L'OUVERTURE

T WAS night. The tranquil moonlight smile,
    Which heaven dreams of earth, shed down
    Its beauty on the Indian isle—
On broad green field and white walled towr.
And island waste of rock and wood,
In searching sunshine wild and rude,
Rose, mellowed through the silver gleam,
Soft as the landscape of a dream,
All motionless and dewy wet,
Tree, wine and flower in shadow met
The myrtle with its snowy bloom,
Crossing the nightshade's solemn gloom—
The white cecropia's silver rind,
Relieved by deeper ,green behind—
The orange with its fruit of gold—
The lithe paullinia's verdant fold—
The passion flower with symbol holy.
Twining its tendrils long and lowly—
The rexias dark and cassia tall,
And proudly rising over all
The kingly palm's imperial stem,
Crowned with its leafy diadem,
Star-like beneath whose somber shade
The fiery winged cuculla played.
Yes—lovely was thine aspect then,
    Fair island of the western sea!
Lavish of beauty even when
Thy brutes were happier than thy men,
    For they at least were free!
Regardless of thy glorious clime,

"Friend of the Negro! fly with me,
The path is open to the sea."

Unmindful of thy soil of flowers,
The toiling Negro sighed that Time
No faster sped his hours.
For by the dewy moonlight still,
He fed the weary turning mill,
Or bent him in the chill morass,
To pluck the long and tangled grass,
And hear above his scar worn back
The heavy slave whip's frequent crack:
While in his heart one evil thought
In solitary madness wrought,
One baleful fire surviving still
The quenching of the immortal mind,
One sterner passion of his kind,
Which even fetters could not kill—
The savage hope to deal ere long,
A vengeance bitterer than his wrong!

Hark to that cry!—long, loud and shrill,
From field and forest, rock and hill,
Thrilling and horrible it rang,
Around, beneath, above—
The wild beast from his cavern sprang,
The wild bird from her grove!
Nor fear, nor joy, nor agony,
Were mingled in that midnight cry;
But like the lion's growl of wrath,
When falls that hunter in his path,
Whose barbed arrow, deeply set,
Is rankling in his bosom yet;
It told of hate, full, deep and strong,
Of vengeance kindling out of wrong;
It was as if the crimes of years—
The unrequited toil, the tears,

The shame and hate which liken well
Earth's garden to the nether hell—
Had found in Nature's self a tongue
On which the gathered horror hung;
As if from cliff, and stream, and glen,
Burst on the startled ears of men
That voice which rises unto God,
Solemn and stern—the cry of blood!
It ceased—and all was still once more,
Save ocean chafing on his shore,
The sighing of the wind between
The broad banana's leaves of green,
Or bough by restless plumage shook,
Or murmuring voice of mountain brook.

Brief was the silence. Once again
　　Pealed to the skies that frantic yell,
Glowed on the heavens a fiery stain,
　　And flashes rose and fell;
And painted on the blood-red sky,
Dark, naked arms were tossed on high;
And round the white man's lordly hall,
　　Trod, fierce and free, *the brute he made;*
And those who crept along the wall,
And answered to his lightest call
　　With more than spaniel dread—
The creatures of his lawless beck—
Were trampling on his very neck!
And on the night air, wild and clear,
Rose woman's shriek of more than fear;
For bloodied arms were round her thrown,
And dark cheeks pressed against her own!

Then, injured Afric!—for the shame
Of thy own daughters, vengeance came

Full on the scornful hearts of those
Who mocked thee in thy nameless woes,
And to thy hapless children gave
One choice—pollution or the grave!
Where then was he whose fiery zeal
Had taught the trampled heart to feel,
Until despair itself grew strong,
And vengeance fed its torch from wrong?
Now, when the thunderbolt is speeding;
Now, when oppression's heart is bleeding;
Now, when the latent curse of Time
    Is raining down in fire and blood—
That curse, which through long years of crime,
Has gathered, drop by drop, its flood—
Why strikes he not, the foremost one,
Where murder's sternest deeds are done?

He stood the aged palms beneath,
    That shadowed o'er his humble door,
Listening with half suspended breath,
To the wild sounds of fear and death,
    Toussaint l'Ouverture!
What marvel that his heart beat high!
    The blow for freedom had been given,
And blood had answered to the cry
    Which earth sent up to heaven!
What marvel that a fierce delight
Smiled grimly o'er his brow of night—
As groan and shout and bursting flame
Told where the midnight tempest came,
With blood and fire along its van,
And death behind!—he was a man!

Yes, dark-souled chieftain!—if the light
    Of mild religion's heavenly ray

Unveiled not to thy mental sight
   The lowlier and the purer way,
In which the Holy Sufferer trod,
   Meekly amidst the sons of crime—
That calm reliance upon God
   For justice in His own good time—
That gentleness to which belongs
Forgiveness for its many wrongs,
Even as the primal martyr, kneeling
For mercy on the evil dealing—

Let not the favored white man name
Thy stern appeal with words of blame.
Has he not with the light of heaven
   Broadly around him made the same?
Yea, on his thousand war fields striven,
   And gloried in his ghastly shame?—
Kneeling amidst his brother's blood,
To offer mockery unto God,
As if the High and Holy One
Could smile on deeds of murder done!—
As if a human sacrifice
Were purer in His holy eyes,
Though offered up by Christian hands,
Than the foul rights of pagan lands!

Sternly amidst his household band,
His carbine grasped within his hand,
   The white man stood, prepared and still,
Waiting the shock of maddened men,
Unchained and fierce as tigers when
   The horn winds through their caverned hill,
And one was weeping in his sight—
   The sweetest flower of all the isle—

The bride who seemed but yesternight
    Love's fair embodied smile.
And, clinging to her trembling knee,
Looked up the form of infancy,
With tearful glance in either face
The secret of its fear to trace.

"Ha! stand or die!" The white man's eye
His steady musket gleamed along,
As a tall Negro hastened nigh,
    With fearless step and strong.
"What, ho, Toussaint!" A moment more,
His shadow crossed the lighted floor.
    "Away!" he shouted, "fly with me —
The white man's bark is on the sea—
Her sails must catch the seaward wind,
For sudden vengeance sweeps behind.
Our brethren from their graves have spoken,
The yoke is spurned, the chain is broken;
On all the hills our fires are glowing—
Through all the vales red blood is flowing!
No more the mocking white shall rest
His foot upon the Negro's breast;
No more, at morn or eve, shall drip
The warm blood from the driver's whip:
Yet, though Toussaint has vengeance sworn
For all the wrongs his race have borne—
Though for each drop of Negro blood
The white man's veins shall pour a flood;

Not all alone the sense of ill
Around his heart is lingering still,
Nor deeper can the white man feel
The generous warmth of grateful zeal.

Friend of the Negro! fly with me—
The path is open to the sea:
Away for life!" He spoke and pressed
The young child to his manly breast,
As headlong through the cracking cane,
Down swept the dark insurgent train—
Drunken and grim, with shout and yell
Howled through the dark, like sounds from hell.

Far out, in peace, the white man's sail
Swayed free before the sunrise gale.
Cloud-like that island hung afar,
    Along the bright horizon's verge,
O'er which the curse of servile war
    Rolled its red torrent, surge on surge;
And he—the Negro champion—where
    In the fierce tumult struggled he?
Go trace him by the fiery glare
Of dwellings in the midnight air—
The yells of triumph and despair,—
    The streams that crimson to the sea!
Sleep calmly in thy dungeon tomb,
    Beneath Besancon's alien sky,
Dark Haytien!—for the time shall come,
Yea, even now is nigh,—
When everwhere thy name shall be
Redeemed from *color's infamy;*
And men shall learn to speak of thee,
As one of earth's great spirits, born
In servitude and nursed in scorn,
Casting aside the weary weight
And fetters of its low estate

In that strong majesty of soul
    Which knows no color, tongue or clime—

Which still hath spurned the base control
    Of tyrants through all time!
Far other hands than mine may wreathe
The laurel round thy brow of death,
And speak thy praise as one whose word
A thousand fiery spirits stirred—
Who crushed his foeman as a worm—
Whose step on human hearts fell firm:—
Be mine the better task to find
A tribute for thy lofty mind,
Amidst whose gloomy vengeance shone
Some milder virtues all thy own—
Some gleams of feeling pure and warm,
Like sunshine on a sky of storm—
Proofs that the Negro's heart retains
Some nobleness amidst its chains—
That kindness to the wrong is never
    Without its excellent reward—
Holy to human kind, and ever
    Acceptable to God.

                            —JOHN G. WHITTIER.

CHALMETTE

MEMORIAL DAY

WREATHS of lilies and immortelles,
   Scattered upon each silent mound
   Voices in loving remembrance swell,
Chanting to heaven the solemn sound.
Glad skies above, and glad earth beneath;
   And grateful ones who silently
Gather earth's flowers and tenderly wreathe
   Woman's sweet token of fragility.

Ah, the noble forms who fought so well
   Lie, some unnamed, 'neath the grassy mound;
Heroes, brave heroes, the stories tell,
   Silently, too, the unmarked mounds,
Tenderly wreathe them about with flowers,
   Joyously pour out your praises loud;
For every joy-beat in these hearts of ours
   Is only a drawing us nearer to God.

Little enough is the song we sing,
   Little enough is the tale we tell,
When we think of the voices who erst did ring
   Ere their owners in smoke of battle fell.
Little enough are the flowers we cull
   To scatter afar on the grass grown graves,
When we think of bright eyes, now dimmed and dull,
   For the cause they loyally strove to save.

And they fought right well, did these brave men,
   For their banner still floats unto the breeze,

And the paeans of ages forever shall tell
    Their glorious tale beyond the seas.
Ring out your voices in praises loud,
    Sing sweet your notes of music gay,
'Tell me, in all yon loyal crowd,
    Throbs there a heart unmoved today?

Meeting together again this year,
    As met we in fealty and love before;
Men, maids, and matrons to reverently hear
    Praises of brave men who fought of yore.
Tell to the little ones with wondering eyes,
    The tale of the flag that floats so free;
Till their childish voices shall merrily rise
    In hymns of rejoicing and praises to Thee.

Many a pure and noble heart
    Lies under the sod all covered with green;
Many a soul that had felt the smart
    Of life's sad torture, or mayhap had seen
The faint hope of love pass afar from the sight,
    Like swift flight of bird to a rarer clime
Many a youth whose death caused the blight
    Of tender hearts in that long, sad time.

Nay, but this is no hour for sorrow;
    They died at their duty, shall we repine?
Let us gaze hopefully on to the morrow
    Praying that our lives thus shall shine.
Ring out your bugles, sound out your cheers!
    Man has been God-like, so may we be.
Give cheering thanks, there, dry up those tears,
    Widowed and orphaned, the country is free!

Wreaths of lilies and immortelles,
  Scattered upon each silent mound,
Voices in loving remembrance swell,
  Chanting to heaven the solemn sound,
Glad skies above, and glad earth beneath,
  And grateful ones who silently
Gather earth's flowers and tenderly wreathe
  Woman's sweet token of fragility.

—ALICE RUTH MOORE.

HIS EXCELLENCY, GEORGE WASHINGTON

(1775)

CELESTIAL choir, enthron'd in realms of light,
    Columbia's scenes of glorious toils I write.
    While freedom's cause her anxious breast alarms,
She flashes dreadful in refulgent arms.
See mother earth her offspring's fate bemoan,
And nations gaze at scenes before unknown;
See the bright beams of heaven's revolving light
Involved in sorrows and the veil of night!
The goddess comes, she moves divinely fair,
Olive and laurel bind her golden hair:
Wherever shines this native of the skies,
Unnumber'd charms and recent graces rise.

Muse! bow propitious while my pen relates
How pour her armies through a thousand gates,
As when Eolus heaven's fair face deforms,
Enwrapped in tempest and a night of storms;

Astonished ocean feels the wild uproar,
The refluent surges beat the sounding shore;
Or thick as leaves in autumn's golden reign,
Such, and so many, moves the warrior's train.
In bright array they seek the work of war,
Where high unfurl'd the ensign waves in air.
Shall I to Washington their praise recite?
Enough, thou know'st them in the fields of fight.
Thee, first in peace and honors, we demand
The grace and glory of thy martial band.
Fam'd for thy valor, for thy virtues more,
Hear every tongue thy guardian aid implore!

One century scarce perform'd its destined round,
When Gallic powers Columbia's fury found;
And so may you, whoever dares disgrace
The land of freedom's heaven defended race!
Fix'd are the eyes of nations on the scales,
For in their hopes Columbia's arm prevails.
Anon Britannia droops the pensive head,
While round increase the rising hills of dead.
Ah! cruel blindness to Columbia's state!
Lament thy thirst of boundless power too late.
Proceed, great chief, with virtue on thy side,
Thy ev'ry action let the goddess guide.
A crown, a mansion, and a throne that shine
With gold unfading, Washington be thine!

—PHYLLIS WHEATLEY.

ABRAHAM LINCOLN

FAR in the West, in forest wild,
  Was born one day, to us, a child;
  A man most truly great to be,
Although of humble birth was he.
No herald the event proclaimed;
No royal scribe wrote down his name.
A hut of logs rough hewn and bare,
With scarce enough of light and air;
A bed of straw, a floor of earth—
Such was the scene, the place of birth
Of him whose name the world reveres;
That grows in greatness with the years

Uncouth, unlettered—yet a prince,
The impious scoffer to convince,
That God vouchsafed no right divine
To man, his fellows to confine;
To mark their bounds, their course dictate;
A royal road to greatness make,
The cabin floor, the pine knots' blaze,
Might be the medium fit to raise
Ambitious man from low estate,
To heights ennobling, truly great;
From raft of logs with peers to stand,
The applause of senates to command.

A grateful nation now in praise,
From loyal heart a song must raise
To God, for those who blazed the way,
For Freedom's universal sway;

For those who prayed on Plymouth's Rock;
For those who felt the awful shock
Of war with savage fierce and wild;
Who gazed in Death's grim face and smiled,
Because from tyranny's haughty sway,
The sacrifice would pave the way.

Yet few were those who rose above
The common trend of thought; and strove
To tear away the pall of shame,
That blurred their country's sacred name;
A sleeping conscience sought to 'wake;
The alien's galling chain to break;
Who braved the scorn of bigots base,
To succor a benighted race.
Foremost among this stalwart few,
Stood Old Abe Lincoln stanch and true
In every fibre of his frame,
He waited 'till the hour came.

Then raised on high the fiery brand,
To scourge the evil from the land,
The awful storm of blood and tears
Did rage and beat for four long years.
The world looked on in blank dismay.
As brothers struggled in the fray.
All reverence for his wisdom fled;
They heaped reproaches on his head.
Foes lurked his pathway, stormed his door.
And wise men deemed his judgment poor.
Yet firm and undismayed he stood;
This rustic lawyer; hew'r of wood!

Although at times defeat he saw,
Yet still, he deemed it Saxon war.

VANITY

Reluctantly he gave the word,
Which called forth the immortal horde.
The alien host unshackled, free,
Rose like an angry, billowy sea—
And grateful for the longed for chance,
To check the sullen foe's advance.
Let Wagner and Fort Pillow tell,
The glorious story, how they fell!
Newmarket Heights—O gory field!
In Freedom's cause they could not yield!

Up! up that rugged steep—and wide,
They climbed to glory side by side,
Or calmly laid them down to rest,
Clasped to a Spartan mother's breast.
Brave chattels from the auction block!
They faced alone the "Crater's" shock,
And changed the scoffer's laugh to cheers,
The skeptic's eyes made wet with tears.

And when 'twas o'er—the strife, the pain,
There lay their great commander, slain!
They raised the blazing torch on high,
To light his pathway to the sky.
Be hushed forever, lips of scorn!
In generations yet unborn,
Parents to children still will tell,
While love and pride their bosoms swell;
The rough backwoodsman of the West,
Was he who served his country best.
And nations still shall gather there,
Around the martyr's sepulchre.

—David B. Fulton (Jack Thorne).

17

CHARLES SUMNER

ON SEEING SOME PICTURES OF THE INTERIOR OF HIS HOUSE

ONLY the casket left! The jewel gone,
 Whose noble presence filled these stately rooms
 And made this spot a shrine where pilgrims came,
Stranger and friend to bend in reverence
Before the great pure soul that knew no guile;
To listen to the wise and gracious words
That fell from lips whose rare, exquisite smile
Gave tender beauty to the grand, grave face.

Upon the pictured walls we see thy peers,
Poet and saint, and sage, painter and king,
A glorious band! they shine upon us still;
Still gleam in marble the enchanting forms
Whereon thy artist eye delighted dwell;
Thy favorite, Psyche, droops her matchless face,
Listening methinks for the beloved voice
Which never more on earth shall sound her praise.

All these remain—the beautiful, the brave,
The gifted silent one—but thou art gone!
Fair is the world that smiles upon us now,
Blue are the skies of June, balmy the air
That soothes with touches soft the weary brow;
And perfect days glide into perfect night,
Moonlit and calm; but yet our grateful hearts
Are sad and faint with fear; for thou art gone.

O friend beloved, with longing tear filled eyes,
We look up, up to the unclouded blue,

And seek in vain some answering sign from thee.
Look down upon us; guide and cheer us still
From the serene heights where thou dwellest now;
Dark is the way without the beacon light
Which long and steadfastly thy hands upheld;
Oh, nerve with courage new the stricken hearts
Whose dearest hopes seem lost in losing thee.

—CHARLOTTE FORTEN GRIMKE.

CRISPUS ATTUCKS

TWAS not in vain he lived and died:
'Twas not in vain his blood was shed;
His spirit still survives:
The brave of every race and clime—
In memory chambers for all time—
The martyr hero lives.

He died? Nay, laid him down and slept:
And angels bright their vigils kept
Around the patriot's bed.
For love he laid his treasure down,
The love of freedom was his crown—
He sleeps; he is not dead.

Brave Attucks! how his honors shine!
We build for him a glorious shrine!
His memory will not fade,
So long as History's pages stand,
Of this our free and favored land,
A tribute shall be paid.

To Attucks for his valiant deed;
To Attucks brave his blood the seed
   First planted in this soil,
To nourish freed and secure
For every man while years endure,
   Freedom in life and toil.

But who was Attucks? Afric's son:
Who toiled for years and never won
   A free man's just reward.
A man of stature strong and brave,
Yet held in bondage as a slave,
   By men who worshipped God.

By men who felt the galling yoke
Of motherland: whose ire awoke
   Against the tyrant's power;
Who cry, Injustice! when the claim
For war is pressed: and loud declaim—
   We're robbed of rightful dower.

To force her claims the motherland
In ships of war moored at the strand
   Of this, her new estate:
She stationed men in old King Street.
These soldiers insolently beat
   The people of the state.

While men of wisdom gathered round,
Seeking to know where might be found
   Deliverance from the foe—
How to throw off the British yoke,
A swarthy Negro fearless spoke—
   And struck the primal blow.

The blow is struck! another sound—
The roar of battle shakes the ground:
    And Attucks is no more!
No more? A *hero's* wreath is thine!
Around *thee* deathless laurels twine,
    And fame from shore to shore!

He lies in state in Faneuil Hall:
Yes; there upon the sable pall
    Lies Attucks true and brave;
And as the people drop a tear,
In gratitude upon his bier,
    They cry—He's not a slave!

'Twas not in vain our hero died:
'Twas not in vain his blood was shed:
    His *spirit* still survives;
The brave of every race and clime—
In memory's chamber for all time—
    The martyr hero lives!

—Rev. Geo. C. Rowe.

NAT TURNER

HE stood erect, a man as proud
       As ever to a tyrant bowed
       Unwilling head or bent a knee,
And longed while bending to be free:
And o'er his ebon features came—
A shadow 'twas of manly shame—
Aye, shame that he should wear a chain
And feel his manhood withered with pain,
Doomed to a life of plodding toil,
Shamefully rooted to the soil!

He stood erect; his eyes flashed fire;
His robust form convulsed with ire;
"I will be free! I will be free!
Or, fighting, die a man!" cried he.

Virginia's hills were lit at night—
The slave had risen in his might;
And far and near Nat's wail went forth,
To South and East, and West and North,
And strong men trembled in their power,
And weak men felt 'twas now their hour.

"I will be free! I will be free!
Or, fighting, die a man!" cried he,
The tyrant's arm was all too strong,
Had swayed dominion all too long;
And so the hero met his end,
As all who fail as Freedom's friend.

The blow he struck shook Slavery's throne:
His cause was just, e'en skeptics own;
And round his lowly grave soon swarmed
Freedom's brave hosts for Freedom's armed.
That host was swollen by Nat's kin
To fight for Freedom, Freedom win,
Upon the soil that spurned his cry:
"I will be free, or I will die!"

Let tyrants quake, e'en in their power,
For sure will come the awful hour
When they must give an answer, why
Heroes in chains should basely die,
Instead of rushing to the field
And courting battle ere they yield?

—T. THOMAS FORTUNE.

(The "Nat Turner Insurrection" was begun August 21, 1831.
Turner was hung at Jerusalem, Southampton County, Virginia, in
April, 1832. Turner was a religious enthusiast and was regarded
as a prophet among his people. His "Insurrection" produced wide-
spread apprehension among the slaveholders of the South, which was
not dissipated wholly for many years after.)

EMANCIPATION

BLEST freedom! 'tis the sweetest strain that fills the
human heart,
Its blessings must delight the soul and sweetest
joys impart;
The feathered songsters of the globe were mute, if
caged in gold,
And, though in rags, the heart, free, beats in ecstasy
untold.

Upon the ocean, calm and deep, a lordly vessel sails.
She bears upon her swelling breast twenty human
slaves;
Far from their native land to dwell, beneath an alien
sky,
Far from that dear and sunny home where Afric's
waters lie.

She landed on Virginia's shore, just where we stand
today,
And gaze upon a lovely group, clad in bright array.
And mem'ries strong and deep arise, and quick the
tear drops spring,
As we think of what today we are, and what we late
have been.

But yesterday, and dark the cloud that hung above our
sky;
Today, 'tis past and full of joy the tears of gladness rise.

The day we longed and prayed for sore at last has
　blessed our sight,
And that we come to celebrate, who can but say 'tis
　right?

E'en in our slavery we can trace the kindly hand of God,
That took us from our sunny land and from our native
　sod,
Where tropic birds their matins sing and sweet the
　streamlets flow,
And kindly Nature sweetly smiles upon the vales below.

Where scented zephyrs fan the cheek and heav'nly
　music swells,
And God's own matchless finger paints the lovely hills
　and dells;
There sweetest music fills the air while beauteous
　Nature smiles,
And every scene delights the soul, but only man is vile.

There, clad in Nature's simplest garb, he roamed a
　savage wild,
Untamed his passions, half a man, and half a savage
　child,
And knew not God, save what in stones the God of
　love revealed,
The blessed Revelation was to him a message sealed.

And God, to teach him His dear will, saw fit to bring
　him where
He learned of Him and Jesus Christ, those lessons rich
　and rare;
He made the savage into man though moulded by the
　rod,

And Ethiopia has indeed stretched forth her hands
to God.

He was a man, and felt as men, his soul with anguish
burned,
His heart with deep pulsations beat and indignations
spurned;
But God still held him to the blast, and still afflicted
sore,
And still he groaned, and still he prayed, yet still his
burden bore.

But, like the cries of Israel old, his prayers ascended
high,
And reached the great Jehovah's throne beyond the
azure sky,
And His own power brought freedom down and broke
the chain despair,
And bade the Negro walk with men as free as Nature's
air.

But was he true? speak, Bunker Hill! and Boston Common say,
Did he defend the British foe on that historic day?
While thousands stood with heaving breast and dared
not strike a blow,
A Negro's voice then cheered the throng and bade them
charge the foe.

His blood was spilled to gain a place in battle's honored
roll,
And Crispus Attucks stands aloof among the heroes
bold,

And when we speak of valiant deeds and love of country fair,
We'll not begrudge his well bought fame, but place a laurel there.

And in the dark and bloody days when thick the battle rolled,
And North and South had gathered arms and called each other foes,
A soldier brave upon the field, a faithful slave left home,
He disdained to mar the name of loved ones left alone.

But as a faithful watch-dog stands and guards with jealous eye,
He watched his master's wife and child, and at the door would lie
To shed his blood if need should rise and one had come to mar
The peace of those whose father went to fight in cruel war.

Today is hushed the cannon's roar and peace reigns everywhere,
And blessed freedom makes our land the fairest of the fair;
Shall we who helped to make it bloom and blossom as a rose,
Be cast aside unworthy of a place upon its sod?

We love her and are loyal as the truest of her sons,
For her our blood was shed, for her so oft our tears have sprung,

We'll strive to have her take her place the first of
  any land,
Stand ready to defend her soil from any alien band.

But God has freed us and to Him we bow in praise
  today,
He'll never leave us nor forsake but will protect alway,
And conscious of a heart that's true with purpose
  brave and strong,
We leave our case in those just hands that cannot do
  a wrong.

'Tis here our eyes beheld the light and here at evening's
  close
We hope to wrap our mantles round and take our last
  repose;
No politicians should divide relationships divine,
No arm should sever friendships formed in "days of
  auld lang syne."

'Tis the blessing that we celebrate and not the cause
  now lost,
For that was dear to other hearts as this can be to us,
And who were right, or who were wrong, we are not
  here to say,
For—still in death—they're heroes all, the blue, likewise the gray.

And now, the din of battle past, they are our friends
  the same,
Not such as come to get our votes, not friends in only
  name,

But friends who deep in honest hearts but wish our
　highest joy,
God grant it may ne'er severed be, but last without
　alloy.

Then let us all with one accord now join the jubilee,
And praise our God the ruler of the new land of the
　free,
And babes unborn in future years will rise to call us
　great,
For fixing now for coming time the "Day We Cele-
　brate."

—D. WEBSTER DAVIS.

FIFTY YEARS *

O BROTHERS mine, today we stand
    Where half a century sweeps our ken,
    Since God, through Lincoln's ready hand,
Struck off our bonds and made us men.

Just fifty years—a winter's day—
    As runs the history of a race;
Yet, as we now look o'er the way,
    How distant seems our starting place!

Look farther back! Three centuries!
    To where a naked, shivering score,
Snatched from their haunts across the seas,
    Stood, wild-eyed, on Virginia's shore.

Far, far the way that we have trod,
    From heathen kraals and jungle dens,
To freedmen, freemen, sons of God,
    Americans and citizens.

A part of His unknown design,
    We've lived within a mighty age;
And we have helped to write a line
    On history's most wondrous page.

A few black bondmen strewn along
    The borders of our eastern coast,
Now grown a race, ten millions strong,
    An upward, onward, marching host.

* Reprinted by permission J. W. Johnson.

Then let us here erect a stone,
    To mark the place, to mark the time;
A witness to God's mercies shown,
    A pledge to hold this day sublime.

And let that stone an altar be
    Whereon thanksgivings we may lay—
Where we, in deep humility,
    For faith and strength renewed may pray.

With open hearts ask from above
    New zeal, new courage and new pow'rs,
That we may grow more worthy of
    This country and this land of ours.

For never let the thought arise
    That we are here on suffrance bare;
Outcasts, asylumed 'neath these skies,
    And aliens without part or share.

This land is ours by right of birth,
    This land is ours by right of toil;
We helped to turn its virgin earth,
    Our sweat is in its fruitful soil.

Where once the tangled forest stood,
    Where flourished once rank weed and thorn,
Behold the path-traced, peaceful wood,
    The cotton white, the yellow corn.

To gain these fruits that have been earned;
    To hold these fields that have been won,
Our arms have strained, our backs have burned,
    Bent bare beneath a ruthless sun.

That banner, which is now the type
   Of victory on field and flood—
Remember, its first crimson stripe
   Was dyed by Attucks' willing blood.

And never yet has come the cry—
   When that fair flag has been assailed—
For men to do, for men to die,
   That we have faltered or have failed.

We've helped to bear it, rent and torn,
   Thro' many a hot-breath'd battle breeze;
Held in our hands, it has been borne
   And planted far across the seas.

And never yet, O haughty Land—
   Let us, at least, for this be praised—
Has one black, treason-guided hand
   Ever against that flag been raised.

Then should we speak but servile words,
   Or shall we hang our heads in shame?
Stand back of new-come foreign hordes,
   And fear our heritage to claim?

No! Stand erect and without fear,
   And for our foes let this suffice—
We've bought a rightful sonship here;
   And we have more than paid the price.

And yet, my brothers, well I know
   The tethered feet, the pinioned wings,
The spirit bowed beneath the blow,
   The heart grown faint from wounds and stings;

LONGING

The staggering force of brutish might,
　That strikes and leaves us stunned and dazed;
The long, vain waiting through the night
　To hear some voice for justice raised.

Full well I know the hour when hope '
　Sinks dead, and 'round us everywhere
Hangs stifling darkness, and we grope
　With hands uplifted in despair.

Courage! Look out, beyond, and see
　The far horizon's beckoning span!
Faith in your God-known destiny!
　We are a part of some great plan.

Because the tongues of Garrison
　And Phillips now are cold in death,
Think you their work can be undone?
　Or quenched the fires lit by their breath?

Think you that John Brown's spirit stops?
　That Lovejoy was but idly slain?
Or do you think those precious drops
　From Lincoln's heart were shed in vain?

That for which millions prayed and sighed,
　That for which tens of thousands fought,
For which so many freely died,
　God cannot let it come to naught.

　　　　　　　　　—JAMES WELDON JOHNSON.

18

BOOKER T. WASHINGTON

TO one of humble lineage sprung
  My harp in duteous strain is strung,
    To order my compliant tongue
  In laudatory lays.
His matchless triumphs I would sing
Till every voice a tribute bring,
And every land and clime shall ring
  With paeans of his praise.

Commissioned by Eternal Fate,
From scorn and shame to liberate
The millions of a race belate,
  He led the struggling van—
Among the nations to contend;
Beneath the common load to bend;
Their full co-operation lend
  The universal plan.

So arduous the task begun,
So tireless the labor done,
So marvelous the triumphs won,
  No page a par records,
For difficulties overstept,
For latitude of service swept,
For heights of duty gained and kept,
  No age a peer affords.

Yet, virtue walks a path obscure,
And honor struggles to endure,
While arrogance and deeds impure
  Adorn the Hall of Fame.

Still, power triumphs over right,
And wrong is victor in the fight;
Greed, graft, and knavery excite
 Vociferous acclaim.

When equity pervades the earth,
When virtue overtowers birth,
And when integrity and worth
 Attain their righteous cause;
When error's baleful era ends
And truth's sublime régime begins;
When might declines and merit wins
 Victorious applause,

Then history's reluctant muse
Both hut and hall alike will use,
And, for his brightest laurel, choose
 The nominee of fate;
And with impartial pen aflame,
Upon the highest round of fame
In gleaming gilt inscribe the name
 Of Washington the Great,

     —JOHN RILEY DUNGEE.

BOOKER T. WASHINGTON *

AS nearly as any man I have ever met, Booker T. Washington lived up to Micah's verse, "What more doth the Lord require of thee than to do justice and love mercy and walk humbly with thy God." He did justice to every man. He did justice to those to whom it was a hard thing to do justice. He showed mercy, and this meant that he showed mercy not only to the poor, and to those beneath him, but that he showed mercy by an understanding of the shortcomings of those who failed to do him justice, and failed to do his race justice. He always understood and acted upon the belief that the black man could not rise if he so acted as to incur the enmity and hatred of the white man; that it was of prime importance to the well being of the black man to earn the good will of his white neighbor, and that the bulk of the black men who dwell in the southern states must realize that the white men who are their immediate physical neighbors are, beyond all others, those whose good will and respect it is of vital consequence that the black men of the South should secure.

He was never led away into the pursuit of fantastic visions; into the drawing up of plans only for a world of two dimensions. He kept his high ideals always, but he never forgot for a moment that he was living in an actual world of three dimensions, in a world of unpleasant facts, where those unpleasant facts have to be faced; and he made the best possible out of a

* From the preface to "Booker T. Washington," by Lyman Abbott and Emmett J. Scott.

bad situation from which there was no ideal best to be obtained. And he walked humbly with his God.

To a very extraordinary degree he combined humility and dignity; and I think that the explanation of this extraordinary degree of success in a very difficult combination was due to the fact that at the bottom his humility was really the outward expression, not of a servile attitude toward any man, but of the spiritual fact that in very truth he walked humbly with his God.

—THEODORE ROOSEVELT.

T HE following programs are not necessarily to be taken as a whole by anyone arranging an evening's or a morning's entertainment. They are merely suggestions which may open up a vista of ideas which may be worked out by any enterprising teacher. Some of the selections mentioned are not in this volume, but may easily be obtained. The music is easily found, and almost everyone will know of other music as appropriate, or of a greater variety. The use of one piece of prose or poetry on the program may suggest another. It is to be hoped that teachers will suggest to their schools other programs which will show to the boys and girls the wide range of the writings of the men and women of their own race.

A. D.-N.

THANKSGIVING

The President's Proclamation
Thanksgiving ....*Brathwaite*
Signs of the Times........................*Dunbar*
The Better Part........................*Washington*
The Boys of Our School..............*Dunbar-Nelson*
The Governor's Proclamation

MUSIC SUGGESTED

Jubilee Songs
Swing Along ....*Cook*
Since You Went Away....................*Johnson*

Young Children's Program

The Birdlet ....*Poushkin*
The Sparrow's Fall.........................*Harper*
The Seedling ....*Dunbar*
The Boogah Man...........................*Dunbar*
Thanksgiving ....*Brathwaite*
The Clock That Gains
The Boys of Howard (name of own school) School

Music Suggested

Little Alabama Coon
The Little Pickaninny's Gone to Sleep.......*Johnson*
Honey Chile ....*Adams*
Li'l Gal ....*Johnson*
Mighty Lak' a Rose..........................*Nevin*

Heroes of the Negro Race

The Unsung Heroes.........................*Dunbar*
Crispus Attucks ....*Ruffin*
Black Samson of Brandywine...............*Dunbar*
How He Saved St. Michaels...............*Stansbury*
Toussaint L'Ouverture ....*Phillips*
The Second Louisiana.......................*Boker*
Fort Wagner ....*Dickinson*
A Negro's Rebuke..........................*Simmons*
How France Received the Negro Soldier.......*Tyler*

Music Suggested

The Young Warrior........................*Burleigh*
Joshua Fit de Battle ob Jericho............*Burleigh*

MEMORIAL DAY

Ode for Memorial Day......................*Dunbar*
When Dey 'Listed Colored Soldiers..........*Dunbar*
Robert Gould Shaw...............*B. T. Washington*
Ethiopia Saluting the Colors...............*Whitman*

Music Suggested

EMANCIPATION DAY

Music Suggested

NEGRO WIT AND HUMOR

MUSIC SUGGESTED

THE YOUNG NEGRO

Use Burleigh's "The Young Warrior" as one of the musical numbers.

LINCOLN-DOUGLASS CELEBRATION

MUSIC SUGGESTED

Sometimes I Feel Like a Motherless Child—Sung from the arrangement by Coleridge-Taylor.

Instrumental Solo—The Bamboula Dance............
.............................*Coleridge-Taylor*

Listen to the Lambs...........................*Dett*

Stainer's Seven-Fold "Amen."

THE LIFE OF PAUL LAURENCE DUNBAR

Told in His Songs and Lyrics

PROGRAM

THE POET'S INTERPRETATION OF CHILD LIFE

Two Little Boots
The Boogah Man
The Poet and the Baby
Lullaby
In the Morning
A Confidence
Little Brown Baby

MUSIC

Li'l Gal ....*Johnson*
De Little Pickaninny's Gone to Sleep.........*Johnson*
Down in Lover's Lane.........................*Cook*
Dawn ....*Coleridge-Taylor*

THE POET'S STRUGGLES

The Poet and His Song
Life
Conscience and Remorse
Keep a-Pluggin' Away

Just Whistle a Bit
Misapprehension
The Warrior's Prayer
Joggin' Erlong
Not They Who Soar
The Poet
Life's Tragedy

MUSIC

A Little Dreaming by the Way............*Carrington*
Joshua Fit de Battle ob Jericho..............*Burleigh*

RACIAL LIFE

A Hymn (O Li'l Lam')
W'en de Co'n Pone's Hot
A Coquette Conquered
A Christmas Basket
Angelina
Puttin' de Baby Away
By Rugged Ways
Limitations

MUSIC

When Malindy Sings.......................*Conrade*
An African Love Song..............*Coleridge-Taylor*
Who Knows ....*Ball*

PRIDE OF RACE

W'en Dey Listed Colo'ed Soldiers
The Unsung Heroes
Frederick Douglass
Black Samson of Brandywine
Booker T. Washington
Slow Through the Dark
The Haunted Oak

MUSIC

A Death Song...................................*Bond*
Steal Away
Swing Low, Sweet Chariot
Good-Night ....*Hebron*

QUAINT PHASES OF THE LIFE OF THE NEGRO

PROGRAM

MUSIC

Memory .... *Burleigh*
Mammy ....*Cook*
An Ante-Bellum Sermon.......................*Cook*

THE OLD FOLKS OF THE PAST

Th' Ol' Tunes.............................*Dunbar*
The Praline Woman.........................*Moore*
Cris'mus on de Plantation..................*Dunbar*
The Goopherd Grapevine...................*Chesnutt*

MUSIC

Since You Went Away....................*Johnson*
Li'l Gal ....*Johnson*
Dawn ....*Coleridge-Taylor*
De Little Pickaninny's Gone to Sleep.......*Johnson*

CITY LIFE

Jimsella ....*Dunbar*
Dat O'l Mare o' Mine.......................*Dunbar*
The Finish of Patsy Barnes..................*Dunbar*

MUSIC

Why Adam Sinned...........................*Rogers*
Deep River ....*Burleigh*

AUTHOR'S INDEX

286

SUBJECT INDEX

287

W. B. C.

THE POET AND HIS SONG

THE A.M.E. REVIEW

THE POET AND HIS SONG

ALICE M. DUNBAR

"OUR NOTIONS UPON THE SUBJECT OF BIOGRAPHY," says Carlyle, "may perhaps appear extravagant; but if an individual is really of consequence enough to have his life and character for public remembrance, we have always been of opinion that the public ought to be made acquainted with all the inward springs and relations of his character. How did the world and the man's life, from his particular position, represent themselves to his mind? How did co-existing circumstances modify him from without; how did he modify these from within? With what endeavors and what efficacy rule over them; with what resistance and what suffering sink under them? * * * Few individuals, indeed, can deserve such a study; and many *lives* will be written, and, for the gratification of innocent curiosity, ought to be written, and read and forgotten, which are not, in this sense, *biographies*."

Thus Carlyle. It would seem then, that if one must write about a poet, the world would wish to know how and in what manner the great phenomena of Nature impressed him, for Nature is the mother of all poets and there can be no true poetry unless inspired deeply by the external world which men do not touch. If the poet was an urban child, if the wonder of star-filled nights, the mystery of the sea, the beauty of sunrise and sunset, the freshness of dewy morns, and the warm scent of the upturned sod filled him with no rapture, then he was no true poet, howsoever he rhymed. So if one wishes to get a correct idea of any poet whatever, he must delve beneath the mere sordid facts of life and its happenings; of so many volumes published in such and such a time; of the influence upon him of this or that author or school of poetry; of the friends who took up his time, or gave him inspiration, and, above all, one must see what the love of Nature has done for the poet.

Mere looking into the printed words may not always do this. Who knows what heart-full of suggestion may lie in one expression? Who can tell in how much one word may be, as Higginson has expressed it, "palaces to dwell in," "years of crowded passion in a phrase," "half a life concentrated in a sentence?" To the banal mind a phrase may be nothing but a sweet rhythm of language, a well-turned, well-chosen expression. To the one who may have had the chance of communion with the creative mind, ere it expressed its longings in words, the phrase may be all pregnant with suggestion.

Your true poet is a child of Nature and lies close to the great Mother-heart. Even though he were born in the city, where his outlook on trees and fields is an incidental and sporadic occurrence in his life, he senses the divine heart pulsing beneath all things, and when he is finally brought face to face with the wonders of out-of-doors, untouched by the desecrating hand of man, he bursts forth into song, released from the conventionalities of other men's verse.

This was true of Paul Dunbar. He was a child of the city, a small city, true, where Nature was not so ruthlessly crushed away from the lives of men. There were trees and flowers near home, and a never-to-be-forgotten mill-race, which swirled through all his dreams of boyhood and manhood. Like the true poet that he was, he reached out and groped for the bigness of out-of-doors, divining all that he was afterwards to see, and in his earlier verse expressing his intuitions, rather than his observations.

Love of nature was there, but the power to express this love was not. Instead, he harked back to the feeling of the race, and intuitively put their aspirations into song. Tennyson and Lowell meant much to him, because they had expressed his yearnings for the natural world, and his soul yearned toward their verse. The exquisite line, "When cows come home along the bars—" how much of the English poet went into that line, and how much of the reminiscences of the earlier life of his family? More of the former, he always confessed.

Children love "The Seedling." It is good for them who are being initiated, city-wise, into the mysteries of planting and growth. It is scientific, without being technical—it is Tennyson's "Flower in the crannied wall," Americanized, brought down to the minds of little folks. The poet loved Tennyson, he walked with him in his earlier years, he confessed his indebtedness to him in his later days; he always praised him, and defended him hotly against the accusation of too much mere academic phrasing.

In the poem "Preparation" we see more of this groping toward the light; the urban child trying to throw off the meretriciousness of city life. Say what you will, or what Mr. Howells wills, about the "feeling the Negro life esthetically, and expressing it lyrically," it was in the pure English poems that the poet expressed *himself*. He may have expressed his race in the dialect poems; they were to him the side issues of his work, the overflowing of a life apart from his dearest dreams. His deepest sorrow he told in "The Poet."

> He sang of life serenely sweet,
> With now and then a deeper note.
> From some high peak, nigh, yet remote,
> He voiced the world's absorbing heat.
>
> He sang of love when earth was young,
> And love itself, was in its lays,
> But, ah, the world, it turned to praise
> A jingle in a broken tongues.

This is a digression. "Preparation" is contemporaneous with "Discovered" and "Delinquent," but in the latter poems, he is feeling his way to make the laughter that the world will like; in the former, he is feeling his way to that true upward expression of the best in him. "A little bird sits in the nest and sings" is too much of Lowell to be true, "But the note is a prelude to better things," reflecting as in solution the thought of the "Vision of Sir Launfal." Our poet cast the poem aside as a thing of no worth, nor is it, except as it glimpses a bit of the soul within, like Lowell's clod "reaching up to a soul in grass and flowers."

Then came the experience on the lake. It was a never-to-be-for-gotten summer. Opportunity and youth combined with poetry and the unsuspected beauty of the inland sea. Nature burst upon him with a surge. He knew now to the full the beauty of the gray days that he had dimly sung; the wind rising along the lake reeds and shivering premonition into them; the moon scudding before the wind clouds like a pale wraith with flung-back hair; the storm, never so swift in its wrath as on the shores of a lake; these things entered into his soul like a revelation. This, then, was what it all meant—these quivering fears and wonders of the early spring. From a little boy, he confessed, the spring filled him with longings, unexpressed, vague, terrible, like the fears of the night, which per-sisted long after manhood. What did it mean, this terrible loneli-ness, this longing for companionship, and disgust with mere human company? He knew now. Nature had called him, and he had not been able to heed her call, until the Lake told him how.

He had sung about "Merry Autumn" in the conventional man-ner; he had enumerated pictures in the "Song of Summah," and he had written many conventional spring poems, dialect and oth-erwise, from the point of view of the spectator, but now began that passionate oneness with Nature, that was not to leave him until he deliberately turned his back upon her.

Beginning with that summer, he began to learn how to store up pictures in the mind as Wordsworth did. He began, mind you, only began to learn how to accumulate experiences that would later burst red-hot in one phrase, one line, one stanza that combined a month's experiences, a season's joy, a year's longing in them. It is only the true poet-heart that can do this. Whether or not it may be able to express it in rhythm, or metre, or music, or painting, or express it at all, is a mere matter of no moment. If these accumu-lated experiences be stifled in the sweet darkness of the heart, that is no matter, they have been; it is enough.

This faculty of stored experiences swiftly phrased may be exquisitely traced in many a poem. There was in Washington a bare, red-clay hill, open to the sun, barren of shade on its highest point, steep of ascent, boldly near the sky—truly, almost a "heav-en-kissing hill." Daily walks on the hill fulminate in one line in "Love's Apotheosis," "the sun-kissed hill." The white arc light of the corner lamp, filtering through the arches of the maples on Spruce street, make for the tender suggestion in "Lover's Lane," where the lovers walk side by side under the "shadder-mekin'" trees. Up in the mountains of the Catskills, where the rain fell often in July days, more often than the lover of out-door sports would relish, there was one little phoebe-bird, who would sing plaintively through all the rain, ending with a mournful chirp when the sun shone out at last. His little song through the disappointing storm was infinitely cheering, and often finds expression in the song of the human bird who listened to him.

> An' it's moughty ha'd a-hopin'
> W'en de clouds is big an' black,
> An' all de t'ings you's waited fu'
> Has failed—er gone to wrack—
> But des keep on a joggin' wid a little bit of song,
> De mo'n is allus brightah w'en de night's been long.

"Keep a Song Up on De Way" enshrines both the little bird and the beloved water-fall that boomed all night under the windows. The first and third stanzas were merrily conceived and merrily written, a "compliment to the persistent bird."

> Oh, de clouds is mighty heavy—

(The cloud wraiths used to creep down the mountain side and literally camp in the front yard, so that one went stumbling about in the mixture of cloud and mist),

> An' de rain is mighty thick;
>   Keep a song up on de way.
> And de waters is a rumblin'
> On de boulders in de crick,
>   Keep a song up on de way.
> Fu' a bird ercross de road
> Is a-singin' lak he knowed
> Dat we people didn't daih
> Fu' to try de rainy aih
>   Wid a song up on de way.

The power of keen observation grows in arithmetical ratio as the soul divests itself of the littlenesses of life, the mere man-made ambitions, the ignoble strivings after place. The poet found new joy in the patch-work greenery of the mountains spread out at his feet; in the lights and shades on the fields of rye and corn and wheat and buckwheat, making the mountains seem as if Mother Nature had cunningly embroidered a huge cover for her summer dress. When he discovered, on the first visit, that the ground of the potato fields was violet, he cried aloud for joy. It had been a hard struggle to see that the light turned violet in the shadows under the vines, but when the realization came home, it was an exquisite sensation, worthy to be enshrined in a tender line. Thereafter, the mountains meant more than they had before, and subsequent visits always held out a promise of new things to be keenly detected and shoutingly announced. The waterfall that droned all night, save when, swollen with pride by the rain, it roared; the rain pouring down slantwise through the skies across the fields; the clouds casting great shadows athwart the mountain sides may have been forgotten those summers, yet, trick-like, they return here and there in unexpected places, showing how deeply they had become a part of "that inward eye, which is the bliss of solitude," of which Wordsworth sings. "The bird's call and the water's drone," and the "water-fall that sang all night," from "The Lost Dream," were but single instances of the stored-up memories expressed years after the summers in the Catskills were themselves fragments of forgotten days.

> In the little poem "Rain-Songs" he sings:
>> The rain streams down like harp-strings the sky,
>> The wind, that world-old harpist, sitteth by;
>> And ever, as he sings his low refrain,
>> He plays upon the harp-strings of the rain.

This came long after the simile of the harp-strings had been discovered, exulted over and laid aside on the tables of his memory.

One more recollection of those days in the mountains is worth recording. The first time the song of the whip-poor-will came to him, he was amused. Plaintive it is to all who hear it for the first time, but to him it suggested tattling, from its nervous haste, its gasping intake of breath, like a little boy trying to clear himself from fault, yet half pleading that his companion in misdeeds be let go unpunished. The poet queried with much anxiety of every one on the place, was the cry "Whip-poor-will" a command, or was it "Whip-poor-will" a pathetic question and hoping of Will's final exoneration? It was a whimsical turn that he gave to the cry of the night-bird, and the shrill insistence of the katy-did in the little poem "Whip-poor-Will and Katy-Did," when he wants to know why one must "Whip-poor-Will," when we know from the song of the insect that it was Katy who did?

This humorous outlook on Nature is a quaint turn of mind that few poets possess. Nature is stern, awful, sweet, sympathetic, lovable, but hardly humorous, so the world thinks. Yet where are there such exquisite manifestations of humor to be found in the man-made world about us? Nature's humor is grim sometimes, tricksy sometimes, dainty ofttimes, and sternly practical many times. To view life with humor is as Nature intended us to do. The gods must laugh, else where did men learn how?

This apropos of West Medford, Massachusetts. Here he visited thrice, and confessed that the place held for him the charm of hallowed association, which all the country near Boston must have for the world born outside Massachusetts, which still rules the minds of the *hoi polloi* with the potent sway of the nearest approach in this country to anything like reposeful ease and culture. But historic spots and monuments and powder mills of Revolutionary fame and battle-fields meant but little after a while to the poet. Middlesex county abounds in rivers—were they fishable? Fishing was his one pastime, which he loved ardently, passionately, with the devotion of the true fisherman. Was there a river? Then the next question, "How is the fishing?" Walton's "Compleat Angler" is all right to read, but better to live. Anyhow it contains too many recipes for cooking. Van Dyke's "Fisherman's Luck" is better, particularly as the book is dedicated to the "Lady in Gray." Fishing and the color gray! His favorite sport and color; an unforgettable combination.

So the streams in the Catskills were deliciously suggestive of mountain trout, and even native indolence and poor health did not prevent him from arising one Fourth of July morning at three o'clock, and taking with him all the valiant souls who would go, to hie them to an over-fished stream, where the most carefully chosen flies only made the trout sniff and flirt themselves arrogantly; and where the unsportsmanlike women, having found a cool pool to use as a refrigerator, were stupid enough to try to tempt sophisticated suckers to bite—and that after a fierce cannonading of firecrackers in honor of their early patriotism.

So West Medford suggested fishing, wonderful possibilities. What though Longfellow had enshrined the Mystic in the Hall of Fame by the lines in Paul Revere's Ride? That was no matter. Anything as brown and dimpled and slow as that river must be fishable. Thus he decided on his first visit and came back to investigate when there was more time, and lo! The result he humorously enshrined in the "Ballade."

> By Mystic's bank I held my dream,
>   (I held my fishing rod as well);
> The vision was of dace and bream,
>   A fruitless vision, sooth to tell.
> * * * * *
>
> Oh, once loved, sluggish, darkling stream,
>   For me no more thy waters swell,
> Thy music now the engines' scream,
>   Thy fragrance now the factory's smell.
> * * * * *
>
> Thy wooded lanes with shade and gleam
> Where bloomed the fragrant asphodel.
> * * * * *

Poor Mystic! "Arcadia now has trolley lines," mourns the poet, and so wends his way home to put up his fishing rod, and pack away the reel until the streams of the Rocky Mountains lure the basket and rod out again.

To the soul born inland, the sea is always a revelation, and a wonder-working experience in the life. The man born near the sea, who has been reared near its beauty and wonder, whose soul has learned early in life to enter into its moods, to understand its gentleness and not to fear its grimness, whose life has been attuned to the roar of the breakers and the purl of its littlest white waves, such a man can scarcely understand the rush and uplift that comes to the inland man who sees the ocean in his maturity for the first time. Such was the tidal wave that swept over the poet when the ocean burst upon his view. And like all those born inland, when once the fascination of the sea possesses them, it becomes more exquisitely a part of the whole nature than even it does in the case of the one born on the shores of the sea. When the sea became a part of the poet's life, it wrapped itself naturally into his verse—but hardly ever disassociated from the human element. Humanity and the ocean melted into one indistinguishable mist, even as Wordsworth's moors were always peopled with one shadowy figure so indistinct that it merged into the grayness of the horizon. There is no hint of the sea, save from the hearsay point, in the first published volume of poems, but before the second came, Narragansett Pier had opened his eyes to the mystic beauty of the ocean, and his soul to its turbulence. The journey to England made him familiar with the gray nothingness of mid-ocean, and life subsequently meant frequent pilgrimages to the seashore. Gray skies and gray sea; these meant most to him; sombreness and gloom seemed part of the real meaning of the ocean. One need not seek in the life of the poet a kinship between love of the serious aspects of nature and a fancied wrong or injury in life. Because Milton always loved the moon veiled in clouds is no reason why we should conclude that early and unfortunate loves left him unable to view skies moonlit and cloudless without sorrow. Because Keats found passionate intensity of emotion in the mere aspect of Grecian beauty, a passion that saddened him, is no reason why we should conclude that Greece had wronged him or that beauty had wrecked his life. A poet is a poet because he *understands*; because he is born with a divine kinship with all things, and he is a poet in direct ratio to his power of sympathy.

Something of this, emanating from his own experience the poet shows in his poem "Sympathy."

"I know what the caged bird feel, alas!"

The iron grating of the book stacks in the Library of Congress suggested to him the bars of the bird's cage. June and July days are hot. All out of doors called and the trees of the shaded streets of Washington were tantalizingly suggestive of his beloved streams and fields. The torrid sun poured its rays down into the courtyard of the library and heated the iron grilling of the book stacks until they were like prison bars in more senses than one. The dry dust of the dry books (ironic incongruity!—a poet shut up in an iron cage with medical works), rasped sharply in his hot throat, and he understood how the bird felt when it beat its wings against its cage.

When he went down to Arundel-on-the-Bay—picturesque name of a picturesque place—he was thrilled as though stepping on hallowed ground. This was the Eastern Shore that gave birth to Douglass. More than the Boston Common, which memorized Attucks and deified Robert Gould Shaw and inspired his best sonnets, this was near the home of the idol of his youthful dreams, the true friend of his enthusiastic youth. The place was wild after the fashion of the shore of the Chesapeake; it seemed almost home to him—and the fishing was excellent. He enshrined it in his memory, and later came the poem "The Eastern Shore." It was written months after the lure of the bay had been forgotten when the skies swirled snow down on a shivering city, and the mind warmed the body as it harked back to the hot days of July under the burning skies and over the clean-washed sands of the Chesapeake Bay. One more poem the eastern shore inspired, "The Memory of Martha." The story "The Memory of Martha" being finished, the poet found himself rushed onward with a mighty sympathy for the man he had created, whose wife had left him for the unknown. It was the poet-heart throbbing in sympathy with the woes of the universe. He *was* the old husband, mourning his loss, even as when he wrote "Two Little Boots"; he *was*, for the time being, the broken-hearted mother, mourning over the little shoes. He wept as he wrote the poem, both poems in fact, and then laughed at his own tears—no immediate animus for either poem, just the overflowing of an understanding soul over a fancied grief.

Sometimes with him the memory of the words of another author commingled with a landscape, and then there is a rare combination of verse. It was when in the dire grip of pneumonia that the oft-reiterated desire, perhaps delirious, certainly comic, came for "A bear story, just one little bear story," to be read aloud to him. Blessed fortune it was then that Ernest Thompson-Seton was just giving to the world his inimitable "Wild Animals I Have Known," and fever or no fever, the poet must revel into forgetfulness of pain in listening to the woes of Raggy-lug, and the too canny wolves and bears. It made a review of the "Jungle Book" a delightful process, and invited a re-persual of Bliss Carman's poems. When the Catskills burst upon his delighted vision a while later, what more natural than that "To the Road," with its hint of Carman should enshrine the little white road winding up the mountain side?

> Cool is the wind, for the summer is waning—
> Who's for the road?
> Sun-flecked and soft where the dead leaves are
> raining,
> Knapsack and alpenstock press hand and shoulder—
> Merriment here, loud and long, because any old dead
> branch when

carried on a walk became dignified by the name of alpenstock, and the leather chatelaine purse of the companion in tramping became a knapsack.

The "Forest Greeting" enshrined both Kipling and Thompson-Seton. "Good Hunting," from the cry of the wood brothers in the "Jungle Book," but the mourning was for the wounded animals, the funeral wail of the little ones left alone to whose sufferings Thompson-Seton was the first to call attention in an unsentimental way.

All this newly-acquired love of the wee things of Nature and life had taught him to let the smallest suggestions find expression in the quaintest turns of comic verse. The east winds from the Massachusetts Bay howl around the houses of West Medford, and their piercing "Woo—oo—ee!" suggested the "Boogah Man," written for the very tiny maiden of two years, who persisted in hugging his avuncular shoes when he wanted to write sonnets about Harriet Beecher Stowe and Robert Gould Shaw. How can one work? he asked fretfully, and then burst laughingly into "How's a poet to write a sonnet, can you tell?" And so dashed off the poem on scrap paper, and read it aloud to the small maiden, who thereupon suggested that the "Woo—oo" of the wind was a "Boogah Man." So that was written immediately, dramatizing it as he wrote, much to her delight.

The dramatic instinct was strong behind the delicate perception of the power of suggestion. One must dramatize the poems as they were written, white hot. So, when "The Dance" and "The Valse" were penned, the metre must be dramatized in order to get it right; anapestic tetrameter admits of no limping lines; so one must waltz, humming the lines in order that there be no faulty rhythm. It was well that there were good dancers in the household to be sure there would be correct metre. "Whistling Sam" was troublesome. All had to whistle Sam's tunes, and then the music teacher must come and play them out on the piano, and transcribe the musical notation to be sure there were no mistakes.

Suggestion—that power of making one idea bring out a poem apparently foreign to the original thought—was never more humorously exemplified than in "Lias" and "Dat Ol' Mare o' Mine," both products of that winter in Colorado. "Dat Ol' Mare" was a weird and eccentric maiden horse of uncertain age and dubious ancestry, whose ideas were diametrically opposed to any preconceived notions one might suppose horses in general and Colorado horses in particular to have. But she would come home "on de ve'y da'kest night," without guidance, even if she did betray doubtful pre-ownership in the day-time when an exasperated and embarrassed woman drove her into Arapahoe street, the end of the ranch road, upon which street she would make frequent, unpsychological and embarrassing stops. But she would come home unguided and sure, hence "Dat Ol' Mare o' Mine."

There never was a "Lias," except generically, but maternal adjurations as to the beauty of the life of the despised early worm, and the "early to rise" maxim generally was greeted with Homeric laughter, and culminated in poor abused "Lias."

Colorado! As much of a revelation of Nature as the sea! But here was a new mother, more stern, less sure, never so capable of intimacy. Magnificent sweep of mountain range visible from the windows of the tiny house on the ranch—one hundred and fifty miles of Rocky Mountains, from Pike's Peak to Long's Peak, with all the unnamed spurs in between! Unsurpassed sunsets, wonderful sunrises that flushed the eastern prairies, and reflected back on the snows of the mountains in the west, so that the universe went suffused in a riotous prismatic color scheme; the meadow lark perched on the eaves of the house, tossing golden liquid sweetness to the high clear heavens; cowboys herding unwilling cattle across the horizon, miles and miles away; clear ozone, thin air which pierced the lungs and made them expand, sharp extremes in January from 60 degrees above to 30 degrees below. Here was Nature, untamed, unconfined, unfamiliar, wild. It went to the head like new wine, and ideas came rushing, fulminating, fructifying. One forgot sometimes, and it became comic when forgetting that the altitude of Denver and the surrounding land of 5200 feet or more was just becoming familiar; one rushed fearlessly into the higher strata of other towns, like Leadville and Colorado Springs, and was brought sharp up against the stubborn fact that rarity of air is not to be tampered with by the tenderfoot.

But the longing for the beloved East persisted, and though two novels and some short stories came forth that winter, the verse halted because the heart was elsewhere. "A Warm Day in Winter" and "Spring Fever" are both suggestive of the East, yet both were descriptive of days in Harmon. In the darkness of the night came the sound of a herd of cattle, padding feet echoing through closed doors, and so the simile of a race struggling slowly through the dark was born, and the poem "Slow Through the Dark" came to life:

> Slow moves the pageant of a climbing race;
> Their footsteps drag far, far below the height—

The spectacle of a small caravan climbing the heights of the mountains in the far distance, up the steep winding road that crept whitely out of sight across the snow-capped boulders, was pregnant with the same suggestion. So came to his mind "By Rugged Ways":

> By rugged ways and through the night
> We struggle blindly toward the light.

These two poems were always among his favorites. The darker side of the problems of the race life was being brought home more and more forcibly to him as he grew older, and the stern ruggedness of nature in the Rocky Mountains forced him to a realization of the grim problems of the world's work.

As the herd of cattle climbing the sides of the mountain suggested something more than insensate animals struggling toward food and shelter, so the trifle of a brick side yard, damp and shut in by high brick walls of the two houses on each side, made for a riot of odd little poems. There were many poems born out of the fullness of the heart, out of a suggestion of long ago, from a picture, from a book, from a chance expression. Many were truly lyrical in that they were the record of the "best and happiest moments," as Shelley puts it. So many were truly poetic in that they were the record of the divine oneness with all mankind and all nature, and so many were like that group of November poems in that they were merely experiments in the power of suggestion.

If a short brick walk between two brick walls of two city houses does not suggest a cloistered walk of a monastery, what, then, does it suggest? And if that walk be damp, as perforce it must be, and if violet beds grow on the side, wild rank things, pushing through the brick crevices and allowed to remain because the inmates of the house are sentimentally fond of violets—even wild ones that grow in city back yards—what more natural than that all kinds of cool, damp, cloistered ideas will emanate from the tiny spot? So in one *dies mirabilis* were born "To a Violet Found on All Saint's Day," "The Monk's Walk," "The Murdered Lover," "Love's Castle," "Weltschmertz," "My Lady of Castle Grand," and "In the Tents at Akbar."

It is a base libel, much advertised and bruited abroad, to label the exquisite "Violet Found on All Saints' Day" as a vulgar premonition. Within the one little flower was all the lesson of "The Seedling," fruition now, less Tennyson, more filled with the understanding of maturity. The poet had been told by those near him, who once had lived in a Roman Catholic community, that on All Saints' Day every one goes to the cemeteries laden with flowers to lay on the graves of the loved lost ones. He had always loved the custom and he remembered each All Saints' Day with a tender sympathy. So he saw in the violet not a premonition of despair, but a sweet effort on its part to bloom in memory of man's sorrows.

The chill November winds, following an unusually riotously beautiful Indian summer, waved the bird's nest in the Virginia creeper on the house next door, and "Weltschmertz" came forth, his deepest sympathy with all the woe of the world—complete universality of the true poet, nothing personal, merely infinite. The line "Count me a priest" betrays its cloister sisterhood. "The Monk's Walk" was near enough to the original idea of a monastery, but it evolved into the "Murdered Lover." The little walk grew to mean cloisters, castles, priests, knights—even "My Lady of Castle Grand," by the process of suggestion comes to life, for what so medieval as a castle with an inverted Lady of Shalott?

The medieval fancy ran riot then, and though it seems a far cry from Tennyson's "Lady of Shalott" to Bayard Taylor's "Bedouin Love Song," yet such a bridge does the poet's fancy make from reality to dreamland, that all strange fancies clustered about that cloistered walk, and his imagination careened out into the desert sands "In the Tents of Akbar," because the "Murdered Lover" of the poem, written in the morning, suggested the murdered dancing girl under the burning skies, and the grief of Akbar rent his heart in the evening. It is the exceptional mind that drags its pitifully methodical way through conventional, well-worn grooves of thought. One who thinks at all thinks by leaps and bounds, ranging all the universe, touching but tangentially the thought suggested by the last thought, and then winging swift flight elsewhere. Else wherefore think? One might as well ruminate. The poet puts wings to his words, as Homer phrases it, "winged words," and lo, a poem is born. And three or four great poems may have the same trivial place of conception, or a great soul-shaking experience may culminate in a line. Else why write poetry?

The power of Mother Nature having once entered into the poet-soul, it could never leave altogether. When the day came that he turned his back upon her deliberately, she did not avenge herself, but persisted in the haunting line, the pregnant phrase, the tender mood, albeit dimmer in each succeeding poem. For she gathers all her children to her breast and croons them melodies that will last through all eternity, if they will have them last; and even when the petulant children stop their ears, the inward ear listens to the great mother heart and heeds its call.

Wilmington, Del.

ABOUT THE EDITORS

Henry Louis Gates, Jr., is the W. E. B. Du Bois Professor of the Humanities, Chair of the Afro-American Studies Department, and Director of the W. E. B. Du Bois Institute for Afro-American Research at Harvard University. One of the leading scholars of African-American literature and culture, he is the author of *Words, Signs, and the Racial Self* (1987), *The Signifying Monkey: A Theory of Afro-American Literary Criticism* (1988), *Loose Canons: Notes on the Culture Wars* (1992), and the memoir *Colored People* (1994).

Jennifer Burton is in the Ph.D. program in English Language and Literature at Harvard University. She is the volume editor of *The Prize Plays and Other One-Acts* in this series. She is a contributor to *The Oxford Companion to African American Literature* and to *Great Lives from History: American Women*. With her mother and sister she coauthored two one-act plays, *Rita's Haircut* and *Litany of the Clothes*. Her creative nonfiction has appeared in *There and Back* and *Buffalo*, the Sunday magazine of the *Buffalo News*.

Akasha (Gloria) Hull is Professor of Women's Studies and Literature at the University of California, Santa Cruz. Her publications include *Color, Sex, and Poetry: Three Women Writers of the Harlem Renaissance* (1987) and *Healing Heart: Poems 1973–1988* (1989). She has also edited *Give Us Each Day: The Diary of Alice Dunbar-Nelson* (1984) and *The Works of Alice Dunbar-Nelson* (1988).